ATHENS *City of the Gods*

κλειναὶ ᾿Αθᾶναι
δαιμόνιον πτολίεθρον

ATHENS

City of the Gods

from prehistory to 338 B.C.

ANGELO PROCOPIOU

photographs by EDWIN SMITH

 STEIN AND DAY / PUBLISHERS / NEW YORK

DF
285
P 72

Stein and Day / Publishers / 7 East 48 Street, New York, N.Y. 10017

Istituto Geografico De Agostini S.p.A. - Novara 1964

Printed in Italy

Contents

MAPS

PLANS

FIGURES

Plates

Jacket illustrations: *front:* Head of a girl in Attic marble *c.* 500, *Acropolis Museum, Athens*

               back: Temple of Athena Nikê from the west, *c.* 427-404

Title page: the obverse (Athena) and the reverse (her owl) an Athenian dekadrachma, struck *c.* 484

Publishers' note

ALL DATES IN THIS volume are B. C. unless it is otherwise stated or except where it was felt that the omission of B. C. might lead to ambiguity. The transliteration of Greek names and words into English does not pretend to be systematic. In most cases it conforms to spellings used by *The Oxford Classical Dictionary;* where this was not possible an accepted usage has been adopted.

The publishers express their gratitude to the following for permission to quote from translations of classical texts of which they hold the copyright:

The Bodley Head Ltd., London, for Rex Warner's translation of Thucydides' *The Peloponnesian War.*

The Clarendon Press, Oxford, for the late Professor B. J. Jowett's translation of Plato's *Dialogues.* The text followed is that of the 4th edition of 1953.

Penguin Books Ltd., Harmondsworth, for E. S. Watling's translation of Sophocles' *King Oedipus* and Aubrey de Selincourt's translation of Herodotus' *The Histories.*

Trinity College, Cambridge, for the late Sir James Frazer's translation of Pausanias' *Description of Greece.*

All the photographs in this volume are the work of Edwin Smith except for those kindly supplied by the following to whom the publishers wish to express their gratitude: – Alinari (Figs. 7, 10 and 20); American School of Classical Studies at Athens (Figs. 1 and 24); British Museum (Fig. 21); M. Chuzeville (Fig. 14); Conzett and Huber, Zürich (Fig. 25, Pls. 54 and 55); De Foscherare (Fig. 9); D. A. Harissiades, Athens (Pl. 20); Hirmer Verlag, Munich (pp. 1 and 2); Laboratoire photographique de la faculté d'architecture d'Athènes (Pls. 19 and 66); National Museum of Athens (Figs. 2, 3, 4, 5, 6, 15 and 16); Soprintendenze Antichità, Florence (Figs. 8 and 19); Stournaras, Athens (Fig. 22); V. and N. Tombazi, Athens (Figs. 17, 18 and 23).

Some of the maps and plans in this volume have been specially prepared, others are based on existing material. Amongst the latter, the publishers would like to acknowledge the following sources: – American School of Classical Studies at Athens (plan 7); A. Furtwängler, *Aegina* (plan 3); C. Glotz and R. Cohen, *Histoire grecque* Vol. 1 (map 7); J. Miliadis, *The Acropolis* (plans 2, 4, 5 and 6); John Travlos, *The Development of Town-planning in Athens* (maps 3, 4 and 6); C. Tsountas, *A History of Ancient Greek Art* (plan 1).

Finally the publishers express their gratitude to the Directors of the National Museum of Athens and the Agora Museum for the courtesy and cooperation extended to Mr Smith in the taking of the photographs and for permission to reproduce the objects in their collections illustrated here.

Introduction

AMONG THE FEW privileged cities of antiquity whose names still retain grandeur and glory in our own age, Athens is pre-eminent. It had the good fortune to be spared conflagration and earthquake and was able to escape destruction by war. Most of the cities of Greece crashed down into ruin and dust as a result of these upheavals. Knossos, Phaestos, Mycenae, Tiryns, Argos, Delos, Olympia, Delphi, Sparta, Thebes and Pella, all perished. But Athens survived and has been inhabited without interruption from neolithic to modern times, a span of more than six thousand years.

But the fame of Athens is not due merely to the fact that it survived physically throughout the ages: it is due to the civilization which developed and flourished there, for Athens was the mother of democracy, of political freedom, of tragedy and comedy, of plastic arts which achieved a unique synthesis between the real and the ideal, and lastly of dialectical philosophy.

The achievements of Athens were treated as a priceless heritage by the cities which succeeded it, Pella, Alexandria and Rome. The influence of Athenian literature and painting continued to be felt in Constantinople until the downfall of the Byzantine empire. Twice in the history of modern Europe, in the fifteenth and eighteenth centuries, nostalgia for Athenian styles in architecture and art was responsible for a classical and neo-classical Renaissance. Rome, Florence, Paris, London, Munich, Berlin, Leningrad, Washington and Philadelphia all have monuments and buildings which can trace their ancestry back to Athens.

Indeed, the influence of Athenian civilization on both the ancient and modern worlds is so extensive that a whole book could be devoted to this subject; my purpose here, however, is to present this civilization in the setting in which it was born, flourished and began to fade.

A great deal of material evidence of Athenian civilization still exists and is accessible to students today. First, there are the texts which have survived, texts which were written in Athens and which discuss the problems of politics and ethics, of natural philosophy and metaphysics, of the psychology of human passions and the rules of logic. These texts may be history such as the works of Herodotus, Thucydides and Xenophon; or they may be rhetoric such as those of Demosthenes and Isocrates; or philosophy such as the dialogues of Plato and the treatises of Aristotle; or poetry such as the tragedies of Aeschylus, Sophocles and Euripides and the comedies of Aristophanes. But they all have one thing in common: they are informed by the same clarity of thought, the same preoccupation with causality and are based on the same concept of the fundamental nature or " measure " of man.

Secondly, there are the examples of Athenian art which have survived: architectural monuments which are still standing or which have been restored on or near the Acropolis, and sculpture, ceramics, vase-paintings, jewelry and coins which can be seen in museums in Greece and elsewhere. These works of art are important in that they amplify and correct the knowledge of ancient Athens which we derive from classical texts; but quite apart from their documentary value, they are also in themselves a source of vivid aesthetic pleasure.

As recently as ten years ago, the history of Athens had as a starting point the year 776 B. C., the date which coincided with the first Olympiad and with the geometric phase of Athenian art. Further back there extended a vague and undefined world, without precise dates or geographical limits, fitfully illuminated by myths and epic poetry. The contrast between this period and the flowering of the fifth century may well be compared to the contrast between the Dark Ages and the Renaissance, in both cases viewed with the same bias by intellectuals of the age of enlightenment.

When in June 1952 the late Michael Ventris found the key to Linear B, enabling the clay tablets of Knossos, Pylos and Mycenae to be deciphered, the temporal limits of Greek civilization were suddenly pushed back a full seven centuries and the history of Athens acquired a new dimension and a new significance.

The mythical and heroic world now began to take shape, with a distinctive social physiognomy. It could be placed with certainty, chronologically and geographically. Its presence in Athens could be studied side by side with contemporary manifestations at Tiryns, Mycenae and Pylos, and the chain of events could be followed link by link from the Mycenaean to the classical and on to the Hellenistic ages. This mythical world became an integral part of the cultural cycle to which the classical and Hellenistic worlds were later to belong, inspired and interpreted by the same Greek intellect.

In the light of this new world revealed by the decipherment of Linear B, we have begun to appreciate the geometric and non-figurative art of the late Mycenaean period, particularly as we have learned to understand its beauty in the school of modern art: we can see today why Plato placed its abstract forms above the realistic works of his own age.

Mycenaean civilization in Athens was not abruptly extinguished as it was in Mycenae, Pylos and Tiryns, although the fact that the latter were destroyed by the Dorian invaders did render one

service to archaeology: the fires which consumed the cities hardened the unbaked clay tablets on which their records were kept and enabled us to decipher their script. No such tablets have been found in Athens, possibly because the Dorians who destroyed the Mycenaean cities appear to have bypassed Athens.

Because it escaped destruction, Athens attracted many refugees from other parts of Greece. Here there were no gangs of helots or slaves as in Sparta and no powerful military or aristocratic caste, simply because there were no extensive tracts of rich soil to be cultivated by slaves and guarded by armed overlords. Social classes existed, but friction between them grew progressively less sharp as inhabitants turned from agriculture to manufacture, commerce and colonization.

The diversity of occupation of its citizens was the cause of the rapid development of Athens and led to the political unity of the scattered settlements and the founding of a single state which eventually became democratic. The immediate causes leading up to the social reforms of Solon are outlined very clearly by Plutarch, but their beginnings date back in fact to Mycenaean times when the monarchy had already started to disappear.

Athens' connection with the sea also had Mycenaean origins. Plutarch describes how the Athenians reverently preserved their first ship with thirty oars, the one that had carried Theseus to Crete to kill the Minotaur and free Athens from its annual tribute. This vessel apparently still existed in the time of Demetrius Phalerius at the beginning of the second century B. C. In the " Catalogue of Ships " in the *Iliad*, Homer records that the Athenians sent fifty vessels to the expedition against Troy.

In their struggle for survival, the Athenians found their salvation by turning to the sea; their journeys to other lands opened new horizons; they came into contact with other peoples and learned new skills from them as well as selling them the products of their own. Herodotus was not only the father of history: he was also the first to give expression to an international outlook. Originating in the merchant class of Athens, this new attitude influenced the legislation of Solon, himself a merchant as well as a politician and a poet. The individual, even if he was a foreigner, was respected and given legal and political rights which had hitherto been reserved to the old patriarchal families. The weakening of the hold of these families and the strengthening of the citizen's position created a sense of individual responsibility within the collective structure of Athenian polity. This blend of individualism and co-operation was seen at work in meetings and assemblies where public affairs were debated. Public discussion gave rise to rhetoric as a special branch of political science and developed a spirit of enquiry in the Athenian citizen.

This spirit found its finest literary expression in the dialogue and in the scepticism of the sophists and presupposed the existence of a new kind of man who rejected static traditionalism and was acutely conscious of his personal and political freedom. The new citizen became the political standard-bearer of democracy in the ancient world; a democracy which produced a moral and intellectual climate of its own within which literature and art flourished and which was responsible for what Renan aptly called " the Greek miracle".

Without political training, the individual Athenian would not have treated the defence of his country against the Persians as a personal responsibility. The victorious wars against the Asiatics freed the sea lanes and opened up for Athens the possibility of maritime control of the Mediterranean. In the fifth century, Athens became the metropolis of a Greek commonwealth and with the funds contributed by allied city states Pericles built on the Acropolis the monuments which to this day reflect the glory of Athenian civilization.

When we speak of civilizations which preceded that of Greece—those for example of Egypt, Mesopotamia or Persia which undoubtedly added much to man's sum of knowledge—,we think of austere-looking kings and high priests who built huge tombs and luxurious temples. These figures obscure the presence of any individuality in the anonymous and disciplined populations over which they ruled. About the civilization of Athens we feel quite differently. The names that immediately come to mind are those of men whose individual achievements—in the field of politics, philosophy, literature or art—pointed the way to a better life, enriching mankind with new ideas and sensations. Even the wars that Athens waged were different from those fought by acquisitive and ambitious kings. Only the war among the Greek cities, so movingly described by Thucydides, is a distressing exception, not so much because of the stark economic and political rivalries which caused it, but because cf the failure of Athens to communicate to other Greek cities the democracy her citizens enjoyed at home. At the very moment when her creative energies had reached their greatest power, Athens' nerve failed and she allowed them to be sapped.

After the Peloponnesian War, optimism gave way to the romantic pessimism of Demosthenes, to Plato's rejection or " devaluation " of reality, to the caustic irony of Aristophanes, to the melancholy of Scopas and the sensual individualism of Praxiteles. Isocrates alone foresaw the solution to the crisis confronting Hellenism in the shape of a unifying campaign against Asia, under a new single leadership, such as that of Philip of Macedon who had defeated the Athenians in 346. But the realization of this aim by peaceful means was not possible in Isocrates' lifetime because of the rivalry between Athens, Sparta and Thebes, the leading cities of Greece.

The ideal of Isocrates eventually became historical fact at the end of the fourth century under Alexander the the Great. The empire which he created out of the old civilizations of Mesopotamia, Egypt and Greece had Athenian culture as its basis. But the history of Athens in Hellenistic times belongs to another book.

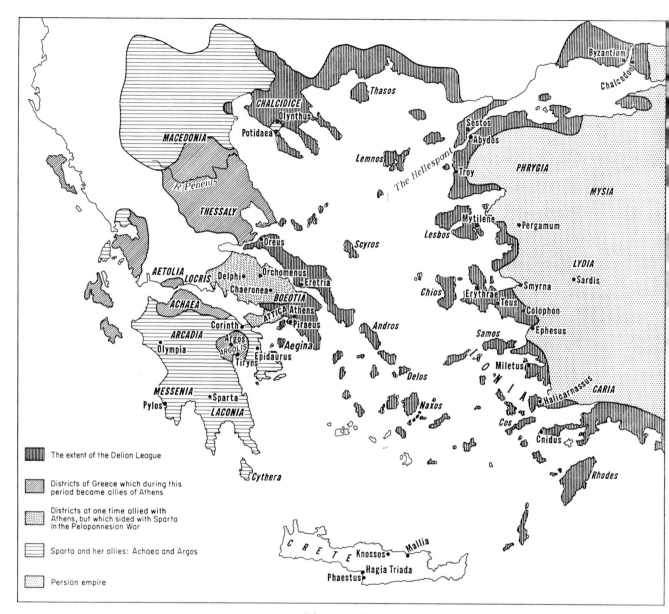

The extent of the Delian League

Districts of Greece which during this period became allies of Athens

Districts at one time allied with Athens, but which sided with Sparta in the Peloponnesian War

Sparta and her allies: Achaea and Argos

Persian empire

Map 1 GREECE AND ASIA MINOR
During the Athenian hegemony and Peloponnesian War

The Birth of Athens

THE LANDSCAPE AND CLIMATE of Attica have changed little since the days of antiquity. When one reads descriptions in the writings of classical authors and compares them with what one can see in Attica today, one is struck by how apposite they still are. The poor soil, the lack of water, the barren mountains, the limited range of agricultural produce in which the olive and the vine predominate, the sparse waters of the Ilissus and Cefissus rivers which become abundant—indeed torrential—only in winter, the dry climate, the clear atmosphere, the blue sky, all have for centuries remained virtually unchanged.[1]

Yet the people who have occupied this land without interruption from neolithic times down to our own day have not remained unchanged. The social and intellectual changes which Athens experienced as it passed from the Mycenaean to the classical ages were as great as the changes which later distinguished the classical from the Byzantine eras. Perhaps modern Athenians, as some writers have claimed, are as excitable, impulsive and individualistic as their forebears but it seems unlikely that they should all be endowed with a uniform character, especially when one remembers that the population of the plain of Athens, numbering today nearly two million inhabitants, is the product of successive waves of migrants and refugees who in the course of its long history have come to Attica from every part of the eastern Mediterranean and the Black Sea.

This contrast between the natural setting of Athens which has remained constant and the human element which has undergone a continuous process of change shows that the physical environment did not determine the history of the city, nor did it impose a specific destiny upon it. However, geography did have important economic and social effects on Athens and on the life of its inhabitants; it provided the context of their activities, something to struggle against and to adjust to.

Athens responded to the challenge of its surroundings in various ways at different periods of its history. The poverty of its soil, for example, was an important factor in Athens' drive toward colonial expansion. From the beginning of the Iron Age (about 1100) when waves of refugees fleeing from the Dorian invaders caused serious overpopulation in Attica, through the archaic and classical ages, the Athenians devoted their energies to colonization.[2] The appearance of numerous independent free city-states, each within the narrow confines of a plain shut in by mountains, is another example of the adaptation of the Greeks to their natural surroundings. The proliferation of governments in ancient Greece was an expression in political terms of the country's irregular geography, just as the centralized administrations of the vast agricultural empires of Mesopotamia and Egypt reflected the most efficient means of exploiting economically the conditions created by the great river systems of the Euphrates and the Nile.[3]

The general features of Greek geography are summarized in Attica herself.

Its shape as seen on a map resembles the head of a horse whose spinal column is formed by the north-western diagonal leading to Boeotia and continental Greece (*see* Map 2, p. 17). The outline of its body is traced rather irregularly by the peninsula of Megara, the northern coast of the Gulf of Corinth and the coast of Attica facing the Euboean straits.

Myriads of islands with jagged coastlines, peninsulas, coves and bays spread out before Attica over the azure expanse of the Aegean towards the south-east. First come the islands of the Saronic Gulf, then the Cyclades and the Sporades like two sets of stepping-stones linking the European shore with Asia (*see* Map 1, p. 14). Athens was to use these stepping-stones, after the Persian Wars, to unite the cities and islands of the Aegean into a confederacy under her leadership. But before she attained the height of her naval power Athens had to struggle within the geographical confines of Attica to unite the small scattered settlements into a single city-state with the Acropolis as its religious and political centre.

The physical geography of Attica determined the centre and extent of the Athenian state. Several hills, among them the Acropolis, rise in the centre of a plain some eighty-five square miles in area. The rock of the Acropolis, with its many natural advantages, became early in history the nucleus of Athens. It rises 495 feet above sea level. The eastern and southern sides of the hill are sheer precipices forming natural walls which were later extended artificially. The northern side is also precipitous and the only possible approach is from the west. A miniature plateau 878 feet long and 306 feet wide extends along the crown of the Acropolis and this, together with the sloping western side, measures 274,500 square feet, an area large enough to accommodate a permanent settlement and in time of war to harbour refugees from the plains below with their flocks. The Acropolis derived its fresh water supply from subterranean streams such as the Clepshydra in the north-west and from springs such as the fountain of Asclepius at the southern end and the spring in the cave of Aglauros.

The other hills near the Acropolis did not possess the same advantages. Lycabettus, though quite high, is so sheer that it offered little, if any, living space. Vrilissos (the modern Turkovounia) is even higher, but stretches out too far for defence and has no central plateau. Mars Hill, the Pnyx, the hills of the Muses, and Ardittus, all lower than the Acropolis, are easily approached from every side and have neither water nor natural foundations on which to erect defensive walls. The choice of the Acropolis, therefore, was a natural one and it is easy to see why it played a vital part in the creation of Athens as a city-state and later became the religious and cultural centre of Athenian civilization.

The plain of Athens or ' plain of the Athenians ' as it was called in antiquity stretches out round the Acropolis and measures about nine miles by thirteen at its furthermost points. Two streams, often mentioned in ancient texts, flow through its western and eastern approaches and enter Phaleron Bay: the Cefissus which rises on Mount Parnes and the Ilissus which flows from the foot-hills of Mount Hymettus and meets the Cefissus below the hill of the Museum. The eastern half linked with Hymettus by the Ilissus is barren, but the western half watered by the Cefissus is full of market-gardens, vines and fruit trees.

The plain of Athens is bounded to the east, north and west by a semi-circular chain of mountains which include Hymettus, Pentelicum, Parnes and Aegaleos. Beyond, there are three plains—the flats of the Mesogeia and of Marathon to the east and the plain of Eleusis to the west—reached by narrow gaps in the mountains which the Athenians guarded with fortresses at Decelea, Phylae and Eleutherae. Eleutherae controlled the pass through the ravine of Cithaeron, linking Athens with Boeotia.

From the Acropolis, only the south-western horizon towards the Saronic Gulf is unobstructed. The distance from the Acropolis to Phaleron, the site of the first port of Athens, is only three miles. Subsequently, at the time of Themistocles, a new port was built behind the hill of Munychia at Piraeus which in earlier times had been a marshy island. A series of three walls connected Athens with Phaleron and Piraeus.

Beyond Piraeus lie two large islands in the Saronic Gulf, Salamis and Aegina. Salamis nearly blocks the entrance to the Gulf of Eleusis and it was here in the narrow strait between the island and the Piraeus peninsula, in one of the most famous sea battles in history, that the fleet of Xerxes was defeated in 480 and Greece saved from Persian rule. Aegina, the second island, set in the heart of the Saronic Gulf, controlled the sea routes to the Argolid and Sunium. Until the fifth century, Aegina with its powerful fleet, hampered the maritime expansion of Athens. Pericles described Aegina as the eyesore of Piraeus and called upon the Athenians to remove it.

The journey by land from Phaleron to Sunium is very easily accomplished today, thanks to the 'corniche' winding its way along the south coast of Attica on the Saronic shore. But in antiquity it was less comfortable, for the way was obstructed by the lower slopes of Hymettus and Paneion. The road from Athens to Sunium and to the rich iron, lead, silver and copper mines of Laurium, from which the Athenians derived the wealth and the incentive to build a large fleet,

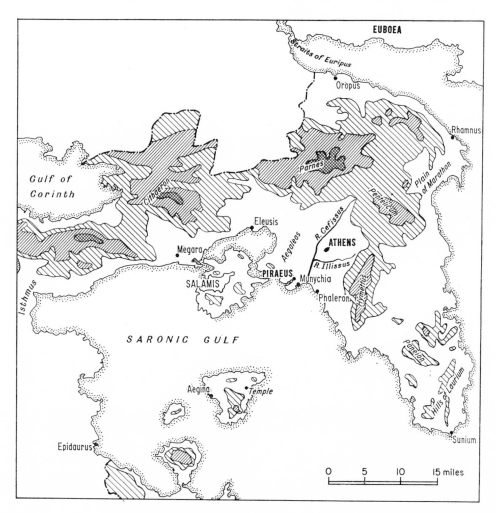

Map 2. Attica

passed through the narrow col between Hymettus and Pentelicum and crossed the inland plain of Mesogeia. Land communications with the plain of Marathon and the port of Oropus from which Euboea exported wheat and cattle to Athens, use a more northerly pass between Pentelicum and Parnes. It was through this pass that the first marathon runner brought news to Athens, in September 490, of the victory which ended Darius' dreams of European conquest. Between the foothills of Parnes and Aegaleos the Sacred Way winds down to Eleusis.

In antiquity the greater part of the plain of Athens, especially toward the Ilissus, was bare of topsoil. Excavations made round Athens confirm that the layers of soil—such as they are today—were formed much later and have some-what modified the character of the ancient countryside. The stratum of clayey schist which then formed the surface of the plain was unsuitable for building purposes and the Athenians were obliged to quarry the hard limestone of the Acropolis and the Pnyx for their constructions. They also used the yellow limestone of Karas, the porous stone of Aegina and the Piraeus shore, and the grey limestone of Eleusis, until they discovered the transparent qualities of the finely-grained marble of Pentelicum for the monuments and statues of the Acro-polis. Pentelic marble contains particles of iron so that its white colour in time takes on tints of gold. The marble of Hymettus, which tends to be blue-grey and finely-grained, was used in the sixth century, as was the marble of Paros of which the archaic Calf-Bearer (Pl. 58) in the Acropolis Museum is made.[4]

If the Athenian plain provided no stone for public buildings and sculpture, it certainly did provide fine clay for pottery. This clay acquired a remarkable lustre and lightness when fired and enabled Athenian pottery to compete success-fully with the pottery of Aegina and Corinth. Athens brought to the potter's art skills of draughtmanship and painting which, matching the material and form of the Attic vase, created a unique aesthetic whole.

From the Acropolis the citizen of Athens could see with the naked eye the whole of his native land, from Hymettus to Aegaleos, from Pentelicum and Parnes to Phaleron and Piraeus, and beyond, in the Saronic Gulf, the islands of Salamis and Aegina. Visibility in Athens extends sometimes as far as thirty miles: and mountains, islands and bays seem nearer than they really are because of the dryness and clarity of the atmosphere. Against the azure background of the sky, the heights of Hymettus and Pentelicum look like the pediments of stone-carved temples which at sunset acquire striking tints of orange and violet.

In Athens the sun shines nearly every day, albeit sometimes only for brief moments, and snow is rare. Statistics show that on average there are only seven-teen sunless days in the year and that on 122 days the sun shines all day.

Towards the end of November begins a period of cold and rain which ceases abruptly about the middle of January and for a fortnight spring comes with its sun-bathed days. This climatic phenomenon is expressed in the ancient legend of Alcyone and her husband Ceyx. Zeus had punished them for their arrogance by changing them into kingfishers or *halcyons* as they are called in Greek. But hearing their plaintive cries as they struggled to escape from the waves on the seashore, he took pity on them and forbade the winds to blow for fourteen days, a period coinciding approximately with the winter solstice which in Greece we still call the halcyon days.

By means of such myths the Athenian explained natural phenomena in terms which his mind could grasp; that is to say, by personifying them he reduced them to the proportions of man and his environment, so that he could live as comfort-ably with them as he did with the mountains, the plains, the seas and the islands which surrounded his native city. These myths are perhaps the best and most appropriate introduction to the natural setting of Athens.

1. Eastern end of the Parthenon (447-432), with a geometric stamnos in foreground

UNTIL 1958 no one could speak with any certainty of palaeolithic settlements in Greece. The discovery of signs of palaeolithic life at Pikermi in Attica by two palaeontologists between 1855 and 1860 was never related to the discovery in 1905 by a pair of archaeologists—one French, one Greek—, Albert Gaudry and Theodore Skoufos, of fossils of animals belonging to the middle palaeolithic age, for they found no trace of human skeletons or implements with them. Neither did the three palaeolithic tools from Greece (now in the Museum of Manchester), one of which came from Piraeus, appear to fit into any recognizable pattern of palaeolithic settlement.

In 1958 Vladimir Milojcic and D. Jurg excavated twelve sites on the Peneius river and brought to light 250 palaeolithic implements and tools made of sardonyx from the Pindus range, forty flute-shaped bone tools and 100 skeletal remains of mammals of the Mousterian age including bones of mammoths and of a hippopotamus. Here at last was proof of a palaeolithic culture in Greece some 40,000 years ago.[5] When in 1960 a skull of Neanderthal Man was discovered in the Chalcidice, the picture of Thessaly in the Mousterian age was complete.

The evidence so far available of a similar culture in Attica is still too meagre to permit us to do more than speculate. But if we compare the objects found at Pikermi and Piraeus with those found in Thessaly and in the Chalcidice, it is not unreasonable to infer that a thriving palaeolithic culture may have existed in Attica as well. But more needs to be done before we can be certain.

Our knowledge of the neolithic age is much greater. Some forty years ago excavations on the Athenian Acropolis and on other sites in Attica brought to light many indications of neolithic life—dwellings, vases, tools, skeletons of sheep— which confirmed the traditions recorded by Herodotus that the Athenians were descended from the Pelasgians, the neolithic inhabitants of Thessaly. Indeed the neolithic vases of Attica date from the earliest neolithic age (5520-4900) like the ceramics from the Thessalian acropolis of Sesclos, as well as from the later neolithic age (4900-3200) like those from the other Thessalian acropolis of Dimini.[6]

The excavations carried out by Milojcic and Theocharis in 1956, jointly at Gremouza (Argissa) and by the latter alone at Sesclos, revealed a stage of neolithic culture in Thessaly which has been called pre-Ceramic to distinguish it from the neolithic age proper which it preceded and to lay emphasis on the fact that ceramic objects were not found in its strata. The dates of this pre-Ceramic age are placed somewhere between 6000 and 5520 and suggest that Stone Age culture in Thessaly was older than in other neolithic settlements in the Balkans. Indeed if we take into consideration the palaeolithic discoveries of the Mousterian age in the Thessalian plain, we must move the beginnings of neolithic culture in this part of the world from the Danubian basin to the valley of the Peneius.

The spread of neolithic culture from Thessaly to the rest of Greece can be traced by discoveries made in Macedonia, in the plain of the Spercheius river, in Chaeronea, Orchomenus, Copais, Attica, Megarid, Salamis, Aegina, Corinth, Nemea, the Heraeum of the Argolid and elsewhere.[7] The theory that neolithic culture spread from northern to southern Greece rests on the fact that evidence of neolithic settlements is more plentiful in the north and becomes progressively more sparse as we move down towards the Peloponnese.

The search for traces of the neolithic age on the Acropolis began in 1922 with the excavations of the Italian Archaeological School near the Aesclepium. Another settlement was discovered in the vicinity of the Odeion of Pericles where many sherds of pottery and a stone axe, both of Sesclos type, were unearthed. Excavations carried out by the American Classical School near the Clepshydra un-

2. The Propylaea (437-432), from below

covered twenty-one wells and countless pieces of handmade pottery, sherds of Dimini type, implements of the later Stone Age and bones of domestic animals and fish. The discoveries reinforced the theory that permanent settlement by farmers with their flocks, their stone and bone tools and ceramic utensils had taken place on the rock of the Acropolis as early as the sixth millenium.[8]

From then onwards, as ceramic remains of the Early Helladic (2600-2000), the Middle Helladic (2000-1600) and the Late Helladic (1600-1100) periods show, life continued without interruption on the Acropolis and in Attica. Excavation made by Dr Theocharis at Néa Macri and at the Ascetarium of Rafina and by Professor George Mylonas at Hagios Kosmas have provided evidence that settlements on the small promontories of the coast of Attica had also begun to be established in the Early Helladic age, fortified on the landward side with ramparts like those which must have been built on the Acropolis. At the same time there was also activity in the hinterland where John Travlos has counted and plotted eighty settlements on a map. He also noted that the network of tracks used by their inhabitants corresponds closely to the roads that exist in Attica today.[9]

The painted and polished pottery (*Urfirnis*) of the Early Helladic age found on the Acropolis come from the southern slope of the rock where the sanctuary of Dionysus was situated, from the area of the Clepshydra and the sanctuaries of Aphrodite and Eros, and lastly from the lowest strata of the embankments. The name *Athenai* (Athens), which is Pelasgian in origin, may well have been used by the first inhabitants, for many Pelasgian place names have survived in Greek.

THE LANGUAGE AND THE PEOPLE

THE VIENNESE PHILOLOGIST Paul Kretschmer [10] who studied the history of the Greek language observed that many proper names of people and places in which the ending *-os* is accented and preceded by a single vowel and a double sigma had been formed from a single root, a phenomenon which cannot be accounted for in Greek. Examples of such proper nouns are Parn*assos*, Halicarn*assos*, Il*issos*, Kef*issos* and Kn*ossos*. We encounter a similar problem with proper names ending in *-issa* such as Lar*issa* and Arg*issa*. Another ending alien to Greek is *-nthos* found for example in Cori*nthos* and Zacy*nthos* and the root *Myc-* from which are formed the place names *Myc*enae, *Myc*alessos and *Myc*arna is equally difficult to explain. The same type of problem occurs with names ending in *-eus* such as Achill*eus*, Tyd*eus* and Atr*eus*.

The survival of these names in the Helladic region is explained by the fact that, prior to Greek, a language which we know as Pelasgian was spoken throughout the area before the Middle Helladic age. Kretschmer believed that the Greek language, which replaced the older Pelasgian, took shape outside the confines of Greece proper, somewhere in the Danube basin, and is derived from a branch of Indo-European which broke away from the main stem of Indo-European languages in about 2000 and was subsequently transplanted to Greece.

John Chadwick [11], the colleague of Michael Ventris who deciphered Linear B, has contested this theory. He maintains that Greek developed within the confines of Greece itself by the fusion of ancient Pelasgian and Indo-European stocks after the year 2000. According to Chadwick's theory, the surviving Pelasgian place names belong to sites which had already been established in the Early Helladic period by peoples who did not speak Greek.

Archaeological evidence shows that an interruption in the growth of Early Helladic culture took place in about 1900 and enables us to date the arrival in

Greece of invaders speaking some kind of Indo-European dialect. Many inhabited sites were then destroyed by fire and when they were rebuilt, the inhabitants used dwellings and ceramic materials of an entirely new kind. In Asia Minor the reconstruction of Troy VI [12] presents certain marked analogies with cities built in continental and insular Greece during the Middle Helladic age and suggests that a similar process had taken place there.

The new race which Schliemann called the Minyans brought with them elements of a new culture which was to grow without interruption until the Dorian invasion. The Minyans appear to have been an energetic and active race, they possessed new techniques (notably the use of bronze) and although their appearance did not result in the complete displacement of the older Pelasgians, they were able in part to impose their language on them. And from this fusion of races and tongues came the Greek people and the Greek language.

Later this basic Greek split up into four dialects which flourished in Greece during the classical age and which philologists once thought to be due to successive waves of invasion. The dialect which predominated in north-western Greece, in central Greece to the west of Thessaly and Boeotia, in the isthmus of Corinth, in the Peloponnese with the exception of Arcadia, in Crete, Melos, Thera, Rhodes and the neighbouring islands of the Dodecanese was known as Doric. It appears that the invading Indo-Europeans or Achaeans first established themselves in the Argolid and from there spread to other parts of Greece.

In Attica and in the Aegean islands from Euboea to Miletus, Ionic was spoken. The Athenians believed that they were Ionians, descendants of Ion, and had not been affected by the Dorian invasion. Yet the dialect of Attica appears to have differed from pure Ionic and perhaps the traditional belief that the Ionian colonies were of Athenian origin should be re-examined.

Aeolic which with certain variations was prevalent in the northernmost part of continental Greece, in Thessaly, in Boeotia and in some islands of the Aegean such as Lesbos is considered to have originated in Thessaly.

The so-called Arcadian dialect was spoken in the heart of the Peloponnese on the Arcadian plateau and maintained its independence in spite of the fact that the plateau was surrounded by people of Dorian speech. A peculiar and puzzling offshoot of Arcadian is found in distant Cyprus. According to a theory once widely held, the Aeolic and Arcadian-Cypriot dialects had roots in a more ancient branch of the language, Achaean, brought into Greece by the Achaeans. But in fact we do not know which of the Achaeans or the Ionians was the first to appear in Greece, nor has the influence of either on the development of Greek been established. But we do know that during the Bronze Age the language spoken at Athens—as at Knossos, Mycenae and Pylos—was Greek, a tongue common to the whole of Mycenaean Greece which was first written during the Late Helladic age in the form of Linear B. [13]

We cannot be certain, however, whether all the inhabitants of Greece who spoke Greek at that time called themselves Greeks or rather Hellenes. Homer designated as Greeks only the men from Phthiotis who were led by Achilles in the Trojan war. Other members of the expedition he calls Danae, Argives and Achaeans. Writers in classical times knew the prehistoric inhabitants of Greece by different names according to where they lived; they called them Pelasgians in Thessaly, Attica and the Peloponnese, Leleges in Laconia, Messenia, Megara and Leucas, and Carians on the islands of the archipelago and on the shores of Asia Minor.

The word Hellene, or Greek, before it was used to designate people who spoke the Greek tongue, was the name of the legendary son of Deucalion and Pyrrha who reigned in Phthia in Thessaly about 1600. According to the myth, the bronze race of men owed its regeneration to Deucalion, son of Prometheus. Zeus had sent a flood which completely destroyed the human race except for Deucalion and his wife. When the waters subsided, the ark of Deucalion came to rest on the mountains of Thessaly. Thereupon Zeus commanded Deucalion and his wife to cast stones over their shoulders from which sprang a new race of men. After this, Hellen was born to them in the normal way.

Herodotus interprets this myth in geological terms to explain how the plain of Thessaly arose from the depths of Lake Boibeis and records a local tradition that the cleft in the Vale of Tempe which released the waters of the lake into the Aegean was caused by an earthquake. In the autumn of 1958, Vladimir Milojcic discovered in the lowest geological stratum of the Thessalian plain artifacts of the palaeolithic age together with remains of fauna and flora which had flourished in Thessaly before the cataclysmic upheaval mentioned by Herodotus and Apollodorus,[14] that is to say, 40,000 years before recorded history.

The myth goes on to describe how the earlier inhabitants of Thessaly had taken refuge on the surrounding mountains after the great flood and from among them Hellen chose a wife who bore him three sons, Dorus, Xuthus and Aeolus. The first was the patriarchal founder of the Dorians and the third of the Aeolians; from the two sons of the second stemmed the Achaeans and the Ionians.[15]

Greek mythology when it places the cradle of Greek civilization in Thessaly has been largely substantiated by the conclusions of modern archaeology. And it seems fairly certain that the ancestors of the Athenians were Pelasgians from Thessaly and that a definite link existed between prehistoric Athens and the earliest neolithic cultures centred in the Thessalian settlements of Sesclos and Dimini.

ART

THE OLDEST EXAMPLES of art so far discovered in Attica date from the earliest neolithic age and consist of pottery and figurines of the Sesclos type. The similarity in technique, shape and decoration of objects from every part of neolithic Greece in which they have been found forces us to the conclusion that Pelasgian potters everywhere came under a common influence emanating from Sesclos. We can therefore speak of a " Sesclian " or early age in neolithic Greece ending in 4900, just as later we shall speak of a " Diminian " or late age ending about 3200.

Neolithic objects were primarily functional; the pottery was intended for everyday domestic use and the figurines had a specific part to play in funerary and magical practices. But they must nevertheless be regarded as works of art because it is clear that the potters and sculptors who fashioned them were concerned with aesthetic as well as practical considerations. Their work shows a truly creative inventiveness in their search for new shapes, new decorative designs and new colours.

During the neolithic age, neither the settlement on the Acropolis nor other settlements in Attica had yet become originators in the field of the arts and crafts. Throughout the period they were dominated by the styles of Sesclos and Dimini. Excavations in neolithic Athens have brought to light a substantial quantity of ceramic remains and sherds, as well as four figurines which we shall discuss later. These give some idea of neolithic art in Attica, but to get a proper picture they must be looked at alongside the more complete finds from Sesclos and Dimini, now thoroughly restored and on display in the museums of Volos, Larissa and Athens.

Vases of the Sesclos age, with their thin walls, are made of pure clay mixed with sand, quartz dust or quartz chippings to withstand firing. The earliest are

3. The Propylaea, from
the north-east

24

Fig. 1. Two neolithic vases, *c.* 3000,
Agora Museum, Athens

monochromes and undecorated. They are cup-shaped, initially without either base or handles, and they have a single polished coating of red colour. The lips are thinner than the sides and turn slightly outwards. In a second stage, the vase becomes more complex, acquiring a ring-shaped base, handle and neck (Fig. 1). Alongside the monochrome variety, spotted vases in two colours appear, usually red and black. A third category is the incised vase: the patterns are cut while the clay is still damp with the finger-nail or some pointed object. These incisions are generally parallel, in horizontal, vertical or diagonal rows, and white or red colouring matter is poured into them to bring out the design against the natural colour of the baked clay. Painted pottery vases constitute a fourth type in which the decorative painting conditions the shape. The middle section of the vase is broadened to accommodate the design and is painted bright red so that the decorative motifs may stand out more clearly. The lines are straighter, more regular and more firmly drawn: diagonals converging to form angles (Pl. 22); horizontals extending round the neck, the middle and the base; and verticals meeting the horizontals to form steps, lattices and zigzags. Within this network of rhomboids, representative themes, animals or birds, stand out, stylized into geometrical shapes.

In the early neolithic age, statuettes or figurines representing male and female begin to appear. The female is usually depicted nude and erect—seated female figures are rare—with hands placed on the breasts. The large buttocks are steatopygous, symbolizing motherhood and fecundity, the neck is elongated (Pl. 23) and the hair falls in plaits over the shoulders. The male figures are also nude, but are usually seated. The neck is elongated and the face is treated with great freedom and variation in the modelling of the nose, the hair, the beard and the eyes.

Four interesting female statuettes come from prehistoric Athens and are the most ancient stone sculptures to have been found there. All four display the realistic style of early neolithic three-dimensional art. Of the first, a standing figure now in the Agora Museum, only the part from the waist to the knees has been preserved. The genital organs are incised with great definition and the buttocks are steatopygous. The second, also in the Agora Museum, is more unusual in that it represents a seated female and is one of the largest neolithic statuettes in existence. The head, the neck, the legs below the knees and the hands are missing. The chest is bent at an angle of ninety degrees to the thighs and the body is recumbent with the left knee sagging outwards, perhaps to allow the right foot to rest against the inside of the left thigh. The steatopygous buttocks and the generous curves of the thighs, the belly and the swelling breasts, all indicate pregnancy. The hands were probably crossed on the breast in the usual posture. Five stylized plaits of hair fall on to the shoulders and the incisions marking the position of the hair on the shoulders suggest that actual hair may originally have been attached to the head after the completion of the sculpture. This particular technique is commonly found in clay statuettes

4. The Temple of Athena Niké (427-404), from the west

27

from Sesclos. The third, now in the collection of the Ashmolean Museum in Oxford, is a marble statuette representing a mother with her child. It was found at Patissia, a suburb of Athens, and is also seated with legs crossed. The fourth (Pl. 23), in the Eleusis Museum, is made of Pentelic marble. It depicts the more common standing female, it is steatopygous like all early neolithic female figures and has the elongated neck of the Sesclos statuettes.

The art of making thin-walled pottery of the Sesclos type was lost in the later neolithic age. About the year 4900 a race of warriors who built large dwellings that presage the palaces of Homeric times appeared in Greece and established fortified settlements in the region of Dimini. Dimini pottery is made of heavier, coarse-grained material and the walls of the vases become thicker as though to compensate for the quality of the clay. But the painting of vases in the Dimini period is enriched by new motifs composed of curves and helices and the drawings are picked out in great emphasis either in black and red on a creamy white background or in black and white on a red background. At the same time, although the technique of thin-walled pottery had been lost, the decorative style associated with it and its rectilinear motifs blended and combined with the new shapes and patterns.

Towards the end of the Dimini period, the black vases of Rachmani and Larissa appear, on which the designs are incised and picked out in white. Marble as well as clay is used for figurines and important changes take place in the manner of representing the two sexes. The female form becomes almost abstract, pointing the way to the violin-shaped figures of the Cyclades, while the male is pronouncedly phallic. Phallicism survived into classical Athenian art and Herodotus tells us that it was a legacy from the Pelasgians.

The tendency towards complete abstraction proceeded even further in Early Helladic sculpture (2500-1900): heads with elongated necks become little more than clay or marble wedges, decorated with incised geometric motifs which symbolize rather than represent the eyes, the mouth or the nose. The bodies lose all distinguishing characteristics and turn into pedestals or the bases of columns.

Early Helladic ceramic work appears sporadically in Athens, at Marathon, at Brauron, at Keratsini and in Aegina: many exceptionally fine examples from Hagios Kosmas and from the Ascetarium at Rafina were discovered and studied, the former by Professor Mylonas, the latter by Dr Theocharis.[16] The lower Early Helladic strata produced monochrome vases coated with a thick layer of red colour, very highly polished, but made of coarse clay clumsily and imperfectly baked. In vases found in the upper (later) strata, the technique of polished coating is replaced by a new polishing technique called *Urfirnis* (primitive lustre ware) and the shape known as the "sauce-boat" makes its appearance. The sauce-boat represents the highest form attained by Early Helladic vase-making. The deep single-handled jugs of this type were seated on ringed bases and coated in reddish-yellow paint which was polished with an aqueous substance. The clay is very

Fig. 2. "Sauceboat„ beaker, *c.* 3000 - 2000, *National Museum, Athens*

pure, the walls thin and fine, the baking good throughout, and the shapes are uniformly full of movement and grace. The beaked jug or "sauce-boat" of Attica (Fig. 2) is the first sign of the refinement which was to characterize later Athenian art.

The Early Helladic age which had begun about 2500 and ended in about 1900 was interrupted by the invasion of the Minyans who destroyed the settlements and centres which had created the art described above. But an even more radical change was the replacement of polished stone by bronze as the basic material for tools and weapons. The beginning of the second millenium in Attica, as in the whole of Greece and the eastern Mediterranean, witnessed the birth of a new civilization which was to reach its height in the Mycenaean age.

THE FORMATION OF THE CITY-STATE

WHEN WE SPEAK of ancient Athens, we think at once of the Acropolis as it is today and of the monuments of the classical age which are preserved there: the Propylaea, the Parthenon, the Erechtheum and the Temple of Athena Nikê. These monuments represent Athenian society at its zenith, but it must be remembered that they were built about seven centuries after the founding of the city-state of Athens.

Thucydides marks the birth of the Athenian state when Theseus founded the Agora, or market-place, and the Prytaneum, the seat of the federated settlements of Attica which made up the city of Athens. The sacred flame which burned eternally on the hearth of the Prytaneum symbolized the determination of the citizens to live thenceforth under common laws, with a common ethical code, in a unified community which would serve the best interests of all its members.

Up to that time political unity of this type did not exist. Attica consisted of widely scattered farming settlements and demes or townships with independent administrative centres, prytanea and assemblies which often fought among themselves. During the Late Helladic period, from about 1580 to 1425, the first kings to establish themselves on the Acropolis, Actaeus, Cecrops and Erysichthon, struggled to fuse these separate elements into a single community. But traditionally the formation of the Athenian state did not finally take place until the reign of Theseus in the middle of the thirteenth century.

It was then that the plateau on the top of the rock of the Acropolis was made level and surrounded (1300-1225) by cyclopean walls similar to those built at approximately the same period at Mycenae and Tiryns. The cyclopean system of construction originated apparently with the Hittites who had fortified their capital Hatousa (Boyazkioy) in this fashion. And it has been suggested that the name of cyclops is due to the large round eyes of stone-masons from the east who had brought the technique of building walls of this type to Greece. The cyclopean system was first used at Mycenae and Tiryns, later on the acropolis of Gla in Boeotia which is the most extensive acropolis of the Mycenaean period, measuring some 3000 yards long, and lastly on the Athenian Acropolis.

With the establishment of the Agora, the Prytaneum and the hearth of the commune of Theseus, the walls, the palace, the dwellings and the graves on the Acropolis, Athens emerged in Mycenaean times as a city-state ready to play its role in history.

Early Athens was one of a group of kingdoms in which the civilization known as Mycenaean developed in succession to the Minoan civilization of Crete. The cyclopean walls of the Acropolis are by no means the only evidence which establishes the connection between Athens and other centres of Mycenaean culture, notably Mycenae and Tiryns. The similarity of grave construction and burial customs, as well as of vases, statuettes, trinkets and weapons, all prove that Athens was part of the Mycenaean world (Pls. 27 and 32). In the heroic myth of Erichthonius we can trace the sources of classical religion back to their Mycenaean and Minoan origin; and in that of Theseus we can glimpse the part played by Athens in the struggles of the Mycenaean-Achaeans against the Minoans for control of the Mediterranean sea-routes and for commercial and political supremacy in the Middle East.

Evidence drawn from archaeological and mythological sources has recently been supplemented by historical evidence derived from inscriptions in Linear B. These provide a great deal of information about the way in which Mycenaean kingdoms were organized in the age when Athens was evolving politically along Mycenaean lines. The history of early Athens can therefore be more fully grasped now that we know so much more about Mycenaean institutions.

Mycenaean civilization was not born in a vacuum. It arose as an offshoot of civilizations which had developed in Crete and in the Cyclades. Both these had mastered the working of copper and bronze as well as other handicrafts and their skills, knowledge and ideas had gradually spread throughout the Aegean. The influence of Minoan (Cretan) and Cycladic civilization can be discerned in the religion and myths of Athens as well as in her political and artistic achievements. Most of the Olympian gods reached Athens from Crete. The Eleusinian mysteries were first enacted in the mountain caverns of Crete and are associated with the melting of bronze. The legend of Theseus which is discussed more fully on pp. 56-65 recounts in heroic terms the struggle of the Athenians to free themselves from the blood-levy exacted each year by the Cretans. The first palaces to appear on Hellenic soil, the first wheels, the first vases of baked clay, the first frescoes, all originated from Crete. And finally, the Minoans were the first to achieve maritime supremacy in the Mediterranean and this tradition of " thalassocracy " as it is called (*thalassa* in Greek means sea) was taken up in turn by the Achaeans, the Ionians, the Aeginetans and, in the fifth century, the Athenians.

THE AGE OF BRONZE

THE SECOND MILLENIUM began with the introduction of bronze into the Aegean brought by the Minyans and ended with the invasions of the Dorians and the destruction of the strongholds of Mycenaean civilization in Greece. Thessaly had ceased to be the centre of activity as it had been in neolithic times and civilization had shifted to the Cyclades, Crete and the Argolid. We distinguish the three types of civilization which developed in these areas as Cycladic (in the islands of the Aegean archipelago), Minoan (in Crete) and Helladic (in mainland Greece).

Sir Arthur Evans[17], whose work in Crete gave a new impetus to the archaeology of prehistoric Greece after Schliemann's great discoveries at Troy and in Greece, proposed a division of the Bronze Age into three periods corresponding to the chronology of the Old, Middle and New Kingdoms of Egypt. Thus in his system, the first period of the Bronze Age, lasting from 2500 to 1900 was called Early Minoan in Crete, Early Cycladic in the Cyclades and Early Helladic in mainland Greece; the second (1900-1580), Middle Minoan, Middle Cycladic and Middle Helladic respectively; and the third period (1580-1100), Late Minoan, Late Cycladic and Late Helladic. Each of these periods was further subdivided into three shorter periods indicated by a Roman numeral I, II or III placed after the initial letters of the period; for example EH I stood for the first third of the Early Helladic period.

With some reservations, notably in the limits of the Minoan periods, scholars have accepted Evans's system. It provided a useful framework in spite of the many modifications which have had to be made to it. The divisions and subdivisions offered archaeologists a convenient method of classifying their finds whose age was determined by the stratum of the soil in which they were unearthed, the material of which they were made, the type of object to which they belonged, their decorative motifs, and lastly their shape.

Early Minoan in Crete is somewhat earlier than Early Helladic and Early Cycladic and begins about 3000. Middle Minoan, beginning in 2200 is likewise earlier for it is the period when Crete played an important part in spreading the use of copper and bronze in the Mediterranean world. It had also traded in metal during the third millenium, although metal was also worked at Troy, at Thermae in Lesbos and at Poliochne in Lemnos from an early date.

THE CYCLADES

ARCHAEOLOGISTS believe that the use of metal was discovered in the plateau of the Caucasus whence it spread to Greece by two routes: one through Troy and Thrace to Macedonia, the other through the Cyclades to Crete, the Peloponnese and central Greece. Excavations at Thermae II in Lesbos and at Hissarlik (Troy II) show that the introduction of metal occurred more or less simultaneously in the Aegean and on the northern coast of Asia Minor.

At Dimini in Thessaly there is an Early Helladic palace which with its large throne room and circular hearth resembles that of Troy II. The examples of goldsmith's work and of bronze casting were found in these two palaces, together with closed kilns for pottery work and evidence of the use of the wheel.

Both the use of metal and the technique of making the older types of vase—those known as " sauce-boats " with beaked mouthpieces and ringed bases as well as the highly polished type (*Urfirnis*)—come from the east. But it is on the island of Scyros in the Cyclades that the spiral motif appears for the first time. It is also encountered at Dimini, but was unknown in Crete until the end of Early Minoan III.

The Cycladic room in the Athens Museum contains the first Greek sculptures in white island marble as well as ceramics of the same period from Scyros, Siphnos, Andros, Melos, Amorgos, Paros, Naxos and other islands. The visitor can follow the development of Cycladic sculpture from the two-dimensional forms of the mother idols in white Parian marble with their simple, nearly abstract shapes to the three-dimensional, truly sculptural figures of the Seated Harpist, the statuette of the naked flute-player and the male heads from Amorgos which are as polished and rounded as pebbles from the beach.

New types of pottery decorated with incised motifs appear in the Cyclades: the " frying pans " of Scyros and the vases of Melos with dark on light decorations. We meet in Cycladic art the first representations of stylized human figures and of boats propelled by oars. It was in boats like these with their high prow and single oar to steer by that the corsairs of the Cyclades sailed forth on their marauding expeditions.

Cycladic styles in sculpture and ceramics spread to the Peloponnese and central Greece. The marble statuette discovered on the Acropolis and the finds from Early Helladic settlements in Attica, now in the Athens Museum (Fig. 3), all bear traces of Cycladic influence.

Fig. 3. Torso of (?) a Cycladic marble figurine, *National Museum, Athens*

THE SHIPS of the Cyclades were too small to venture out on the open seas, but the Minoans who built the first large vessels in the Mediterranean were able to cover great distances and thereby to link the centres of metal production with the metal markets. Situated at the crossroads of Europe, Africa and Asia, Crete became the dominant naval power at a period when the use of metal was beginning to spread and develop in the three continents of the ancient world.

The Minoan royal dynasties appear to have been descendants of the rulers of Troy II which according to Professor Blegen was destroyed in about 2300 and the first great palaces of the king-priests of Crete, roundw hich the cities of Knossos, Phaestos and Mallia grew, were built during the Middle Minoan period (2000-1700). The high level of civilization attained by the Minoans is shown by the fact that they used the potter's wheel and the kiln, built four-wheeled chariots and had learnt the art of writing—Linear Script A which has not yet been deciphered.

The influence of Early Minoan civilization spread far and wide by ship or by merchant caravan to Cyprus, the Syrian coast, Egypt, Mesopotamia, the plateau of Iran and the valleys of India. The discovery in Crete of many Egyptian scarabs and statuettes made of diorite and of numerous Cretan vases in Egypt confirms that trade relations existed between Crete and Egypt.[18] The Cretans whom the Egyptians called *Keftiu* probably learned the art of wall painting and the firing of clay in the workshops of the Nile valley. A strong Cretan influence may be discerned in wall paintings of the eighteenth dynasty at Tel el Amarna (1350-14).

Contacts between Crete and Mesopotamia are shown by the architecture of the mass burial tombs of Messara whose circular shape recalls their Mesopotamian origin.

A recent theory[19] based on certain affinities between the neolithic pottery of Crete and vases found on the eastern coasts of the Mediterranean, principally in Syria, suggests that even as early as neolithic times trade relations existed between Crete and the neighbouring coasts. This theory gained strength from the results of a dig carried out in 1960 by archaeologists of the British School at Athens in the neolithic strata of Knossos. Besides the numerous hand querns used to grind wheat, they also found two bone ladles similar to some which had been unearthed in neolithic strata in Asia Minor. A few pieces of malachite and azurite came to light which could only have been of Asiatic origin and the diggers observed certain similarities in ceramic objects.[20] As a result of these discoveries archaeologists are now convinced that the first builders of Knossos reached Crete from the coast of Asia Minor.

Tha palaces and settlements of central Crete were rebuilt during the Middle Minoan period after their destruction in 1700, apparently by earthquake and fire. Among the new buildings some palaces built on a comparatively smaller scale have been found which may have been residences of officials at the Minoan court. In its turn this second stage of Minoan civilization was destroyed in about 1500 and Professor Marinatos connects the catastrophe which brought it to an end with the seismic upheavals of Theara.

It has always been difficult to distinguish Late Minoan (LM II and III) Cretan history (1450-1100) from Mycenaean, not only because the art forms present such marked similarities—the most significant works of sculpture and painting of this period are in the Heracleion museum—but also because by the middle of the Late Minoan period (1400-1100) Linear B had been taken into common use at Mycenae and Pylos as well as at Knossos.

5. The Temple of Athena Nikê, 'from the east

6. The Acropolis, from the Hill of the Muses

32

48685

48685

Now that Linear B has been deciphered, the dividing line between the history of Late Minoan Crete and that of Greece virtually disappears. Written records add their testimony to the silent evidence of archaeological remains on which scholars had previously had to depend in reconstructing the social, political and religious life of Late Minoan Crete. Many problems have been resolved and errors corrected. Some of these stemmed from the all-too human vanity of Sir Arthur Evans whose wish to enhance the importance of his discoveries led him to ascribe the objects found at Late Minoan Knossos to a period 200 years earlier than their true date. But a recent work,[21] based on a comparison of the clay tablets of Knossos with those of Pylos, has rectified the early dating of Evans and has shown that the so-called last palace of Minos at Knossos belongs to the Mycenaean age. The new system also makes it possible to accept the account in the *Iliad*[22] of the participation of Knossos in the Trojan expedition with eighty ships under the command of Idomeneus and Meriones which took place in about 1200.

Considering the important role played by Crete in the eastern Mediterranean during the Bronze Age, Herodotus and Thucydides give surprisingly little information about it. But it must be remembered that the Greeks of the classical age knew far less about Crete than we do today; for them Minos, Daedalus, Theseus and Ariadne were simply characters from picturesque legends of prehistoric date. It was only at the beginning of this century, when the spade of Evans brought the labyrinth to light, that scholars started to entertain the notion that these legends might be founded on historical fact. Archaeologists were quick to appreciate the significance of Evans's work and they began exploring every part of the island. The palaces of Phaestos, Hagia Triada and Mallia supplemented or corroborated the information unearthed at Knossos and soon the traces of one Minoan city after another were uncovered and studied.

In primitive societies clans often claimed descent from an animal which was deemed to be at once benevolent and fearsome and by whose name the clan was known. At a later stage in its development when the clan invested its power in the person of a king-priest, it also passed on the name and magical powers of its totemic ancestor. Cretan society appears to have conformed to this type for we know that the Minoan kings of Knossos, like the pharaohs of Egypt who were descended from a falcon, claimed to be the heirs of a bull, the Minotaur. The blood of the sacred beast was thought in animal-worshipping societies to reside in the female bosom, for it was women who transfused it from the sacred body of their mythical husband to the human body of their offspring. Cretan society had begun as a matriarchy. Among his few references to Crete, Herodotus tells us that Cretan children took their names from their mothers and traced their descent through maternal lineage. It appears that the communal banquets held by the men, women and children of the Cretan clan of Caunia had their origin in the ancient totemic dinners of the clan.[23]

THE MYCENAEANS

EVANS'S EXCITEMENT at the discovery of Knossos led him seriously to underrate Mycenae and the Achaeans of the Argolid. However, the work of John Papadimitriou who between 1951 and 1953 discovered a second cycle of shaft tombs outside the walls of Myceanae, earlier in date than the cycle found by Schliemann and Stamatakis (1876-7) within the Mycenaean acropolis, has redressed the balance. It showed that the Achaeans of Mycenae had as early as the seventeenth century created an original culture older than the Mycenaean culture of the

7. The Parthenon, north façade

37

tholos tombs and the Minoan culture of last Knossos. It is therefore impossible to regard Mycenaean civilization as the work of Minoans of the Late Minoan period.

Furthermore, to account for traces of destruction which he had noticed in the Cretan palaces of the fifteenth century, Evans proposed the theory that a " new dynasty of aggressive character " had seized power in 1450, had destroyed Phaestos and Hagia Triada and had imposed its rule over the whole of Crete. This oppressive dynasty was in turn overthrown by the Minoan people in 1400 and the palace of Knossos was destroyed in the process. In Evans's view, the Achaeans of Mycenae can have played no part in these upheavals, for they arrived in Crete a full century later.

Alan Wace rejected this theory with convincing archaeological arguments. He drew attention to the many similarities between Knossos and the Argolid of the Achaeans before Late Minoan II. These can be seen, for example, in the separate throne-chamber at Knossos, something quite unknown in the rest of Crete, but of which there are examples in the palaces of Mycenae, Tiryns and Pylos; in the fluted column, like those at Pylos and Mycenae; in the type of tholos tomb which originated in Mycenae; in vases with dark patterns on a light background found at Knossos among ceramics of clearly Cretan origin; and in the new writing of Linear B which had displaced Minoan Script A in the palace of Knossos. This last piece of evidence is of particular interest because the writing on the tables which Blegen and Koutouniotis found in 1939 at Pylos and those which Wace found in 1952 in buildings outside the walls of Mycenae is Linear B, as is the script used on the inscribed Mycenaean vases of Tiryns, Orchomenus, Thebes and Eleusis (Pl. 26).

Thus Evans's theory has been discarded in favour of Wace's, for the latter not only offers a satisfactory explanation of the presence of Mycenaean influence on the architecture, vase decoration and painting at Knossos; but it can also be made to account for the destruction of the palace of Knossos in 1400, for it was against Mycenaean overlords that the Cretans were in revolt.[24]

The moving story of how the late Michael Ventris finally succeeded in reading Linear B has been told by his colleague John Chadwick and together they have summarized their conclusions in another important work which appeared under their joint authorship.[13] The deciphering of Linear B is not only of importance to philologists in that it has enabled them to study the archaic form of the Greek language, but it also permits us to understand the social structure, the institutions and the economy prevalent in Mycenae, Tiryns, Pylos, Knossos, Athens and all other centres within the orbit of Mycenaean civilization.

In 1150 or thereabouts, on the eve of the destruction of Pylos by the Dorians, Chadwick observed that a sinister atmosphere of uneasiness and foreboding pervaded the city. The tablets contain many references to troop movements, to the departure of ships from Pylos to Pleuron in Aetolia, to the formation of special guards and sentry-posts along the coast; some even list the names of the commanders (or *hepetai*) of the varous military units. These officers belonged to the household of the king (*wanax*) and performed liaison duties between the guard units and headquarters, using chariots to move from place to place. But these military preparations were not enough to resist the invaders and to prevent the destruction of Pylos which, unlike Mycenae, Tiryns and Athens, had no acropolis fortified by cyclopean walls.

Light fast chariots were not only used in Pylos but also in Cretan and other Mycenaean cities, as their paintings show. They carried two men and were drawn by a pair of horses. They were used in peace as well as war and a wall painting of Tiryns shows a chariot being driven by two women (Fig. 5, p. 45).

The armour of the Mycenaeans is listed on the Knossos and Pylos tablets. It appears to have been made of hides or skins, sometimes decorated with boars' teeth like the helmets in the Mycenaean room in the Athens Museum. The warriors wore visors called *pariai* and a breast plate or *thorax* consisting of thirty or more plates, made perhaps of metal. Their shoulders and arms were covered by the *epomia* to which various protective appendages were attached. They were armed with spears with bronze heads and wooden shafts, broad two-edged swords (*phasgana*), narrow-bladed swords (*xiphoi*) and long arrows. No mention of greaves or shields has been discovered on tablets so far studied: this is curious because we know from Homer as well as from excavations in Cyprus that the Achaeans used them in battle.

The form of government at both Knossos and Pylos was monarchical and it seems likely that Mycenae was a monarchy of the same type too. The supreme ruler was known as the *wanax*, a title which belonged also to the gods. The rank of *basileus* was inferior to that of *wanax* and carried only local importance. The administration was carried on by a powerful and well-developed bureaucracy and by a military organization under the control of a commander-in-chief called the *lawagetas*. Only the *wanax* and the *lawagetas* had the right to keep personal households and to possess landed estates which were known as *temenoi*.

The great landowners constituted an important and powerful social class and are referred to in the tablets as the *tereta* which corresponds, probably, to the *telestai* of the classical period. Palmer compares them to barons in feudal times, but Chadwick feels that their function was more likely to have been religious. Ownership of land existed in two forms: the communal domain known as the *kekemena* and the private domain known as the *ktimena*. Land was measured as in Babylon by the quantity of seed required for sowing and not by its actual area.

Every settlement or township was administered by a kind of mayor, the *ko-re-te*, and at one time possessed a kind of council of elders referred to as the *gerousia*. The lowest social class consisted of slaves—men, women and children—who were recruited to the administrative centre from distant colonies, from the slave markets of the east and from prisoners of war.

Division of labour had progressed quite far and agriculture, the rearing of live-stock, the timber trade and various artisan activities were all separate occupa-pations. The carding, spinning, weaving, bleaching and sewing of woollen stuffs were done by women. Men worked as carpenters, masons, shipwrights, caulkers, bronze-smiths, gold- and silversmiths, bow-makers, jewellers, perfumiers or potters. At Pylos there is even mention of a doctor in practice. In the list of occupations that of scribe does not appear, but scribes must have existed as specialized workers since all the data we possess on the organization and functioning of Mycenaean society were recorded by them.

Neither copper, tin nor gold were mined in Greece and they may well have been acquired by piracy and plundering, although Professor Marinatos believes that Mycenae obtained its gold in a more legitimate manner. He has suggested that the Egyptians paid the Achaeans in gold for military assistance in their war of independence against the Hyksos. He bases his theory on the presence of Egyptian influence in the funerary habits of the Mycenaeans: the large burial chambers and the objects found in the tombs which include weapons, jewelry, trinkets and utensils; the rudimentary process of embalming and the covering of the faces of the dead with gold masks and of their bodies with gold leaf.

Coinage was unknown in the Mycenaean age (it did not come into use until the seventh century), nor was any other commodity regularly used as a standard of value. The absence of transactions involving payment in the official records can be accounted for by the one-sided character of such transactions in a primitive monarchical society: the monarch levied taxes from his subjects, but was under no obligation to make payments in return. The tax liability of the subject was assessed by the number of head of sheep or cattle he possessed and the taxpayer preferred to make payment in the form of male animals since they were less useful for the increase of his herds. The large number of herds indicates how vital was the role played by animal husbandry in the economy of Mycenaean society.

Most of the gods of the classical age have been identified in one form or another in the Mycenaean tablets: Zeus, Hera, Poseidon, Hermes, Athena, Artemis, Paian-Apollo, Enyalios-Ares, Eileithyia. Aphrodite is missing, perhaps because her cult was not introduced from Cyprus until a later date. The word *Dionysoio* particularly interested scholars because of its resemblance to the Greek Dionysus.

The name *Damate*, found in a text at Pylos, has presented certain difficulties which the Mycenaean ivory group (Fig. 4) of two goddesses standing guard over a small child may help to clear up. Charles Picard claims that it represents the theme of the famous relief of Eleusis which depicts Demeter, Persephone and Triptolemus (Pl. 96). If he is right, it follows that Demeter was known in Mycenaean times and that Damate may be identified with her. But perhaps the most interesting name to have been found is that of *Potnia* which occurs in a dedication at Knossos. Potnia was the mother-goddess of the Greeks who tamed the snakes in Crete and the wild beasts in Greece and was represented in the classical era by Demeter.[25]

The Mycenaean tablets do not record dates; they give the names of months but refer to years only in relative terms, such as this year, last year, or next year. The problem of dating finds is therefore not one which the philologist can help the archaeologist to solve.

The Mycenaeans, or Achaeans as Homer calls them, established an aristocracy based on the private ownership of land in the territories which they had conquered from the Pelasgians. Before their descent into Greece, their ancestors had learned in their native steppes to domesticate and ride horses, a skill unknown to the neolithic and Early Helladic inhabitants. The horse appeared with the civilization of Troy VI, built about 1900. The light chariot, drawn by two trained horses and large enough to accommodate a driver and two warriors, reached Mycenaean Greece from the east much later, about 1600. A funeral stele from Mycenae executed some time between 1580 and 1500 depicts a warrior standing

Fig. 4. Ivory trio from Mycenae, *National Museum, Athens*

40

in a racing chariot. It was introduced in turn from the Argolid into Crete during
Late Minoan I (1580-1450) and became a theme of religious art.

It appears that the high reputation for horses and woven fabrics acquired by
the Troy (VII) of Priam aroused the cupidity of the Achaeans, for it provided
one of the motives for their expedition under Agamemnon. In much the same
way, the fame of the Golden Fleece of Colchis had earlier inspired the Mycenaean
expedition of the Argonauts under Jason of Iolcus [26] which is described in the
poems of Apollonius of Rhodes and Apollodorus. An epic of the Argonauts existed
in a form which has not come down to us before the *Odyssey* was composed, for
the latter bears traces of its influence.

When the ancestors of the Achaeans descended into Greece, they were organized
into clans, each with its own leader. For a long period the clans retained their
traditions of communal land ownership, even after they had changed from a nomadic to a settled mode of existence. They continued the habit of communal
meals which were supposed to perpetuate their blood kinship derived from a
mythical common ancestry. They drank milk from the same vessel and ate from
a communal dish. The clan was like a single family unit and had religious, economic and political cohesion. It administered its own unwritten law and chose its
own judges and leaders. The farms, pasture lands, olive orchards, vineyards,
altars and tombs all belonged to the clan collectively and this communal property,
the *kekemena* of the later clay tablets, was handed down from generation to generation undivided. The unity of the clan appears even in the working of its unwritten
penal code by which guilt for a felony or a crime was shared by all members of
the clan, as were penalties, obligations or punishments which the code prescribed.
When a doubt subsisted the clan would appeal to the gods for judgment and
their decision, transmitted by the judges, was absolute and irrevocable. A verdict
of guilty in such circumstances entailed a sentence of *atimia;* that is to say, the
clan would " excommunicate " the offender by withdrawing its protection and
goods. This amounted to expulsion from the clan and in most cases must have
resulted in death.[27]

We have discussed earlier the change that had taken place by the time of the
tablets; how out of the primitive clan structure described above had emerged the
political, military and religious hierarchies of the Mycenaean monarchy and how
within the framework of communal land ownership an aristocratic class had grown
up based on the private ownership of land. The pattern was further modified
by the growth of small manufacture and commerce which took place in the Aegean
during the Bronze Age. Alongside the agrarian aristocracy, a new class arose
which derived its livelihood from the practice of these new occupations. Its
members no longer lived in the countryside among the farmers or on the acropolis
where the palace and the residences of the leaders were located. They established
themselves in communities that possessed no walls or citadels and which were sited
at the crossroads of commerce between the farmlands, the coast and the acropolis.
These communities eventually coalesced to form the *asty* whose focal point was
the agora or market-place. Thus the residences of the nobility, the walls and the
immediate perimeter outside the walls constituted the *polis* proper whilst the *asty*
or citizen body was centred round the agora.

The struggle which inevitably took place between the *polis* and the *asty* was
destined to become the driving force in the political evolution of Athens from
a monarchy of Mycenaean type to the democracy of the classical age.

The Athenian *asty* appears with its first agora during the final phase of the
Mycenaean period, in the thirteenth century. It was part of the policy of Theseus
to concentrate as many of the inhabitants of Attica as possible into one deme or
township so that they could hold assemblies more readily and in order to put

an end to the " phratricide " and strife that so often occurred between the widely scattered settlements and communities. Thucydides and Plutarch both describe how Theseus visited the various demes and clans of Attica to persuade them to move to Athens while continuing to exploit their land holdings. The poorer people fell in readily with his wishes, but the rich and powerful would do so only after he had promised them a form of government without a king, in which he reserved to himself only the right of declaring war and administering justice. He then set about putting his programme into practice: he abolished all the prytanea, the *bouleteria* (assemblies) and administrative bodies of the various individual demes and set up the Athenian *Asty* with a single prytaneum and a single assembly for all citizens. He called the new city he had founded Athens and he established a religious ritual, the *Synoekia*, to commemorate the creation of his commune. The Agora of Theseus, of which the most important building was the Prytaneum with its hearth and eternal flame, was founded at the same period as the building of the cyclopean walls of the Acropolis.[28]

It is significant that no trace of an agora has been found in Mycenae and Tiryns, but that on the acropolis of both cities foundations of royal palaces have been uncovered. This is in marked contrast with Athens where in spite of certain indications (*see* p. 48) no definite evidence of a palace has yet come to light, though it seems certain that during the Mycenaean period one must have existed there. Mycenaean palaces differed considerably from those of Crete (Plan 1). There was first of all no courtyard dividing the buildings into two sections,

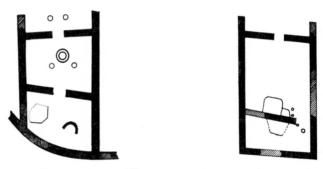

Plan 1. TWO TYPES OF THESSALIAN II MEGARON FROM DIMINI

public and private. Instead, before the main façade, there was a portico with a door between two central columns. The *prodomus* or vestibule led to the main body of the *megaron* which as a rule consisted of a large square chamber dominated by a circular hearth in the centre. The hearth had a base and a grating, very much like the hearths of the Byzantine monasteries of Greece. The altars of the classical Erechtheum on the Acropolis which were used for sacrificial purposes were a survival of this Mycenaean type of hearth and a forerunner of the Roman *arula* (from the Latin *ara* meaning grate, hearth or altar). The Byzantine *photanama* or hearth probably developed from the *arula*. The circular hearths at Mycenae, Tiryns and Pylos were surrounded by four pillars which supported the roof. All the palaces faced south as did the neolithic palaces of Thessaly.[29]

The king's throne was placed opposite the hearth and the walls of the throne chamber were decorated with painted friezes depicting scenes of hunting and battle. Fragments only of wall paintings from Mycenae, Tiryns, Thebes, Pylos and Orchomenus have survived, all executed during Late Mycenaean III (1425-1300). From them we learn that women took part in hunting in two-wheeled

8. The Parthenon, from the east

42

chariots (Fig. 5), that men used a lance (but not a helmet) to kill wild boar, that single combat and chariot battles played a decisive part in siege warfare much sa Homer says, and that demons and fantastic monsters were frequent spectators of the military and hunting exploits of the Mycenaean warriors. These wall paintings in which the faces and legs of the figures are shown in profile while the eyes and bodies are painted front view show that Mycenaean artists were more preoccupied with the decorative interplay of blue with red and ochre and with the general composition of their work than with expressing in realistic terms the tragedies which disturbed the lives of the inhabitants of these palaces.

Had we never read the plays which the ancient tragedians set in these palaces and were we to try and visualize Mycenaean society solely from the brilliant works of art which have survived—the wall paintings, the vase decorations, the gold cups, the inlaid daggers—we would see it quite differently from the sombre and fate-ridden picture created by the tragic poets of the classical age. Perhaps life in Mycenaean times lay somewhere in between these two extremes.

Monumental stone sculpture, destined to play such a dominant role in Athenian art, appeared first at Mycenae. The columns of the royal tombs are carved in relief and the monolithic lintel of the gateway to the Mycenaean acropolis supports a triangular pediment decorated with two huge lions. In the centre of this latter composition, a Minoan pillar is set on a triglyph base. To the right and left, two lions are poised erect with their forelegs resting on the base of the pillar and their heads level with the capital. The whole work has balance and power and is perfectly adapted to the architecture of the pediment which is here to serve two purposes: to lighten the load of the lintel which has to support the full weight of the cyclopean structure and to decorate the façade of the gateway with the heraldic emblem of the royal house of Mycenae. Just as the kings of Knossos were descended from a sacred bull, so at Mycenae lions were the mythical progenitors of the royal line.

The Lion Gate, the cyclopean walls made of huge blocks of hard local stone, the cluster of buildings round the palace, the tunnels in the walls, the subterranean spring hewn out of the rock—only at Mycenae and at Athens has a water-supply system been found on the acropolis—, all are impressive achievements; but most impressive of all are the tholos tombs discovered outside the walls of the acropolis. The best preserved examples are the famous Treasury of Atreus and the Tomb of Clytemnestra. The former has a striking stone vault, conical in shape and originally richly decorated on the inside face with bronze and gold plaques and rosettes. It is forty-seven feet in diameter and more than forty-two feet high. The monolithic lintel over the gateway is twenty-four feet long, over sixteen feet thick and just over three feet high; it weighs 100 tons. The façade of the vault gives the deceptive impression of being that of a two-storied building and is decorated with carved panels of red porphyry and alabaster. A passage-way 117 feet long, cut into the side of the hill along the axis of the gateway and lined on either side with identical walls made of worked blocks of stone, connects the facade with the entrance.

Of all the cities of the Mycenaean age, Mycenae itself holds the greatest fascination because of the astonishing treasures (Fig. 6, p. 46) found in its tombs by archaeologists from Schliemann onwards, visible evidence of its legendary wealth. It was also from the palace at Mycenae that Agamennon set forth to the Trojan war to take command of the Greek host. It was also the scene of his return and tragic death which have excited the imagination of poets of every age and provided the theme and the characters for some of the most moving tragedies of Aeschylus, Sophocles and Euripides. The history of Mycenae provided the poets and artists of Athens with an inexhaustible source of inspiration.

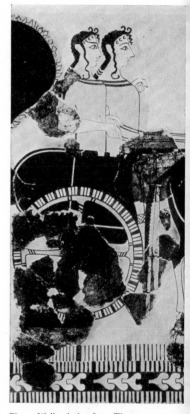

Fig. 5. Wall-painting from Tiryns (detail), *National Museum, Athens*

9. The Erechtheum (421-407), from the west

45

THE MYCENAEAN type of monarchy was the final stage of an historical development started by migratory peoples who had entered Greece, the islands and Asia Minor at the beginning of the second millenium. The destruction of Early Helladic centres such as Orchomenus in Boeotia interrupted the normal transition from Early to Middle Helladic civilization. The invaders who first settled in Orchomenus and then moved on to occupy the islands as well were called Minyans by Schliemann. The Minyans can be identified by their pottery of which the distinguishing features are the colour and the fact that it was shaped either in moulds or on the potter's wheel and baked in kilns. The monochrome grey colour was an attempt to imitate silverware and the outside surface to which the pigment was applied is so smooth and highly polished that the vases do indeed give the impression of being made of silver. Meanwhile the continued existence of the old unpolished Helladic and Cycladic vases is an indication that the earlier industry—stemming from neolithic times—had survived alongside the new industry of the Minyans.

The break caused by these migratory movements can be observed on the Acropolis of Athens if one compares Early Helladic with late Middle Helladic finds. This is the only hiatus to have occurred in the history of the Athenian Acropolis from neolithic times onwards; after the late Middle Helladic period, activity in the arts and crafts proceeded without interruption and fostered in the Athenians the belief that they were an indigenous race.

Another innovation introduced into Greece by the ancestors of the Achaeans was the interment of the dead within their dwellings or within the walls of their acropolis. The oldest Achaean graves found at Mycenae within the confines of the acropolis itself (five by Schliemann in 1876 and one by Stamatakis in 1877) were shaft graves sited in a circular compound. Apparently the wall of the acropolis which lies beyond these six graves is later in date, since its builders adapted its course so as not to disturb the sacred burial ground. Wace believed that these graves belong to an older royal family which he calls the " Shaft Grave Dynasty " and which Tsountas calls the " House of Danaus," in order to distinguish it from a later dynasty which built the tholos tombs and the many sculptured tombs beyond the walls and which Wace calls the " Tholos Tomb Dynasty " and Tsountas the " House of the Achaeans." [30]

According to Wace, the shaft tombs were built in the sixteenth century, that is during Late Helladic I (Mycenaean I, 1580-1500), the tholos tombs during Late Helladic II (Mycenaean II, 1500-1525) and the palace of Mycenae and the later tholos tombs during Late Helladic III (Mycenaean III, 1425-1100). During the last period Mycenae was fortified with cyclopean walls, the Lion Gate was built, the tholos tombs of Atreus and Clytemnestra were constructed, the palace was rebuilt (1250-1200) and the subterranean cistern was installed.

The Acropolis of Athens enters the cycle of Mycenaean civilization with the reign of Cecrops who according to a Parian marble inscription came to the throne about 1573. Thucydides informs us that before the settlement of Theseus the city of Athens was confined to the Acropolis with some dwellings extending to the southern slope. In later times the Athenians continued to regard the Acropolis as their city, for it had been the place of residence of their forefathers from the age of Cecrops onwards. Pausanias credits Cecrops with the introduction of the worship of Zeus and the founding of an altar to him at the entrance of the Erechtheum; he also says that he instituted the ritual offering of sweetmeats known as *pelanoi* in place of human sacrifice. Strabo tells us that Cecrops created an alliance of twelve cities, the Cecropia, to defend Attica against invasion by

Fig. 6. Mycenaean gold mask, *National Museum, Athens*

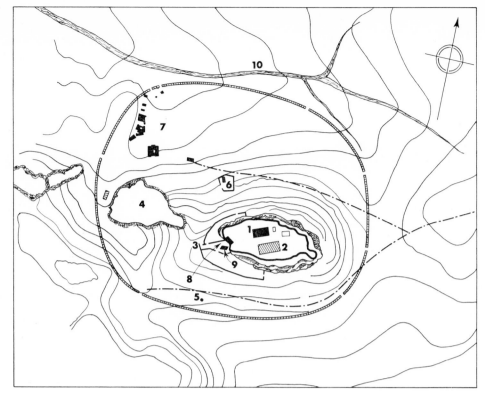

Map 3.   ACROPOLIS AND AGORA IN THE TIME OF SOLON

1 Old temple of Athena
2 Site of the Parthenon
3 Enneapylon
4 Areopagus
5 Temple of Nymph
6 Eleusinium
7 Agora
8 Mycenaean gateway
9 Mycenaean tower
10 Eridanus river

Carians from the sea and by Boeotians from the land.   Apollodorus records the story that Cecrops witnessed the planting of the olive by Athena on the Acropolis and says that his evidence in the judgment of the gods was instrumental in making Athena the protectress of Athens.

The grave of Cecrops was preserved until the fourth century B. C.   It was situated *within* the Acropolis at the south-west corner of the Erechtheum beneath the " Shelter of the Caryatides " and is mentioned in an inscription (known as the Chandler inscription) on a column of the Erechtheum.   George Mylonas [31] takes the view that this grave was a shaft tomb, contemporary with and similar to the sixteenth-century shaft tombs of Mycenae.   On the death of Cecrops' only son Erysichthon, the family of Cranaus succeeded to the throne.   One of Cranaus' daughters was called Atthis and it is from her that Attica derives its name.   The dynasty which followed was closely related to that of Cranaus and bore the name of its founder Amphictyon, Cranaus' son-in-law.

However in 1510 a revolution took place and a new dynasty started, founded by Erichthonius.   Erichthonius was not of Athenian origin.   Pausanias relates that he was not the offspring of mortals, but of Hephaestus and Mother Earth, which may be taken to mean that he was a foreigner.   Mylonas has advanced the theory that the accession of Erichthonius coincided with a change in Athenian burial customs, corresponding to the change which had occurred at Mycenae, and that thenceforth the Athenians interred their dead *outside* the walls of the Acropolis.   And this seems to be borne out by Shear's discovery in the Agora of a sculptured royal tomb.   Thus the Shaft Grave Dynasty at Mycenae appears to correspond to the dynasty of Cranaus at Athens and the Tholos Grave Dynasty to the royal house of Erichthonius.

The correspondence in date of the first dynasties of Mycenae and Athens, the resemblance of their burial customs and, later, the introduction of tholos tombs

47

into both Attica and Mycenae at the same period, taken in conjunction with the statement of Pausanias that Erichthonius was a foreigner, would seem to indicate that these changes were brought about by migratory tribes which had descended into Greece as far as the Argolid, seized power by force, expelled the previous kings whether these were members of the house of Cranaus or Danaus and established themselves in their place. Mylonas further believes that the new dynasties were Achaeans and Ionians.

To this new phase of the Mycenaean period belong the tholos tombs of Attica found at Menidi, Therikos, Eleusis and Spata which have some of the architectural features of the tholos graves of Mycenae. At Menidi and Spata, the passageway is uncovered like the Treasury of Atreus; at Eleusis and Thorikos it is covered. The burial chamber is circular at Menidi and Eleusis and eliptical at Thorikos, whereas Spata has a conical vault.

The only important remains which have come down from Mycenaean Athens are all on the Acropolis (Map 3, p. 47). They are few in number and poorly preserved, but they correspond closely with features at Mycenae and Tiryns [32] and suffice to give a clear picture of the Acropolis in Mycenaean times. Like Mycenae and Tiryns, the Acropolis was used as a place of habitation during the Late Helladic period (1580-1100) and was built on three times, in 1500, in 1300 and in 1225, but it appears to have acquired its walls somewhat later than them. In 1300 the Athenians copied their system of terraces, not for purposes of fortification, but to level off the rock, and it was not until 1250 that the Acropolis was entirely encircled by walls. These were of cyclopean type as at Mycenae and Tiryns and used the same advanced building techniques in their construction. The Athenians felt the need of fortifications for the same reasons which had prompted Mycenae and Tiryns to extend their defensive systems and to reinforce their older ramparts with towers. As the city prospered, it became more tempting to invaders and plunderers, as is borne out by the expedition of the Amazons during the reign of Theseus. Though later in date, the fortifications of the Acropolis did not fall short of their models; in many ways they surpassed them. The walls themselves were more like those of Tiryns than Mycenae, but the entrance which stood near the site of the later Temple of Nikê resembled the Lion Gate and even imitated its tower.

The Acropolis had a well within its ramparts, whereas the cistern of Perseia at Mycenae was only included within the defensive system by a special extension of the main walls. The construction of the steps leading down to the northern spring shows architectural skill equal to that of the builder of the Mycenaean cistern, not in the manner of working the natural rock since the Athenian steps were of wood, but in the management of the successive downward turns which descended to a very great depth within the dark cleft of the rock.

The cyclopean walls of the Acropolis were built of large blocks of stone worked in somewhat rudimentary fashion and fitted tightly together. The small gaps were filled with stones without the use of mortar or mud. At Tiryns and Mycenae the walls were hollow and contained tunnels which are one of the marvels of the stone architecture of antiquity.

A tower guarded the main entrance to the Acropolis just as at Mycenae, but there was another smaller entrance on its north-eastern flank. The palace, if there was one, must have been visible from the tower but only the base of a column of Mycenaean type and two large flagstones survive on the site where the Erechtheum now stands.

Below the top of the rock and on its north-western slope, remains of an outer defensive system can still be seen, although standing beyond the classical walls they are in a bad state of preservation. They once formed part of the famous

10. The Erechtheum, east porch. The Ionic order

48

"Pelargian" or "Pelasgian" Wall (*see* Map 3, p. 47) which completely encircled the Acropolis and communicated with the main defences only from the north-west. This outer ring was intended to prevent enemies from coming in close enough to use the caves at the base of the Acropolis as strongpoints during a siege and to provide protection for refugees from the outlying countryside; in its latter capacity it was much used during the Peloponnesian War. It was built at the same time as the main wall and had nine gateways. Perhaps an extension included the northern cistern and it may have stretched southwards as far as the site of the Roman theatre of Herodes Atticus.

It has been suggested [33] that the main purpose of the Pelasgian Wall was dictated by the nature of Mycenaean economy which was based on animal husbandry. As we have already seen from the tablets, herds and flocks constituted an important source of wealth and both in mythology and in Homer there are stories of raids and battles in which livestock are plundered. An outer defensive system was therefore extremely necessary to protect and preserve livestock in time of war.

ERICHTHONIUS

IF THE MYTHOLOGICAL ancestor of the kings was a bull at Knossos and a lion at Mycenae, at Athens it was a serpent. The gateway to the Acropolis which resembled the Lion Gate at Mycenae has not survived and the heraldic relief which adorned its pediment is lost. Nevertheless the sacred serpent found a place on the shield of Athena in the classical age and it continued to be worshipped at the Erechtheum which was built between 420 and 407. The Athenians regarded the "Domestic Serpent" as the guardian of their Acropolis and nourished it every month with offerings of sweetmeats. Herodotus relates that in September 480 the Athenians were convinced, when the sacred serpent of Erechtheus refused to touch its food, that Athena was expressing her wish that they should abandon the Acropolis to escape the Persian invaders.[34]

But what precisely was this serpent? In about A. D. 150 Pausanias saw the gold and ivory statue of Athena which used to be in the Parthenon. He describes it as "standing erect, robed in a chiton down to the feet, with the head of Medusa carved in ivory on its breast. In one hand the goddess holds a Niké nine feet tall and in the other, a spear. Next to her feet and near the spear there is a serpent, and this must be Erichthonius." [35]

There is reason to believe [36] that the serpent, as well as being the progenitor and patron of the royal house, was also the Minoan form of the goddess Athena and in classical times became at once her symbol and faithful follower. But more recently it has been suggested that the serpent was an infernal deity identified with Erichthonius, the local hero of the Acropolis, who assists Athena, patron goddess of the city, in protecting Athens.

In the ancient texts Erichthonius is often identified with his grandson Erechtheus so that it is sometimes difficult to distinguish them, but under one name or the other he was the legendary founder of the dynasty which succeeded the house of Cecrops. From him were descended the foremost heroes of Athens, including Pandion, Erechtheus, Aegeus and Theseus. He was born of the seed of Hephaestus which had fallen to the ground when Athena rejected his advances and had taken root. When Erichthonius sprouted from the earth, Athena put him in a box which she entrusted to the three daughters of Cecrops, Aglauros, Herse and Pandrosos, commanding them not to open it. Only Pandrosos obeyed her; her two sisters could not restrain themselves from looking inside, but when a snake emerged and crawled to the shield of Athena, they were so frightened

11. The Parthenon:
The Pronaos and the eastern colonnade, from inside

51

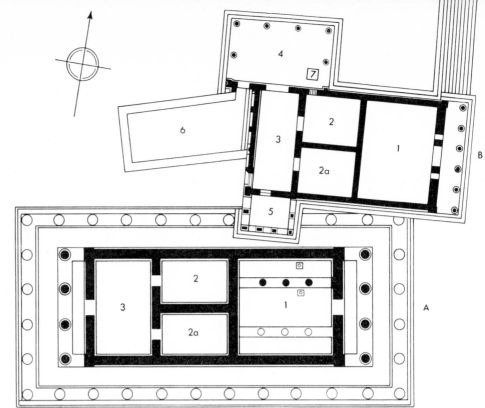

A. The Archaic temple of Athena (Dörpfeld temple) built between 529 and 520 on the south side of the Erechtheum

1 Cella
2 and 2a Treasuries
3 Adytum

B. The old Erechtheum

1 Eastern secos of Athena
2 and 2a Western shrines dedicated to Erechtheus and Poseidon
3 The Erechtheum sea
4 Northern porch
5 Porch of the Caryatides
6 Shrine of Pandrosos
7 Marks of Poseidon's trident

Plan 2

that they went out of their minds and leapt to their deaths from the highest ledge of the Acropolis. Athena then brought Erichthonius into her temple where she reared him and where every year Athenian youths offered sacrifices of rams and bulls " for the delight of his soul ".

The myth of the rearing of Erichthonius by Athena and the annual sacrifices to him are mentioned by Homer in the *Iliad*; but in the *Odyssey* he says that Athena used to visit the Athenian dwelling of Erechtheus. Homer refers to the house of Athena as a temple in the *Iliad*, whereas in the *Odyssey* he calls the palace of Erechtheus a *domus* or residence.[37] This suggests that in Homeric times there was a temple of Athena as well as a palace of Erechtheus on the Acropolis. Memories of this simultaneous existence of temple and palace were revived in the classical age, for when Philocles of Acharnae and Archilochus of Agryle were commissioned to build the Erechtheum, they provided for two separate precincts within the structure, each with its own entrance. The eastern precinct was dedicated to the worship of Athena and the western, in which altars were installed, to the memory of Erechtheus. And these altars consisted of grates like the hearths which we have already seen in the palace of Mycenae (Plan 2).

According to Apollodorus, Erechtheus was interred in the Erechtheum.[38] His tomb was generally considered to be the natural cleft in the rock in the north stoa of the Erechtheum. The cleft had originally been caused by a blow of Poseidon's trident or by one of Zeus' thunderbolts, brought down on Erechtheus because he had slain Poseidon's son Eumolpus in a battle against the Eleusinians. After the death of Erechtheus, the two gods who had killed him installed themselves in the Erechtheum and shared the honours with their victim.

Zeus, Poseidon and Athena are deities of Mycenaean origin and their names occur in the Linear B tablets. Worship of the snake came from Minoan Crete where the many snake-goddesses testify to the honour in which the snake was held. The attitude of the Mycenaean gods towards the snake, alternating between friendship and hostility, symbolizes the ambiguous relationship which existed

12. The Erechtheum: the eastern and northern porches, from the east

52

between the more ancient worship of infernal deities and the later heroic Olympian religion. The snake transferred its magical powers to the hero Erichthonius, founder of the dynasty under which the city of Athens took shape as a conscious political entity. The hostility between the snake and the Olympian gods ended with the building of the Erechtheum in which the snake, Erichthonius, Zeus, Poseidon, Athena and Hephaestus all resided in harmony.

As late as the second century A. D. Pausanias still regarded the Erechtheum as a symbol of religious concord. " There is," he writes, " a building known as the Erechtheum. In the front entrance there is an altar to Almighty Zeus where no animal is sacrificed, but only sweetmeats are offered up. Nor do they use wine in the sacrifices... Within this edifice there are also altars to Poseidon at which sacrifices are offered to Erechtheus as well, in accordance with the oracle; and altars to the hero Butes and to Hephaestus. The walls are decorated with paintings of the clan of Butes. The edifice is a double precinct and in the well sea-water is found. But this should not cause astonishment because others who reside inland have wells of sea-water too, for example the Aphrodisians of Caria. However this well is remarkable because when the wind blows from the south, it emits the sound of breaking waves. On the rock is imprinted the form of a trident in witness of Poseidon's participation in the struggle for possession of this land. Callimachus made a gold lamp in honour of the goddess (Athena) which is filled with oil every year on the same day, and the quantity of oil is sufficient to keep the lamp burning throughout the year, day and night. Its wick is made of Carpasian flax which is not consumable by fire." [39] In drawing attention to the altars dedicated to Erechtheus' brother Butes and to the wall paintings of his clan, Pausanias is underlining the fact that, together with the other gods, the snake clan of Erichthonius was an object of worship in the Erechtheum.

Herodotus' description of the seizure of the Acropolis by the Spartan Cleomenes sheds a new light on this aspect of the Erechtheum. " When Cleomenes climbed the hill to seize the Acropolis, he was just going into Athena's temple to say a prayer when the priestess, before he could get through the door, rose from her chair and cried: ' Spartan stranger, go back. Do not enter the holy place. No Dorian is permitted to come in.' Answering that he was not a Dorian but an Achaean, Cleomenes paid no attention to the warning." [40] As an Achaean Cleomenes could enter the sanctuary, for the Achaeans and the Ionians were descendants of Creusa, daughter of Erichthonius and mother of Achaeus and Ion by her husband Xuthus. The exchange between the priestess and Cleomenes shows that the right to enter the sacred precinct of Erechtheus was not bestowed on all Greeks, but belonged only to the race of Erichthonius, for whom it served as a kind of ritual clan centre.

The placing of marble seats at the sides of the north-western sanctuary seems to confirm this,[41] for in most Greek temples there was scarcely any provision for a " congregation " and few had the right to attend. The absence of a statue of any deity suggests further that it was not an ordinary temple, but rather a centre for enacting mysteries which kept alive memories of the palace on the Mycenaean Acropolis; not only because it had been the residence of the Athenian hero, but because it still contained the grates of its ancient hearth and housed the ancestral grave of Cecrops.[42]

From the information provided by Pausanias and Herodotus, we are able to infer that, in the precinct barred to those who were not of the race of Erichthonius, there were four symbols representing the Sea (*Erechtheis*), the Wind (*Echos*), Fire (altar grate) and Earth. The symbol of the last was the living snake of the Acropolis. The presence of symbols of the four elements leaves us in no doubt as to the nature of the mystery cult practised there.

13. The Erechtheum: the little porch of the Caryatides, from the south

Fig. 7. Rayet vase: Theseus and the Minotaur, *Louvre, Paris*

THESEUS

POPULAR IMAGINATION created about Theseus a heroic tradition which inspired Athenian artists and writers throughout the city's history. The vase paintings of the archaic and classical periods, the sculptures on the west pediment of the temple at Olympia and the metopes of the Parthenon, the *Odes* of Bacchylides, the Sophoclean tragedy *Oedipus at Colonus*, *Hippolytus* and *The Suppliant Women* by Euripides, Thucydides' introduction to his *History*, the first of Plutarch's *Lives*, Pausanias' *Attica* and many other works deal either directly or in passing with the legend of Theseus.

In which period of Greek prehistory should the origins of the legend be placed? Theseus' name like the names of Erechtheus, Aegeus, Achilleus, Tydeus, Odysseus and other heroes which have the same ending and—from an etymological point of view—equally obscure roots leads us far back into the Pelasgian age. And it is possible that, before the epic poetry of the Mycenaean age was composed, there already existed a more ancient local tradition sung by epic poets of the Early Helladic age. The Mycenaeans adapted this older tradition to their own and added their own characters to the legends, much as they had assimilated into their pantheon gods who had originated in Crete.

Though the epic poets of the Mycenaean age regarded Theseus as belonging to the world of the Achaeans, the legend continued to grow and to be enriched in subsequent periods, even as late as the age of Plutarch (A. D. 47-125). Furthermore emphasis on various aspects of the legend shifted from generation to generation. Bacchylides, for instance, in his *XVIIth Ode*, the first of two which he devoted to Theseus, describes his regeneration in the sea palace of his father Poseidon and makes little mention of his Knossos adventures which have greater historical significance.[43] In the classical age, on the other hand, Thucydides, Euripides and Isocrates attributed to Theseus the virtues which their contemporaries looked for in the leader of a democratic state and make no reference to the miraculous or marvellous aspects of the legend. Influenced by the historical methods of his own day, Plutarch concentrates on his political achievements,

14. The Temple of Hephaestus (Theseum), 449-444. The Doric order

Fig. 8. François crater, *c.* 570, *Archaeological Museum, Florence*

his wars and his amorous adventures. The way in which Athenians of every period were able to project their feelings and ideals on to the myth of Theseus indicates how closely the stories of their heroes reflected their own lives. When the Athenians fought against the Persians at Marathon, they felt the presence of Theseus fighting in their ranks. Their victory was his victory, for Theseus epitomized the courage of the people of Athens and his victories over the Amazons and the Centaurs symbolized for them their own victories over the barbarians of Asia.

Theseus was the hero of popular ballad and the stories of his exploits were preserved through the centuries by the epic poets, rather as the incidents of the Trojan expedition were eventually brought together and preserved in the *Iliad* and the *Odyssey*. The Theseus myth was known to Homer and Hesiod and is alluded to both in the *Iliad* and in Hesiod's *Shield*.[44] The earliest episodes are probably those which deal with his struggles with the Minotaur and with the Centaurs, for these are the first themes to be treated by vase painters. The Rayet cup in the Louvre (Fig. 7) and the François crater in the Archaeological Museum at Florence (Fig. 8) which date from the second quarter of the sixth century both depict scenes from these stories. Further episodes, some mythical, some historical, some both, were added at subsequent periods and altogether comprise the cycles of the Theseus legend which Plutarch preserved in his biography written early in the second century A. D.

The first cycle of the Athenian myth, according to Plutarch, is devoted to the birth and early years of Theseus. And as in all heroic myths, the initial theme is concerned with the misfortunes attending the hero's birth.[45] Theseus, in Plutarch's version, was born against the wishes of the gods. His father Aegeus, king of Athens, was childless and the fifty sons of his brother Pallas awaited his death to seize the throne. Aegeus consulted the Delphic oracle as to what he should do to get a son of his own, but being unable to make sense of the reply, he visited Pittheus, king of Troezen, who was famed for his wisdom. Instead of giving him an interpretation, Pittheus made him drunk with wine and when night fell put him on a couch with his daughter Aethra who became pregnant. Aegeus abandoned her, but left behind a pair of sandals and a sword under a massive boulder.

15. The Temple of Hephaestus (Theseum), from the south

59

If she should bear him a son, these were intended for him as soon as he was strong enough to lift the boulder. These were the recognition signs which are a constant element of nearly every heroic myth. Another version of the story relates that Aegeus abandoned Aethra because she was already pregnant by Poseidon when she shared his couch.

Uncertain of his paternity, abandoned before birth by Aegeus, spending his childhood years at Troezen ignored by his father, he grew up with all the classical ingredients of an " inferiority complex " which may account for some of his subsequent actions.[45] In his treatment of Ariadne, for example, who had helped him to escape from the labyrinth at Knossos and whom he abandoned pregnant at Cyprus or Naxos, Theseus re-enacted the callousness of his father towards Aethra.

His sense of inferiority grew even greater when he heard about Heracles who had achieved fame after accomplishing twelve formidable tasks. Theseus was seven years of age when he first met Heracles at the court of his grandfather Pittheus. And so to claim his place in the ranks of royal heroes and to be recognized by his father as heir to the throne, he determined to imitate the labours of Heracles. When he was sixteen, his mother led him to the rock under which lay the sandals and the sword left by Aegeus. He lifted it without difficulty and decided to proceed directly to Athens, travelling by the overland route which was the most fraught with dangers. On the road he confronted alarming monsters and bloodthirsty brigands, but emerged victorious from every encounter. The feats of Theseus on his journey from Troezen to Athens, together with his slaying of the Minotaur are depicted by an unknown artist of the early fifth century on the interior of an Attic calyx now in the British Museum.

The twelve exploits of Theseus, matching the labours of Heracles, have a double significance: one psychological, showing the gradual ascent of Theseus to heroic status; the other, political, symbolizing his struggle against hostile clans that strove to bar his way to power or to obstruct his plans for uniting the demes of Attica into a single city-state. As the sons of Jacob personified the tribes of Israel, so the names of Theseus' twelve enemies correspond to opposing clans and not merely to individuals. Cercyon, for example, was regarded by local tradition as king of Eleusis and Megara.

When Theseus reached Athens, his father Aegeus was living with Medea, whom Euripides made the heroine of one of his tragedies and who had fled to Athens from Corinth after she had murdered her two children to revenge herself against Jason who had abandoned her. Suspecting who Theseus was, Medea persuaded Aegeus to invite him to a banquet, planning to poison him. Theseus accepted the invitation, but in the course of the meal, he drew his father's sword to cut the meat. Aegeus at once recognized him, dashed the cup containing the poison to the ground and banished Medea to Asia together with the son she had borne him. He then proceeded to destroy the sons of Pallas to make sure he had no rivals to the throne. Later he captured the bull of Marathon which Heracles had brought from Crete and sacrificed it to Delphic Apollo. The first cycle ends with his recognition by his father as heir to the throne of Athens and by his contemporaries as the equal of Heracles.

The second cycle, consisting of the oldest elements of the legend, deals with his expedition to Crete. The sacrifice of the bull is the first hint of the humiliation in store for Minos, for the bull was sacred in Crete and symbolized the power of of the royal house of Knossos. In former times a son of Minos had been murdered in Attica and as a punishment Minos had imposed a blood-levy on the Athenians. Every nine years they were compelled to send seven youths and seven maidens to be sacrificed to the Minotaur, a monster half bull and half man which

Fig. 9. Bologna crater, *c.* 400: Theseus and
Poseidon, *Museo Civico, Bologna*

Fig. 10. Red-figure bowl by Euphronios:
Theseus and Amphitrite, *Louvre, Paris*

lived in the heart of the labyrinth at Knossos from which no one had ever escaped
alive. A milder version of the story relates that in honour of his son's memory,
Minos had instituted games and bull-acrobatics at Knossos in which Athenian
hostages participated. Archaeological evidence supports the tradition that Crete
exercised hegemony over Attica in the Early Cycladic period. Excavations carried
out by Theocharis at the citadel of Sunium and on the neighbouring island of
Helen (Macronessos) revealed the existence of an Early Minoan settlement there.

In one version of the legend Minos used to come to Athens personally to collect
the tribute, selecting his victims from among the fairest maidens and handsomest
youths and taking them back to Crete on his ship. On the occasion described by
Bacchylides,[46] when Theseus was among the hostages, Minos stretched out his
hand to caress the cheek of one of the maidens. Theseus intervened angrily declaring that he was the son of Poseidon. But Minos did not believe him and to
make fun of him cast his gold ring into the sea, telling him to recover it from
the kingdom of his father. Theseus dived into the water, was borne by dolphins
to the palace of Poseidon where Amphitrite gave him a crown which subsequently
lit his path in the labyrinth, and returned to the boat re-invigorated. This episode was used as the decorative motif on two vases of the fifth century: one, a
crater by the painter of Cadmus, now in the Museo Civico at Bologna (Fig. 9);
the other, a red-figure vase by a painter of the workshop of Euphronios, now
in the Louvre. The latter version depicts Amphitrite seated on a throne, while
Athena stands nearby armed and helmeted, symbolizing the protection which
she extended to Theseus as to all Athenians (Fig. 10).

When the ship arrived in Crete, Theseus would have to face the Minotaur.
The struggle could not possibly be easy, for even if he overcame it unscathed,
he would still not be able to find his way out of the labyrinth. Fortunately,
however, Ariadne, Minos' daughter, fell in love with him and came to his assistance. She provided him with a sword to slay the monster with and a ball of
thread by which he could find his way out again. By these means and with the
crown of Amphitrite, Theseus emerged safely with the other Athenian hostages.

The Archaic black-figure Rayet cup in the Louvre (Fig. 7, p. 56) is decorated
with a scene depicting the death of the Minotaur at the hands of Theseus,
watched by Ariadne and the fourteen young men and women of Athens. The
François crater at Florence (Fig. 8, p. 59) shows the arrival of the ship at Knossos,

61

the disembarkation and the procession of the hostages towards the labyrinth led by Theseus. A second frieze on the same vase treats the theme of Theseus' battle with the Centaurs which in the middle of the fifth century was to inspire the sculptures of the west pediment of the Temple of Zeus at Olympia.

In the harbour of Knossos Theseus cut down the masts of Minos' ships and departed from Crete in the night with Ariadne and the Athenian youths and maidens. But he soon abandoned Ariadne either at Cyprus or Naxos. He then called at Delos, the island of Apollo, to dance the circular dance of the cranes with his companions and thence returned to Phaleron. His return route, as described by Plutarch, includes the islands of Naxos, Cyprus and Delos. These islands became part of the zone of influence in the eastern Mediterranean into which the Achaean-Mycenaeans expanded after 1450. They were the successors of the Cretans and gradually took over the markets and spheres of activity which the ancient Minoan sea kingdom had created. The islands singled out would seem to have been the share which fell to Athens in the carving-up of the Minoan heritage.

When Theseus had left Athens, his ships had carried black sails, but he had promised his father that he would replace them by white ones if he returned safely from Crete. Alas, he forgot and when Aegeus sighted the black sails on the horizon, he cast himself from the cliff from which he had been watching and was drowned in the sea which has borne his name ever since.

The role of liberator, which is one of the attributes of all heroes of legend, established Theseus' popularity once for all. But it is possible that the importance of the Cretan cycle in Athenian traditions and art was also due to other events —or perhaps another rather different version of the same events—recorded by Cleidemus and quoted by Plutarch.[47] Daedalus, a descendant of Erechtheus and builder of the labyrinth, escaped from Crete and took refuge at Athens. Minos pursued him, but a storm arose which drove Minos' ship to Sicily where he perished. His son demanded that Theseus surrender Daedalus to him, or he would slay the Athenian hostages held in Crete. But Theseus kept spinning out negotiations until he managed secretly to build a fleet at Salamis and Troezen. When the fleet was fitted out, Theseus and the Athenians, together with Daedalus and other political refugees from Crete, surprised and overcame the fleet of Knossos, disembarked at the port and fought their way to the palace where they killed the king and his guard, ceasing operations only when Ariadne assumed the throne and sued for peace.

It is just conceivable that the events recounted in this version of the myth may have something to do with the sack of the palace of Minos by the Achaeans in 1400. According to Plutarch, Theseus was fifty years of age when Helen was a young girl. If the fall of Troy occurred in 1200,[48] Theseus' expedition would have taken place in about 1240, that is to say, little more than 160 years after the sack of Knossos. In view of the uncertainty of all chronology in prehistoric times, is it too fanciful to see a connection between the two events?

The third cycle of the myth concerns the expedition of Theseus and Heracles against the Amazons, a race of warrior women living on the Euxine Sea and using males as slaves. They lived by war and to perpetuate the ascendancy of their sex exposed all their male offspring. They taught their daughters to fight with the spear and the bow from a very early age. Heracles, Theseus and Achilles all had military encounters with Amazons and each fell in love with an Amazon at one time or another.

In his expedition with Heracles, Theseus captured the Amazon Antiope and brought her back to Athens. This incident was often treated in the vase paintings of the classical age and the best known examples are the calyx at Oxford, the amphora at the Louvre and the crater in the Museo Civico at Bologna. Theseus

16. Caryatides of the Erechtheum

later abandoned Antiope to marry Phaedra, but not before she had borne him a son, Hippolytus. On the day of his marriage to Phaedra, Athens was attacked by an army of Amazons which according to one version of the legend could only be beaten off after he had sacrificed Antiope on the altar of Phobus (Fear). Although there is mention of human sacrifice elsewhere in mythology, for example the episode of the twelve Trojan prisoners burnt on the funeral pyre of Patroclus,[49] it does not appear in fact to have been widely practised in Greece and the Linear B tablets give no hint of it. The story of Phaedra and Hippolytus has been a frequent theme in literature from Euripides onwards and is too well-known to be told here.

The friendship of Theseus and Pirithous, the hero of the Lapiths, led to fresh adventures which constitute the fourth cycle of the Theseus myth. The first exploit involved the kidnapping of Helen as she danced in the sanctuary of Artemis Orthia at Sparta. Then, to please Pirithous, Theseus agreed to assist him in his attempt to abduct Persephone from the kingdom of Hades. But the watchdog of the underworld, Cerberus, tore Pirithous limb from limb while Theseus, thanks to the intervention of Heracles just managed to escape. The figures on the famous Orvieto crater in the Louvre (Pl. 68), formerly thought to be those of the Argonauts or the heroes of Marathon, are certainly correctly identified by Jan Six as Theseus, Pirithous and Heracles in the underworld.[50]

During Theseus' absence, Castor and Pollux, the twin brothers of Helen, seized the opportunity to invade Attica with Lacedaemonian and Arcadian troops to recover their sister. Academus revealed Helen's hideout in Aphidna; the two brothers captured the village, rescued Helen and seized Theseus' mother Aethra whom they bore off to Sparta with them. The romantic escapades of Theseus and the wars they occasioned gave his political enemies like Menestheus the opportunity to raise the Athenians in rebellion against his rule. He was forced to seek refuge in Scyros, but Lycomedes, the king of the island, to please Menestheus had Theseus pushed off a rock to his death.

After the Persian Wars in the classical period, the Pythian priestess commanded the Athenians to bring back the bones of Theseus to Athens and to bury them there with honour. In spite of the difficulties put in his way by the inhabitants of Scyros, Cimon occupied the island and was led by an eagle to the grave which contained Theseus' bones, his sword and the bronze tip of his spear. These he brought back to Athens in his trireme. The reburial took place in the centre of the city, near the Gymnasium, and the new grave was declared a sacred place of asylum for slaves and others who sought refuge from harsh masters. In classical times Theseus was regarded as the founder of Athenian democracy and in *The Suppliant Women* Euripides has him explaining to Creon's herald the advantages of a system of government without a tyrant, under which powerful and weak alike are subject to the same written laws.

THE END OF MYCENAEAN CIVILIZATION

AT THE END OF THE SECOND millenium, the Mycenaean Acropolis of Athens loomed large on the historical horizon of Greece and the Aegean, as the peak of Ararat rose from the waters of the Biblical flood. Wave upon wave of invaders had swept down from the north along the two shores of the Aegean to overwhelm the peoples who until then had held sway in the eastern Mediterranean—the Hittites and the Mycenaeans. These dominant powers of the middle of the second millenium were finally submerged in about 1100 under the ebb and flow of migrations which made themselves felt throughout the Middle East from Epirus to the Dardanelles and as far as Syria, Cyprus and Egypt.

17. The Temple of Hephaestus and the Acropolis, from the west

Egyptian sources refer to these migratory tribes as " Peoples of the Sea "; Greek sources call them the " Heraclidae " and the " Dorians ". This great upheaval coincided with the burning of the Mycenaean palaces at Pylos, Mycenae, Tiryns, Orchomenus and Iolcus and indicates that it stemmed from one and the same source.

The Egyptian poem of the scribe Pentaour, written on papyrus and inscribed on the walls of the temples of Karnak, Luxor and Abydos, provides evidence that a great battle took place at Quadesh in the valley of the Orontes in Syria in the middle of May 1294 at which the pharaoh Ramesses II defeated a combined force of invaders from Asia Minor and the Aegean seeking to move down into Egypt. The recorded names of the defeated enemy include the peoples of Troy, Caria, Cilicia, Mysia and Lycia, in short, the " Peoples of the Sea."

Ramesses II, who had signed a treaty with the Hittites in 1278, lived to witness the latter's decline. Before their kingdom collapsed, the Hittites had maintained friendly relations with Achaeans with whom they had kept the balance of power on the two shores of the Aegean. The exact date of their fall is not known, but we do know that their country was in Phrygian hands by 1170. We also know that it brought to an end their monopoly of iron, for in about 1200 the use of iron had spread to the Aegean.

In the fifth year of the reign of Ramesses III (1195), a fresh attack on Egypt took place,[51] recorded on an inscription at Medinet Habu. Military units from Libya had concentrated with hostile intentions to the west of the Nile Delta, while to the east the Philistines (who had come originally from Crete) had taken the initiative on the coast. These latter, armed in the manner of the Achaeans, had landed in Caria and had then moved down the Syrian coast towards Egypt. They were accompanied by the race of Zekal who had also originated in Crete. But the expedition met with disaster at the hands of Ramesses III who claimed that 12,000 of the invaders had been slain.

In the eighth year of his reign (1192), pressure from over the sea and the Syrian coast became even more acute. Further migrants from the islands, including Philistines, Zekals, Danaans and Trojans, had advanced into Asia Minor, Cyprus and the Syrian coast, plundering as they passed through. They arrived in Egypt with their fires with them and laid siege to the Delta by land and sea. Evidence of their arrival is provided not only by inscriptions but also by Egyptian bas-reliefs. One of these reliefs depicts the attack on Egypt by the tall race of Philistines, accompanied by their womenfolk and children loaded on ox-carts. Another scene shows a great naval battle between the Egyptian and the Aegean fleets, the first naval engagement in history to be recorded on the monuments of antiquity.[52]

Where had these Homeric peoples—Trojans, Danaans, Achaeans—come from when they arrived at the gates of Egypt? Egyptian inscriptions provide part of the answer when they identify the origin of the " People of the Sea " as the islands of the Aegean. A further answer is given by the seventh-century elegiac poet Callinus of Ephesus in his tale of the adventures of the Achaean seer Calchas who also appears in the *Iliad*. Accompanied by his aide Amphilochus after the destruction of Troy, Calchas and a body of Achaeans reached Colophon in Lydia. Then joining forces with his rival seer Mopsus he marched into Lycia where he took his life: he had made a prophecy to the king which events had proved wrong and he was unable to overcome his sense of shame. After his death the Achaeans dispersed throughout Pamphylia, Cilicia and Syria. The presence of Achaeans in Cilicia and Syria is further confirmed by a bilingual inscription in Phoenician and Neo-Hittite which was discovered at Karatepe in Cilicia. It records that the area belonged to the Danaans and that its king, a certain Azitawadda, was a descendant of Mopsus.[53]

18. The Theatre of Dionysus

ON THE GREEK side of the Aegean, contemporary evidence of the turmoil of the period is provided by the clay tablets of Pylos. John Chadwick has described the thrill he felt when the texts conveyed to him the sense of tension prevailing at Pylos on the eve of its destruction. The tablets contain directives for the defence of the coastline and for the mobililization of oarsmen and ships. The meaning of these military measures was clear to Chadwick: Pylos had been alerted to expect an attack by invaders from the sea.[54]

These invaders set fire not only to Pylos, but also to Mycenae, Iolcus and other Mycenaean centres. They had not come initially to conquer a kingdom and to impose a dynasty. Like the early Norse invaders of the British Isles, they attacked by surprise, set fire to their objectives and departed. Had they been a mountain people, they would scarcely have confined their military activities to coastal areas and have left uplands such as Arcadia untouched. Nor would mountain people have had sufficient experience of seafaring to conquer the Cyclades, the Sporades, Cythera, Crete, Carpathos and Rhodes; in short, to invade the islands of the Aegean and to spread as far as Cyprus.

Is it possible, then, that the destruction of the Mycenaean centres in 1100 was the work of Aegean islanders returning piratically to their former possessions and that the Dorians never came down from the heights of Epirus into the Peloponnese as we have hitherto been led to believe? Is it possible that they came in fact from Crete and that the legend of the "Return of the Heraclidae" should be interpreted as the revenge of the Minoans for the murder of Heracles by Eurystheus, king of Mycenae? For Heracles, with the consent of Minos, had brought the bull of Knossos—and with it Minoan civilization—from Crete into Attica: the same bull, or Minotaur, which Theseus was later to slay.

The theory which postulates a Cretan origin for the Dorians rests on certain events which took place after they had established themselves in the Mycenaean world. Except for Sparta where the Dorian conquerors confined their activities to guarding their helots in the plain of the Eurotas, the other Dorian centres such as Corinth and Aegina very soon became proficient in piracy and merchant trade, indicating a certain previous familiarity with the sea. But in other respects Sparta had marked affinities with Crete. According to Plutarch, Lycurgus, the legendary law-giver of Sparta, made a special voyage to Crete to study its political institutions with a view to introducing them into Sparta. He also persuaded Thales, one of the wise men and political leaders of Crete, to visit Sparta and to educate the Dorians with his melodies and verse. Several ancient authors state that Lycurgus even died in Crete where his body was burned and the ashes scattered in the sea. In common with all Minoan cities, Sparta had no walls round it. The Spartans themselves used to say that their fighting men were the walls of their city. The communal meals and kitchens of the Spartans as Plutarch describes them are also a feature of Cretan life. The position of women in Spartan society offers marked analogies with Minoan society. Spartan women took part in public debates and had the right to vote, so that women in the rest of Greece said of their Spartan sisters that "only the women of Lacedaemon could govern their men". To which the women of Sparta used to reply that "only they could give birth to them". Sparta was ruled by a dual monarchy like Crete, where Minos and Rhadamanthus reigned jointly, just as they acted jointly as judges in the underworld. Possibly the double axe, emblem of royalty at Knossos, symbolized dual monarchy. Lastly the naked games, which Sparta first introduced into continental Greece and which amazed the ancient Middle East, had only been seen before in Minoan Crete.

19. The Temple
of Poseidon at Sunium

In contrast with the Dorians of Sparta who were oppressive to their helots (the Mycenaean population which they had subjected) and who showed unwavering hatred towards all non-Dorians, the Athenians, who believed that they had never been conquered during the Dorian invasions, gave refugees the same political rights and privileges which they enjoyed themselves. Already in the age of the migrations the difference in character and outlook between Athenian and Spartan had become evident.

Thucydides ascribes the preservation of Attica from the Dorian conqueror to the barrenness of its soil. Herodotus records that a Dorian attack launched from Megara actually took place during Codrus' reign.[55] He is probably referring to the legend which describes how Melanthus king of Pylos and his son Codrus fled to Athens in the wake of the invaders. Melanthus' heroism on the Athenian side in a war against Thebes resulted in his becoming king. His son Codrus succeeded him and reigned during the critical period of the Dorian invasion of Attica. The Delphic oracle had announced that the salvation of Athens could only be brought about by his death at the hands of a Dorian. He therefore disguised himself as a beggar, got into the enemy's camp, challenged two Dorians to combat, slew one and was in turn slain by the other. When the Athenians begged to be allowed to bury the body of their king, the Dorians, realizing that the oracle had been fulfilled and that any hope of capturing Athens had disappeared, at once raised the siege.

Whatever may have been the starting point of the Dorians, whether in the mountains of Epirus or in the islands of the Aegean and Crete, their Greek origin is not disputed. Their language and religion were the same as those of other Greeks and, as Professor Wace observed, their arrival in Greece did not bring about any significant anthropological or cultural changes.[56]

COLONIZATION

THE MIGRATIONS of the twelfth century in European Greece released an outburst of colonizing activity on the part of the Greeks in the eastern Aegean (*see* Map 1, p. 14). Unlike the invaders who burned down the Mycenaean cities, the colonists consisted of organized political communities, nuclei of new city-states, setting forth from the prytaneum of their mother-city armed with the god's oracular utterance and an eternal flame kindled at its hearth. Though they were not dependent economically or administratively upon their city of origin, they nevertheless took with them its customs, language, religion and political ideology. In their new home the colonists divided up the land between them by lot and made permanent settlements.

Apart from the Dorians who occupied the islands of the southern Aegean, the mainstreams of colonization consisted of Aeolians and Ionians from the ancient Mycenaean cities. The Aeolians left Iolcus, Aulis or Orchomenus to escape the Dorian invaders. First settling on the nearest islands, Lesbos and Chios, they later crossed over to the coast of Asia Minor between Smyrna and Troy, where memories of the Trojan war were to fire the imagination of their poets. As we shall see, the *Iliad* was conceived opposite the plains of Troy.

The Ionians set forth from Athens. The claim of the Athenians to be Ionians rests on two considerations: firstly their dialect, Attic, whose connection with Ionic has been noted earlier and secondly the myth of Ion, the eponymous founder of the Ionians.

We have already discussed (on pp. 23-4) the story of Hellen and his three sons. When Hellen's family broke up, one of his sons, Xuthus, went to Athens where he married the daughter of Erechtheus, Creusa, who bore two sons Ion and Achaeus from whom stemmed the Ionians and the Achaeans. In his *Ion*, Euripides describes [57] how the four traditional " tribes " of Attica derived from the sons of Ion—the Geleontes, the Hopletes, the Argadeis and the Aigikoreis. Etymologically these names suggest that the four tribes were in fact social classes or castes: the aristocracy, the military, the labourers and the shepherds. Aristotle regarded the division of Attic society into these four strata as the primitive form of the Athenian constitution and it is interesting to note that their names have been found on inscriptions in certain Ionian colonies, notably Teos and Ephesus.

Traditionally the founding fathers of the Ionian cities were the Codridae or descendants of Codrus; they had come to Athens as refugees from Mycenaean Pylos and later went on to colonize Asia Minor. There they are said to have established the twelve cities of the pan-Ionian confederacy: Miletus (founded by Neleus), Myous, Priene, Ephesus (founded by Androclus), Colophon, Lebedos, Teos, Erythae, Clazomenae, Phocaea, Samos and Chios, to which must be added a thirteenth, Smyrna. Athens strove constantly to maintain close political and economic ties with the Ionian colonies and eventually converted them into bases for her empire.

It seems doubtful that Athens' part in colonizing Ionia was in fact as great as she claimed; indeed Michael Sakellariou [58] holds the view that of the twelve (or thirteen) cities only Miletus, Teos and Smyrna were actually founded by Athenians or by people coming from Attica. But wherever the colonists came from physically, their dialect, political ideas and patterns of culture derived from Athens. Carrying on the traditions of the Minoans and the Mycenaeans, the Ionians engaged in trade and entered into relations with the peoples of the east. They were thus able to blend elements of culture from both sides of the Aegean into a new civilization which became the basis of a renaissance of Hellenism in the post-classical age.

HOMER

THE ESTABLISHMENT of colonies in the east brought the Greeks into contact with the Phoenicians from whom they borrowed a version of the Phoenician alphabet. Adapting it to the needs of their own tongue and supplementing it with symbols of their own, they created a phonetic script for the Greek language. Linear B continued to exist side by side with the new alphabet until the ninth century when it gradually fell into disuse. The primitive form of the Greek alphabet (Pl. 35) which closely resembled its Phoenician prototype has been found on inscriptions in Crete, the southern Cyclades and Rhodes dating from about 800. The acquisition of a phonetic alphabet opened the way for a written literature for which Linear B had apparently not been used.

Epic poetry was born in Aeolis, but its final form (the *Iliad* and the *Odyssey*) was composed in Ionic. At Delos, the religious centre of the Ionian cities, a festival was held to which Ionians from every part flocked with their wives and children. They took part in athletic contests and in musical and choric rituals at which they chanted the Homeric *Hymn to Apollo* which Thucydides quotes.[59] Before Homer systematized them, the epics consisted of a series of folk songs and ballads which were recited by bards accompanied on a phorminx, a kind of stringed instrument resembling a harp. It is possible that the recitation of the verses also went with staged performances of the great scenes. The stories were enriched from generation to generation with new incidents till the Aegean, Ionian and Aeolian contributions were welded together into a universal Greek epic.

71

This was the great achievement of Homer. He assembled these stories and in rearranging them round a central theme, with a beginning, a middle and an end, created a unique artistic whole. With his sense of drama, his narrative skill, his astonishing insight into human character, his flashes of humour and his moments of sombre reflexion, he transformed a string of old legends into one of the great unifying forces, not only of the Hellenic world, but of the whole of European culture as well. In most countries today, translations of the *Iliad* and the *Odyssey*, issued in paperback, command sales which are the envy of many novelists.

During the last hundred years or so, much controversy has centred round what is called the " Homeric question," that is to say, whether Homer really existed or not. But nowadays most authorities agree that he did and that he lived about the year 800. He not only breathed the life of his genius into the *Iliad* and the *Odyssey;* he also himself composed a large number of narrative poems which were preserved by a company of rhapsodes in Chios, the Homeridae, who, rather like the troubadors of the Middle Ages, used to recite his work at the banquets of the ruling class or at public festivals. Ancient writers were in no doubt about his existence. The passage which Thucydides quotes from the *Hymn to Apollo* ends with these lines:

> Maidens, I say farewell to you all, and I pray that the favour
> Light on you of Apollo and Artemis. Then in the future
> Think of me, and whenever some other man among mortals
> Weary of travel comes to this place and questions you, saying
> " Tell me, maidens, the name of the man who is sweetest of singers.
> Tell me the name of the one in whom you have chiefly delighted,"
> Then, in your gentle way, you must all together make answer
> " Blind is the singer. He lives in the rock-bound island of Chios."

And Thucydides does not question that the " sweetest of singers " is Homer. Herodotus who is the first to mention the epics by name says that Homer and Hesiod were contemporaries and lived about four centuries before his own time.[60]

According to Plato,[61] the poetry of Homer was first brought to Athens by Hipparchus, eldest and most cultivated of the sons of Pisistratus. He compelled the rhapsodes to recite the entire epic integrally at the Panathenaean festival. At about this time, in the middle of the sixth century, the first written version of the Homeric cycle was made, but we have Cicero's authority [62] for believing that this was simply a record of existing texts to which nothing new was added. This Athenian version became sacrosanct and any variation from it was forbidden. Later, Aristotle prepared a special edition for Alexander the Great which he took with him in a small case on his expedition into Asia. A third very important edition was that of Aristarchus of Samothrace (185-125) which became the basis of all subsequent editions.[63]

It can be said without exaggeration that the *Iliad* and the *Odyssey* were to the education, art and literature of the Greeks what the Bible was to the Christian world. But to the Athenians they were particularly important. They were composed in the Ionic dialect which resembled so closely their native Attic. Moreover of the entire Greek-speaking world, only Athens and Cyprus had survived the Dorian destruction of Mycenaean civilization. Memories of the Mycenaean period stirred Athenians more intimately than Dorians, for they identified them with their own heroic traditions. In the classical age, they paid tribute to their Mycenaean heritage when their tragic poets revived the heroes of the Trojan War on the stage of their theatre. The Homeric epics thus recorded and preserved for Athenians the " lost paradise " of the Mycenaean age.

20. The Temple of Aphaea at Aegina

21. Neolithic red polished pot, *c.* 4000-3500. *Agora Museum, Athens*

22. Middle Helladic bowl with a single handle and spout decorated in white against the red ground of the clay, *c.* 2000-1550. *Agora Museum, Athens*

21

22

Archaic Athens

THE ARISTOCRATIC STATE

FROM THE END of the migrations until the beginning of the Persian Wars in 490, Athens, like other Greek city-states, enjoyed about five centuries of comparative peace. No great events such as the Trojan War or the Dorian invasion occurred to disrupt or disturb their steady growth. Little change took place in their social systems which remained predominantly agricultural and aristocratic.[64]

In Athens monarchy of the Mycenaean type had disappeared under the encroachment of the landowners whose economic and military strength enabled them to concentrate political power exclusively in their own hands. They alone could afford the upkeep of horses and the cost of military equipment and were able therefore to control the defence and government of Athens. Until the reforms of Solon and Cleisthenes at the beginning of the sixth century, they virtually monopolized the estates, the slaves and the herds of Attica and the fate of tenant- farmers, farm-labourers, artisans and soldiers depended on them.

But from the eighth century onwards, we can discern in the coastal settlements of Attica the beginnings of commercial and maritime activity which was to bring into existence a new social class in Athens. This class derived its wealth, not from the land, but from the profits made by its commercial undertakings. Its power began to be based more and more on money. During the seventh century, it organized itself politically and was able to demand concessions from the landed aristocracy. The struggle of these two classes constituted the driving force in the social development of Athens.

Apart from the limited gains of the " coast-people " embodied in the legal reforms of Solon and Cleisthenes, no sweeping social changes took place until the ten years between 490 and 480, the date of the first and second Persian Wars. During that crucial decade the economic and naval armament of Athens took place and as a result power passed from the landed to the mercantile class, that is to say, from the soldiers to the sailors. The victory of Marathon (490) was the last military success of the oligarchy just as Salamis (480) was the first of Athenian democracy. The end of archaic Athens coincides with the transformation of the state from an agricultural to a maritime one and with the beginning of its domination of the Mediterranean.

Any discussion of the political and social institutions of aristocratic Athens, particularly in its earliest times, must necessarily be conjectural. The evidence which has come down to us is too unsatisfactory to support a clear interpretation. Sources which are anything like contemporary are extremely scanty; where they are more abundant they are either too late in date or too inconsistent to be accepted without grave reservations. The principal source is the *Constitution of Athens*, written during the last years of Aristotle's lifetime, probably by him. Furthermore, there is no measure of agreement between scholars who have studied this period as to how the evidence should be evaluated or interpreted. All we can

23. Neolithic figurine, *height* 9³/₈ in., *c.* 3000. *Eleusis Museum*

24. Middle Helladic two-handled spouted bowl, *height* 4³/₄ in. *Agora Museum, Athens*

25. Middle Helladic long-spouted single-handled bowl, *height* 6¹/₄ in. *Agora Museum, Athens*

77

hope to do here is to try and present a coherent hypothesis in general terms, knowing full well that for every person who finds it acceptable, there will be others who do not.

Even if the evidence were more conclusive, the subject would remain complex, because two systems of social organization appear to have existed side by side in the aristocratic state, one based on divisions and subdivisions of a tribal nature, the other on divisions by economic class. The two systems at certain points are in conflict, at others they coincide; but it is clear that control of the government and the priesthood was determined by class.

Athenian citizens were divided into four tribes (*phylae*), traditionally regarded as descendants of the four sons of Ion. As we have seen (p. 71), the etymology of their names has suggested the theory that they were survivals of a primitive caste-system, but their origins may equally well have been territorial. Each tribe was divided into three *phratries*, making twelve in all. The phratry had certain religious functions and was responsible for recording the birth, coming of age and marriage of its members. It was in turn subdivided into clans: thirty clans made up a phratry and each of the 360 clans had thirty members. Traditionally these divisions went back to a period before the unification of Attica and corresponded to the seasons, months and days of the year.

Parallel to the tribal structure, the citizen-body was also divided into classes: the nobles (*Eupatridae*), the farmers and the craftsmen. Later when the dominance of the aristocracy started to cause serious and increasing economic dislocation, a class of landless poor (*thetes*) developed. Most authorities now accept that the clan and the nobility coincided; that all clansmen were nobles and that all nobles were members of clans. This is illustrated by the marked cohesion of the Eupatridae as a class, for they appropriated the mystical prestige of the clan cult. Each clan constituted a kind of secret blood-brotherhood and claimed descent from a mythical and heroic ancestor whose name it often bore. The clan had a common altar and burial place and the succession of certain priesthoods passed by hereditary right within some of the clans.

It is interesting to note that there was no professional priesthood in Athens as we understand it today: religious duties were performed at specific times by ordinary laymen. Their functions however were simply ritual and they had no power to examine or pronounce on problems of a theological nature. The great "theologians" of the Greeks were the poets and philosophers—Homer, Hesiod, Thales—and the close association of religion with philosophy, poetry and science explains why Greek cosmology reached heights in this field unattained by the professional clergy of the ancient and medieval worlds.[65]

By this period the clan had become patriarchal, the clansmen being members of their father's clan, not their mother's. It retained from its nomadic past, at any rate in theory, the communal ownership of land and, with it, equality of political rights, though this latter tended to become increasingly confined to the leading families within the clans.

Outside the clan organization, but nevertheless members of the citizen-body, were the other classes: the farmers, the craftsmen and the *thetes*. Whether they were artisans, tradesmen, farmers or hired labourers in the fields or workshops, they were economically dependent upon the great landowners who were members of the clans. The farmers, of whom some were crop-sharers and some indentured, surrendered one-sixth of the gross yield of their lands to their masters. Until the reforms of Solon, they were allowed to pledge their persons as a surety of this rent: if they failed to pay it, they and their children became slaves of the landowners.

It is a commonplace today that Greek civilization was based on slavery and one can see from Aristotle's treatment of the question in his *Politics* that the Greeks themselves were uneasy about it. When one has read the various passages in which Aristotle discusses it, one is left with the impression that he regards it as a necessary evil: evil, because try as he will he can find no satisfactory philosophical distinction between the slave and the freeman; necessary, because given the general level of technical know-how prevailing in ancient Greece it was the sole condition whereby *some* members of society could fulfil their roles as citizens. The slave had no legal or political identity and was considered as chattel, on a level with his master's plough or livestock. But in Athens his situation was nothing like as harsh as that of the Spartan helot, for the Athenian slave was entitled to shelter, food and protection from the family to which he belonged. In some ways, Aristotle regards his position as more favourable than that of the hired labourer engaged in menial tasks. In terms of production, the hired labourer is in the same position as the slave, but socially he is " on his own " and cannot claim the protection of a master in time of adversity. The master's *amour-propre* was bound up with the well-being of his slaves as it was with the condition of his horses, whereas the hired man was a stranger to him, and most masters must have realized " that in household management the people are of greater importance than the material property, and their quality of more account than that of the goods that make up their wealth". Furthermore in aristocratic Athens, not only the labourer, but the independent farmer and craftsman as well, were as firmly excluded from the administration of the state as the slave.

If we compare the institutions of the aristocratic *polis* as described in the *Constitution of Athens* with the monarchic institutions of the Mycenaean age which Chadwick was able to reconstruct from the Linear B tablets (*see* p. 39), we see that despite some similarities a considerable change has occurred. The *wanax* or king had vanished from the Athenian scene after the Dorian invasions. The title of *basileus* survived, but its functions had become almost exclusively religious. The polemarch, the Areopagus and the *thesmothetai* seem to have corresponded closely to the *lawagetas*, the council and the *tereta* of the Mycenaeans. The only office that we do not find in the tablets is that of the eponymous archon.

The three highest public offices were originally held for life, but were subsequently restricted first to ten years, later to one. The most important was the archon. The epithet *eponymous* was taken into use after his tenure of office had been limited to one year, for like the Roman consuls he gave his name to the year in which he governed. He was the executive head of state in charge of civil administration. He guaranteed the security of private property and had special jurisdiction over cases involving the rights of parents, orphans and heiresses. Protection of the integrity and interests of the family was therefore one of his main duties. His supreme importance is suggested by the fact that his official residence was the Prytaneum which housed the sacred hearth of Athens.

The polemarch was in charge of the army and the police. In time of war he seems to have had some responsibility for the mustering of ships, for it was not until much later that Athens had a navy of fighting vessels. He resided at the Polemarcheion, also known as the Epilyceum after the polemarch Epilycos who rebuilt it.

The *basileus* controlled the state religion. He officiated at religious feasts, administered the temples and presided over the court of the four tribal leaders which tried religious disputes or violations. During the Panathenaean festival, his wife went through a mystical marriage ritual with the god Dionysus. This ceremony took place at the Bucoleum where it is assumed the *basileus* lived.

In addition to these three principal magistrates, there were also six *thesmothetai*, whose office was annual and whose functions were purely judicial. They tried

79

cases, probably independently rather than as a board, and so long as there was no written code, their judgments gradually built up a body of common law.

After their term of office, the nine administrators, or nine archons as they are sometimes called, became life members of the *Boulê*, the council in which the ultimate responsibility for public affairs was vested. The council installed the magistrates, presumably by some kind of elective process, and kept an eye on their activities. Members of the council were recruited solely from the ranks of the retiring archons and no one could serve a second term of office until every suitable candidate had had his turn. Eligibility for office seems to have been confined not only to the Eupatrid class, but to the wealthier members of it. The council also acted as a penal court for murder. In this function it convened on the hill of Ares and was therefore known as the Areopagus.

The struggle to remove homicide from the jurisdiction of the clans to which it traditionally belonged and to bring it within the province of the Areopagus is ascribed to both Draco and Solon. But it had almost certainly been going on much earlier and a passage in his Oresteian trilogy suggests that even in Aeschylus' day the issue was still alive, at least in the minds of his audience. The only way in which a murder could be atoned for was if the guilty party were himself murdered by a member of his victim's family or clan. Clytemnestra had murdered Agamemnon: therefore she in turn had to suffer the same fate. But when the Areopagus began to function as the supreme court, relatives of the victim were no longer allowed to mete out retributive justice. The sentence of the court was final and an endless chain of ritual murder was avoided.

THE PROTO-GEOMETRIC STYLE

WHILE THE IONIANS on the eastern shore of the Aegean were creating a culture of which the *Iliad* and the *Odyssey* represent the highest achievements, Athens developed a style of vase decoration known as proto-geometric. It flourished for about three centuries, from 1100 to 800, and was centred on the Cemetery of the Dipylum. The Athenian origin of the proto-geometric style has been convincingly demonstrated by Desborough,[66] but its influence on the aesthetic traditions of Athens has still to be fully examined.

Proto-geometric is the first sign of a cultural revival after the collapse which succeeded the destruction of the Mycenaean cities by the Dorian invaders in the twelfth century. The royal palaces and their inhabitants were not the only sufferers. The workshops were also burnt and the artists and craftsmen who worked there perished or were dispersed. Pottery, vase-decoration and painting, like the use of Linear B, entered a period of decline. The funeral statuettes and the vases which have survived from the period immediately following the destruction show a marked lack of creative originality and skill (Pls. 27-31). The so-called sub-Mycenaean style continued to use the old motifs and methods, but in a rudimentary form in which circles and wavy lines are drawn in brown or red on the natural surfaces of the vases.

The first signs of new vitality after the decline occurred in the potters' workshops attached to the Dipylum cemetery. It coincided with the introduction of cremation into Attica and while cremation was a contributory factor in the decline of funerary architecture, it inspired a new art form: the ceramic grave monument. A large amphora was placed on the urn which contained the ashes of the dead and replaced the commemorative stele. The amphorae of the proto-geometric cemetery of Athens were perforated at the base so that libations offered by relatives and friends of the dead could penetrate the ashes (Pl. 42).

26. Mycenaean false-necked amphora, with Linear B script, 14th century, *height* 1 ft. 4 in. *Agora Museum, Athens*

27. Brauron: figure, terracotta, *c.* 1300 *height* 5$\frac{1}{4}$ in.

28. Mycenaean pot, *c.* 1250 *height* (of the figures) 4$\frac{1}{2}$ in. *Agora Museum, Athens*

29. Mycenaean figures and pot, terracotta, early 13th century, *height* (of the figures) 4$\frac{1}{2}$ in. *Agora Museum, Athens*

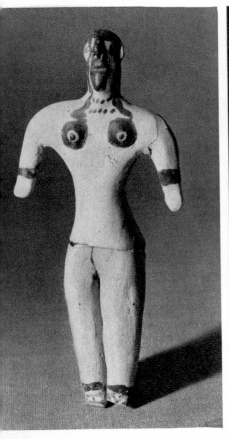

27   28

29

30 31

32

Cremation was practised by the Hittites and the Trojans. The ritual of the funeral pyre so impressed the Achaeans during the siege of Troy that they too adopted the custom for their own dead. In the *Iliad* Homer describes not only the cremation of Eëtion, Sarpedon and Hector on the Trojan side, but also that of Patroclus, the friend and squire of Achilles. However archaeological findings do not support the view that the Mycenaeans practised cremation when they returned home. With the exception of Grave XLI discovered by Blegen in the Argolid, no evidence of cremation has so far come to light in continental Greece. But this may be due to the fact that limited supplies of wood, reinforcing the ancient burial traditions of the Mycenaeans, precluded its introduction except in exceptional circumstances.

It is conceivable that it was introduced into Athens at the time of the Dorian invasions for reasons similar to those which led to its occurrence during the Peloponnesian War. Conditions in Athens in both instances must have been very much the same, with floods of refugees pouring into the city for safety. We know that in 431 the swollen population together with an outbreak of plague posed serious problems in disposing of the dead and Thucydides records that the Athenians began violating their burial customs by cremating their dead on wood piles.[67] In the same way, congestion and disease may have been responsible for the introduction of cremation in the earlier period.

The proto-geometric graves at Athens were situated on either side of a road which left the Dipylum, passed the Agora of Theseus, continued along the western side of the Areopagus and ended where the Roman Odeion now stands. The sites of these graves enable us to trace the road system which existed inside and outside the city, for their long strung-out arrangement is in striking contrast with the dense concentration of the sanctuaries and public buildings of the Agora of Theseus.[68] The dwellings and workshops of the potters who supplied the neighbouring cemetery covered the area to the north-west of the temple of Hephaestus and must have been very numerous indeed, judging from the quantity of proto-geometric and geometric vases found in Attica and elsewhere.

For many centuries pottery was the principal art practised in Athens—at all times it was an important industry—and it may be helpful if we interrupt our discussion of proto-geometric works for a moment to define and describe the forms or shapes which are common to many styles. We shall have to refer to these forms by their names in later sections and the plates illustrate examples of most of them from every period.

All vases were essentially utilitarian and their shapes conform on the whole to the uses for which they were intended. Even the *amphora*, the most characteristic form of Attic vase, which began in proto-geometric times as a funerary object, was later taken into domestic, and even commercial, use as a wine container. It is a large vase with two handles and a ring-shaped base (Pl. 65). As time went on it tended to become more and more oval (Pl. 33) and the neck got longer and narrower, so that it reminds one of the steatopygous figurines of the neolithic age with their elongated necks (Pl. 23). The *hydria* (Pl. 63) is a variation of the amphora, used for carrying and storing water. It is smaller than the amphora and has, in addition to the two lateral handles, a third one at the mouth to enable women to manipulate it more easily when going to the well to draw water. The *loutrophoros* is a special type of hydria used to contain water for bridal lustrations. The *stamnos* or jug (Pl. 1) is another variant of the amphora with broad handles and a cap fitting into the mouth. It held the wine that was drunk on the feast days of Dionysus.

The *crater* (Pl. 34) has a tall bell-shaped foot, a semi-spherical belly and a very wide mouth. It was used for mixing water with wine. The *oinochoe* or *prochus*

Amphora

Hydria

30. Mycenaean oinochoe, *height* 10³/₄ in. *Agora Museum, Athens*

31. Brauron: Mycenaean oinochoe, *height* 7 in.

32. Ivory box from a Mycenaean Chamber Tomb, *c.* 1400, *height* 5³/₄ in. *Agora Museum, Athens*

33. Funerary amphora depicting *prothesis* (laying-out) and lamentation over the dead. Found in the Dipylum. An example of geometric style at its best, *c.* 800. *National Museum, Athens*

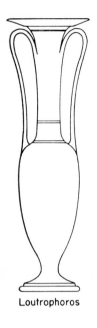

Loutrophoros

Stamnos

Calyx crater

(Pls. 35 and 41) is a small jug with a single handle and a long neck. The mouth is pinched in so that wine can be conveniently poured from it into a *skythos* (Pl. 40), a *kylix* or cup (Pl. 79), a *kantharos* or flask, that is to say into the smaller vessels which were used for drinking. Oinochoai sometimes take the form of a bird or animal (Pl. 38).

Aromatic perfumes were kept in a *lekythos* (Pls. 77-8), a kind of tall thin pitcher with a long neck, a bell-shaped mount and a single handle. The circular *pyxis* (Pl. 39) was a small shallow container with a lid, usually used as a trinket or jewel box.

Most of these shapes go back to the Mycenaean age and we have had to use some of the terms already in describing vases of that period. Wace has shown that the basic decorative motifs which characterize the proto-geometric style— the wavy lines, the concentric circles, the treatment of the vase handles—also have their origins in the sub-Mycenaean style.[69] But although there was no stylistic interruption between the two, proto-geometric nevertheless represents a considerable advance and it does not need a trained eye to observe the difference in technique and feeling between them.

In proto-geometric pottery we see the embodiment of a new conception of form. The realistic themes of the Minoan tradition in painting are abandoned. The subjects which are used to decorate the new vases are all abstract; the forms become geometric and bear no relation to the forms of nature. It is as though the vase painter, who was trained to work with the straight edge and compasses and to prepare a plan of decoration for each vase, was striving to express by means of geometric symbols concepts beyond the reach of mind. In his hands the process of vase decoration becomes as solemn and austere as a religious ritual (Fig. 11, p. 88). It is a sacred exercise in logic, an expression of human thought in its purest and highest form. This is a constant pre-occupation of Athenian art which we meet for the first time in the proto-geometric style.

Proto-geometric amphorae are decorated in horizontal bands, alternately dark and light. The widest band which encircles the greatest circumference (the belly) is divided into sections vertically much as a frieze is divided into metopes. In the example in the Kerameikos Museum (Pl. 42), the number of white concentric circles drawn in the square metopes of the belly is precisely the same (six) as the successive triangles and diamonds which fill the vertical stripes between the metopes. The repetition of this number is almost certainly of religious significance; but the plan is not rigidly followed. Here and there a slight variation occurs: for example, a half diamond instead of a whole one, two triangles instead of one, in the vertical stripes. This variation within a highly organized formal plan gives the composition its inner life, its " latent motion ".[70] We see therefore that proto-geometric decoration achieves harmony more from the contrasts in the decorative elements than from their regularity. In the example we have been studying, we feel this in the alternation of dark and light bands, the variations of theme, the squares which frame the concentric circles and the reversed rotation of the two sets of fishbone motif which form the base of the metopes. The tension due to the absence of symmetry in detail within an overall rhythmic symmetry and the achievement of harmony by means of scarcely perceptible dissonances constitute another constant of Athenian aesthetics present in the proto-geometric style.

We do not know what symbolic meanings the vase-painters attached to the motifs they used. But if we consider the meander which occurs in various combinations to cover the surface of a monumental amphora of the geometric period from the Dipylum (now in the Archaeological Museum of Athens) and study it in relation to the human figures in the funerary scene which forms the principal decorative theme, we notice that the vertical lines of the meander correspond to the erect figures of the living and that the horizontal lines correspond to the reclining figures of the dead. It is possible therefore that the meander had a symbolic significance relating to man's death and rebirth.

Much later, when Greek art was becoming increasingly realistic, Plato, who regarded the imitation of the natural world as an artistic aberration, expressed the view in his *Philebus* that when mathematics is removed from art nothing remains. Plato ranked architecture above any other art form because of its precision. For him, clarity and purity were the characteristic of art. He only regarded painting as beautiful when the lines were rectilinear or the shapes circular and when certain set canons were observed in drawing. The geometrical figure was beautiful because it was abstract. It was unrelated to any object and therefore induced spiritual happiness, whereas realistic representation caused sensual excitement. Plato wanted the same purity in the use of colour. The pure white surface he deemed the most beautiful. The aesthetic self-sufficiency of abstract art or, to use more modern philosophical terminology, " the ontology of plastic space," was another contribution of the proto-geometric style to the aesthetic heritage of Athens.

THE GEOMETRIC STYLE

By 800 THE PROTO-GEOMETRIC style had evolved into the geometric, in which curves were abandoned and only straight lines and their combinations occur. Meanders, triangles, squares, crosses, diamonds and fishbone motifs cover the entire surface of the vase in consecutive friezes, as though the painters were afraid of empty spaces (Figs. 12 and 13, p. 88).

In the midst of the network of geometric motifs, the first human scenes are depicted, usually including chariots and ships. But all the figures—human beings, birds or animals—are reduced to stylized symbolic signs, so that the drawings, which are usually narratives, come to resemble hieroglyphic inscriptions. The head of a man is represented by a dot, the chest by a triangle, the shield by a violin-shaped motif which derives from the Cyclades and Crete, the hands by fine lines. Women are distinguished by their hair and breasts, men by their swords.

This manner of representing people and objects was governed by the kind of intellectual realism with which we are familiar in the drawings of children. For example, a horizontal couch is presented in an inclined position, as is a corpse (Pl. 33); human figures are drawn, chests and eyes *en face*, faces and legs in profile. The artist does not try to depict things as he sees them, but as he knows and remembers them to be. A two-wheeled chariot drawn by two horses (Pl. 34) is not painted in strict profile, because that would only show one wheel and one horse: the painter wants to present his chariot analytically, so he paints the two wheels of the chariot separately and the legs of the two horses as though all eight belonged to a single horse; he inclines the chariot so that we can see that it is rectangular and he suspends the charioteer in the air so that we can distinguish him. In the same way he detaches the dead man from his couch as though each were floating in space. In short his purpose is as much didactic as aesthetic. Since his art, like most children's paintings, is predominantly narrative, he is as much concerned with imparting information as with causing delight.

The technique of inclining corpses so that they can be clearly distinguished is essentially adapted to a two-dimensional medium; but we nevertheless meet it again in certain archaic reliefs, for example in the battle scenes on the friezes

Oinochoe

Skyphos

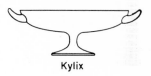

Kylix

Kantharos

Lekythos

Pyxis

Fig. 11. Proto-geometric amphora, *c.* 950, *Kerameikos Museum, Athens*

Fig. 12. Geometric jug found at Brauron, *National Museum, Athens*

Fig. 13. Geometric pot, *Agora Museum, Athens*

at Delphi and the pediments of Aegina, where the wounded warriors are treated in this way.

In the century in which the geometric style flourished, pottery was not a secondary art as it had been in the Mycenaean age and as it would again become in classical times. It was the primary form of artistic expression which completely eclipsed and surpassed architecture, monumental sculpture and painting. From Athens the geometric style spread throughout the whole of Greece and its colonies to become the universal Greek style.

THE PROTO-ATTIC STYLE

THE TRADITION which had arisen in Athens of making very large vases—originally for funerary purposes—continued throughout the seventh century during which the proto-Attic style flourished. At the same period Corinth, Aegina, Rhodes and Miletus were producing elegant, highly coloured vases whose small size gave them an advantage over Athenian ware in the international market. But Athenian potters remained loyal to their traditional sizes and from our point of view it is happy that they did, for the large surfaces were ideally suited to the new decorative style.

Two main differences distinguish the proto-Attic from the geometric style. On geometric vases the greater part of the surface had been covered by geometric motifs, with human figures filling in, as it were, the areas between. In proto-Attic vases the position is reversed: geometric motifs are confined to narrow bands or to the gaps between the figures of human beings or animals. These latter become the dominant decorative themes and occupy the broadest friezes on the vases.

Fig. 14. Flying Gorgon from a Proto-Attic lebes, *Louvre, Paris*

34. Geometric crater, depicting a funerary cortège and horse races. Late geometric style, *c.* 750, *height* 4 ft. *National Museum, Athens*

35. Oinochoe with the oldest known inscription in Greek, *c.* 750. *National Museum, Athens*

Many of these new themes—for example those depicting the slaying of monsters—came from the east, especially from the Ionian colonies and the vigour and realism with which they are executed have something of the impact of the Homeric epics. The curved line which the geometric style had totally excluded, even from the representation of figures, returned to vase-painting and imparted to the treatment of the new themes a movement and a drama which had been missing from Greek art since the wall paintings of the Mycenaeans and the Minoans. It was as though the vase-painters, after the constraining discipline of cerebral geometric abstractions, were athirst for life in its most violent and dynamic forms.

A large Athenian amphora in the Eleusis Museum exemplifies very clearly what we have been saying about proto-Attic vase-painting. Three separate scenes are depicted on it: on the neck, Odysseus and his companions put out the eye

36   37

of the cyclops Polyphemus after they have made him drunk; on the shoulder a lion is pouncing on a wild boar (Pl. 49); and on the belly the Gorgons Stheno and Euryale are pursuing Perseus who has just cut off the head of their sister Medusa.

The figure of Odysseus is drawn with quick powerful strokes while those of his companions and Polyphemus presage the silhouettes of the archaic black-figure style. Although the tradition is continued of representing the legs sideways, the chest as a triangle, the face in profile and the eye *en face*, the scene has immense vitality and drama.

The theme of the Gorgons is as new as the manner in which it is treated (Fig. 14). Their faces are drawn frontally and resemble totemic masks with fully rounded eyes and large mouths. They fly over the sea; one leg, emerging from the robe which covers the other, is bent to convey an impression of flight. This pose was to become standard in archaic representations of the winged Victory of Ionia and we can trace a further step in its development on one of the last proto-Attic amphorae of the seventh century, known as the Heracles vase (Fig. 16, p. 97), now in the National Museum of Athens. Here the theme of the two Gorgon sisters appears again, but this time they are depicted in exactly the same posture as, for example, the Ionian sculpture of the Winged Victory of Delos attributed to Archermos (Fig. 15). It is also interesting to note that the presence of curved motifs denotes movement, for on the neck of the same amphora there is another animated scene in which Heracles kills the centaur who has tried to rape his wife.

The proto-Attic style marks the last stage of the flowering of the Athenian school. During the seventh century the effective centres of Greek ceramic art lay elsewhere, mainly on the shores of the Aegean. On the Ionian side the vases of Miletus and Rhodes attained a high degree of perfection; on the western side those of Corinth and Aegina were pre-eminent. Indeed Aegina was known as the pitcher-capital of the Saronic Gulf. Farther afield, Etruscan Italy, where Greeks from Asia Minor had taken refuge, was also producing fine ware. Flourishing ceramic industries do not exist in isolation: the displacing of proto-Attic ware by the pottery of the other centres was due to social, economic and political factors rather than to purely artistic and commercial ones. Corinth, Rhodes, Miletus, Aegina and Tyrrhenia had become mercantile and maritime cities while Athens remained imprisoned within the outworn structure of her agricultural and aristocratic institutions. The decline of her pottery industry expressed her inability to adapt herself to new conditions. If Athens was to reclaim a place in the first rank of artistic and intellectual activity, she had first to break the fetters of her own heritage.

Fig. 15. The Winged Victory of Delos, *National Museum, Athens*

POLITICAL EVOLUTION FROM DRACO TO SOLON

THE MIDDLE of the seventh century witnessed the first changes in the oligarchic system in Athens. In 621 the nobles, under the pressure of mass discontent, accepted the mediation of Draco the lawgiver who is credited with abolishing the traditional laws of the clans and substituting in their place a written code which laid down procedures and fixed penalties. He is supposed to have defended the harshness of the latter—which have become proverbial in every language—by saying that small crimes ought to be punished by death and that he had not been able to think of any severer penalty for great ones. He made no changes in the form of government, but his legal reforms represented a concession on the part of the governing class which was thenceforth no longer able to apply

36. Late geometric tripod, *height* 7 in. *Kerameikos Museum, Athens*

37. Terracotta head, 7th century, *height* 2¹/₂ in. *Kerameikos Museum, Athens*

38. Late geometric zoomorphic oinochoai, *c.* 720, *height* 4³/₄ in. *Agora Museum, Athens*

39. Geometric pyxis from a grave, 8th century, *diameter* 11 in. *Agora Museum, Athens*

93

and interpret the laws in its own interest. His work did not affect the social and economic foundations of the system. All the functions of government remained in the hands of the nobles, even if they could no longer exercise them quite as arbitrarily as before. Cultivable land continued to belong to the great landowners and their tenants still remained heavily in their debt. The gap between rich and poor continued to widen and the situation cried out for a leader, or *tyrant*, to seize power and break the monopoly of the Eupatridae.

The word *tyrant* as it was used by the Greeks did not necessarily imply oppressiveness or cruelty. They meant by a tyrant a dictator who achieved power by unconstitutional means and imposed his rule by might rather than right. Greek history abounds in examples both of beneficial tyrants and of tyrants in our modern sense of the word. When tyranny became institutionalized as it did in certain instances, it is indistinguishable from monarchy.

The first attempt to establish a tyranny in Athens was the Cylonian conspiracy, of which there are accounts in Thucydides and in Plutarch's *Life of Solon*. Cylon was an Athenian of noble birth who had married a daughter of the tyrant of Megara. His successes in the Olympic Games of 640 had earned him popularity with the Athenian populace. He seems to have been of an ambitious and headstrong nature, but before making a move he consulted the Delphic oracle about the chances and timing of an uprising. The reply encouraged him to make the attempt, but refused to specify a date. So Cylon decided to act on the anniversary of the Olympic games which had gained him his reputation.

But either the economic distress was not as grave as Cylon had calculated or the people were alienated by the presence of Megarian troops among his supporters. They rallied to the defence of the aristocracy and laid siege to the Acropolis. Supplies of water and food soon ran short and Cylon fled, leaving his followers to make the best terms they could. Megacles who was in charge of the operation was a member of a powerful Eupatrid family, but he also had the support of the growing mercantile interest of the coast. He persuaded the followers of Cylon who had sought refuge in the temple of Athena to come down into the city to be tried. Before agreeing, the Cylonians attached a long thread—the symbol of supplication—to the base of the statue of Athena which they clung to as they moved down the Acropolis to the temple of the Eumenides to surrender. But the thread snapped and Megacles and his followers falling on the suppliants slew them to a man. This act provoked a reaction on the part of the populace which Cylon's supporters exploited and a period of civil strife ensued.

To bring it to an end the warring factions accepted the mediation of a new arbitrator, Solon. He persuaded Megacles and his followers to stand trial by a special court consisting of 300 citizens. The court found Megacles and his entire family, the Alcmaeonidae, guilty, condemning the living to perpetual exile and the dead to be exhumed. By the standards of the old clan laws, the punishment was lenient, for murder could only be purged by death, not exile. But the finding of the court satisfied another tradition of the clan justice: the corporate responsibility of the whole family or clan for the crime of one of its members. Solon's aim appears to have been to appease public opinion without destroying the Alcmaeonidae family which as a member of the mercantile middle class himself had his support and whose policies offered the greatest possibilities for social peace and economic development.

The banishment of the Alcmaeonidae was a setback for the coast-people, but their economic growth had already given them a certain independent bargaining power. Though they did not possess the military strength of the landowning class of the plains, they controlled commerce, shipping and manufacture. They were not, however, the only new element on the scene: another party, repre-

40. Late geometric skythos, *height* 3 in. *Kerameikos Museum, Athens*

41. Late geometric oinochoe, *height* 9 in. *Agora Museum, Athens*

94

40

41

senting the " men from beyond the hills," began to demand a voice in public affairs. The leaders of this group were landowners, but their lands had been incorporated in the Athenian polis in more recent times. In spite of their wealth they were not regarded as Eupatridae and were therefore excluded from government office.

In 594-3 new disorders broke out. Since the three parties were equally powerful, they were unable to settle their differences and again called on Solon to arbitrate, investing him with powers to draw up a new constitution. His laws were inscribed on stone slabs in the Basilian Stoa of the Agora and the citizens swore to abide by them for a hundred years. Should an archon deviate from them, he would become liable to a fine equal in value to a gold bust of himself.

The new constitution was drawn up on a basis of wealth rather than of birth. Henceforth Athenian citizens were divided into four classes according to the size of their annual income. First in the land were those who had incomes of 500 *medimnoi* of corn a year or the equivalent in other produce or money. The second category, the *hippeis*, had incomes of from 300 to 500 *medimnoi*. Although their name means cavalryman—in Sparta there was a *corps d'élite* of *hippeis*—it seems likely from the relatively low level of their income that in time of war they were each required to equip a hoplite, the heavily armed infantry soldier who was beginning to challenge the supremacy in the field of the heavy cavalryman of the Eupatridae. The third class of *zeugitai* (originally their name meant owners of a pair of oxen) had incomes ranging from 200 to 300 *medimnoi* and ultimately comprised the majority of the farmers and craftsmen. Under the constitution of Solon they were only eligible for the minor magistracies, though as time went on they acquired full rights. The fourth class, the *thetes*, were not liable for taxation but were also excluded from all public office.

The *medimnos* on which revennes were calculated was a measure of volume, used for solids or liquids. It is impossible to give a monetary equivalent of its value in terms of modern currency, because standards have changed so radically, but it has been calculated that 43 acres of land would have produced an income sufficient to qualify its owner as a member of the *zeugitai* and that 110 acres would have put him in the first category. Furthermore it is doubtful if more than one-fifteenth of the citizen body belonged to the first two groups taken together. These facts may serve to remind us that when we use the term aristocracy in the context of ancient Greece we mean, in economic terms, something very different from, say, the *noblesse* of pre-Revolutionary France.

Solon is credited with creating an assembly of 400 members of which 100 were chosen from each of the tribes, for the tribal structure continued to exist alongside the new class divisions. The task of the assembly of 400 was to prepare the business which came before the Areopagus. The Areopagus continued to function as before, but it acquired the new task of hearing cases of a political nature, notably those involving subversion or attempts to establish a tyranny. It was still recruited from the ranks of retiring magistrates, but the new classifications by wealth necessarily opened the magistracies to members of the community who had previously been excluded on grounds of birth. To increase the political consciousness of Athenians and to encourage a sense of civic responsibility in them, Solon introduced a law whereby any person who did not take up arms when a revolt occurred in the city and join one of the opposing sides was deprived of his political rights (*atimia*) and was barred from participating in the administration of the state.

The legislation of Solon opened the way for the liberation of the individual from the economic and political domination of the oligarchy. He cancelled all existing debts and proscribed the practice of offering or accepting personal

Fig. 16. Heracles vase: Heracles slaying Nessus, *National Museum, Athens*

42. Proto-geometric amphora, *c. 950, height* 2 ft. 3 in. *Kerameikos Museum, Athens*

freedom as a guarantee of debt. This last law was known as the *seisachtheia* of Solon, a word meaning that the burdens which had caused the people such anguish were lifted from their shoulders. He is said to have strengthened the *ecclesia*, the mass assembly of all citizens with political rights, and to have allowed even the *thetes* to take part in its meeting. He thus made it possible for any Athenian to denounce an injustice or to contest the decision of an archon before it. The Athenian citizen became in theory the arbiter of the city's affairs, having the right to recall the actions of the magistrates. But in fact many years were to elapse before this right became effective.

Solon was the first member of the middle class to wield power in Athens. As a merchant he had travelled widely in the Mediterranean and in Ionia. His political sense was sharpened by his experience of business, but his talents for practical action did not prevent him being a philosopher and a poet of considerable merit. His policies were based on moderation and a belief in social justice. As a businessman he believed in hard work and increased production. He ruled that a father who did not give his son the opportunity to learn a trade could not claim that the son should support him in his old age and he empowered the Areopagus to punish those who were idle and to investigate the sources of any citizen's wealth.

According to Plutarch, who devoted one of his *Lives* to Solon, his career began in an original way. Exhausted by a long and inconclusive war with the Megarians for the possession of Salamis, the Athenians had passed a law which forbade any citizen from making new proposals for its capture. Solon disapproved strongly of this measure and secretly composed the *Salamis*, a poem of 100 lines which he recited in the market place. To escape the penalties of the law he feigned insanity. But the poem so stirred the imagination of Athenians that in 610 they decided to mount a new expedition and put Solon in command of it. He succeeded by means of a trick. He dressed up some of his soldiers in women's clothing. When the Megarians saw them, they rushed amorously out of their ships, leaving their arms behind. The Athenians who had weapons concealed in the folds of their dresses set upon them and the island of Salamis became a possession of Athens.

Solon was tempted neither by the wealth of the oligarchs nor by the blandishments of the " men from beyond the hills " to establish a tyranny. Having accomplished his reforms, he retired into private life, where he looked after his business, wrote poetry and launched a ship for the navy. Then he asked permission to absent himself from Athens for ten years to allow his fellow-citizens to accustom themselves to the new form of government which he had initiated. But after his departure Athens was only able to enjoy the fruits of his work for four years: in the fifth a fresh political crisis broke out which called for more drastic measures.

43. Ivory statuette from the Dipylum. *c.* 750, *height* 9¹/₂ in. *National Museum, Athens*

44. Terracotta plaque from a votive offering depicting a goddess, 7th century. *Agora Museum, Athens*

45. Detail of an archaic votive relief depicting Athena, *c.* 530, *height* 1 ft. *Acropolis Museum, Athens*

46. Fragment of a stele showing a child's head held by his mother's hand, *width* 6¹/₂ in. *National Museum, Athens*

THE TYRANNY OF PISISTRATUS

ALL OVER GREECE the sixth century was the century of tyrants. In many cities dictatorial regimes were established and by no means all of the tyrants deserved the harsh criticisms which later writers levelled at them. The career of Pittacus, for example, the tyrant of Mytilene, has certain affinities with that of his contemporary Solon. He seized power in order to reform the constitution and when his work had been accomplished retired into private life. Social and economic growth, stifled by institutions too rigid to be changed by moderate means, made some kind of explosion unavoidable and favoured the rise of leaders who, deriv-

43

44

45

46

47

ing their power from popular support, were able to cut through the vested interests of those who had hitherto monopolized the direction of public affairs.

In Athens, as we have seen, three more or less equally powerful parties struggled for power: the people of the plains representing the old oligarchic families who wanted to maintain and increase their hold on the state; the coast-people, led by the Almaeonidae, who felt that their economic importance entitled them to a commanding voice in state policies; and the mountain people, a group of disaffected landowners from eastern Attica, led by Pisitratus, who obtained the support of the poorest and most numerous sections of Athenian society by promises of social and economic reform. In 560 Pisistratus was able to seize the Acropolis and although he was twice expelled from power for brief periods ruled until his death in 527, when he was succeeded by his son.

The methods of Pisistratus were exactly the opposite of those of Solon whose achievement he respected. Solon was an arbitrator, appointed as a compromise between the three parties. His situation therefore obliged him to concentrate on legal and constitutional measures, but he was powerless to attack or curb the people who would put them into practice. Pisistratus appears to have cared little for the forms of government. There is no record of any constitutional change due to him; on the contrary he treated the Solonian institutions with the most scrupulous respect. But he made sure that he used them in his own interests and in the interests of those whose support kept him in power and that all positions of command which the law prescribed were in the hands of people devoted to his cause.

Aristotle, who in general was not an admirer of tyranny, says of Pisistratus that he ruled as a citizen rather than as a tyrant, showing moderation, clemency and concern for the public good. His policy of firmness and peace abroad favoured colonial expansion and commercial development. Under his rule Attic black-figure ware and Attic currency dominated the markets of the eastern Mediterranean. By sending judges on circuit in the outlying districts of Attica, and by visiting them regularly himself, he broke the local power of the oligarchs and gave Athens a new unity and cohesion. His dictatorial powers enabled him to attack in a practical way the economic problems which lay at the root of Athens' social ills and which Solon's legislation had only touched on in general terms. He instituted measures of land redistribution and settled landless peasants on plots of their own. He advanced state loans to them and to poorer members of the farming community so that agricultural productivity rose, as did the yield of taxation. To provide work for the unemployed he embarked on an extensive programme of public works in Athens, maintaining and repairing existing buildings, installing new water supply and drainage systems, constructing roads and building two temples. One, dedicated to the goddess Athena, was erected between 529-20 on the south side of the Erechtheum where its foundations can be seen today (see Plan 2, p. 52). It was a Doric peripteral with six columns on its short sides and twelve on its long. It had a prodomus or vestibule and an opisthodomus, a shrine with three compartments and an adytum with three section, perhaps for the worship of more than one deity. The other temple was built earlier, about 570-66, probably at the north-west corner of the later Parthenon. It was known as the Hecatompedon, because it was 100 feet long (the Greek foot was slightly shorter than ours). Its position is conjectural as no trace of it has survived. Pisistratus must also be credited with the repair of the Pelasgian wall. On the south side of the Pelasgian wall and within the walls the fountain of Asclepius was built. Beneath the Acropolis the first temple in the sanctuary of Dionysus was erected. The first marble Propylaea which altered the old Mycenaean entrance to the Acropolis as well as the temple of Athena Nikê near the Mycenaean gate-tower were formerly thought to have been built under Pisistratus. But

47. Stone relief of a running hoplite, revetment of a tomb.
Found in Athens near the Temple of Hephaestus, 6th century, *height* 3 ft. 4 in.
National Museum, Athens

48. Archaic statue of a Kore dressed in Ionian style, *c.* 500.
Acropolis Museum, Athens

recent research has shown that they date from the period between Marathon and Salamis when the first white marble Parthenon was built.[71]

Pisistratus and his sons, particularly his younger son Hipparchus, appreciated the important role which entertainment and cultural activities can play in a society deprived of liberty. During their rule, the Panathenaean festivals which commemorated the unification of Attica were greatly extended and Hipparchus made public recitals of the Homeric epics a part of them. He is also credited with instituting the first dramatic performances at the feast of Dionysus.

After Pisistratus' death, his elder son Hippias ruled for seventeen years. He seems to have inherited the ability and moderation of his father, but a regime which had done so much to remedy the causes which had brought it into existence could not hope to remain indefinitely in power. Even so, it could only be overthrown by foreign intervention. The Alcaeonidae who had taken refuge at Delphi when Pisistratus seized power prevailed on the oracle to order Sparta to liberate Athens. At first the Spartans were unsuccessful, but finally Cleomenes at the head of a large army was able to dislodge Hippias from the Acropolis. Hippias fled to the court of the Persian king Darius and twenty years later when he was an old man he took part on the Persian side in the campaign which culminated in the battle of Marathon.

THE AGORA OF SOLON

THE EVOLUTION of an oligarchic rural community to a centralized urban one, begun by Solon and completed under the tyranny of Pisistratus and his sons, marked the city of Athens physically. From a collection of peasant dwellings straggling along the waysides, it became during the sixth century an organized city with its economic, political and intellectual centre in the new market place of Solon. It acquired water and drainage systems, a wall and a network of roads linking it with the demes of Attica; it was embellished with temples on and round the Acropolis, public buildings in the Agora and gymnasia outside the walls.

The temples, public buildings and walls which were erected during the sixth century were destroyed by the Persians in the invasion of 480, but the foundations of most of them have survived. Excavations carried out by the American School have identified the sites of the buildings which stood in the Agora, and sculptures which had been preserved from the general destruction of the temples on the Acropolis have also come to light: they had been buried in pits on the south side of the Parthenon and are now in the Acropolis Museum.

The site on which Theseus had founded his Agora to the northwest of the Kerameikos was abandoned by Solon. The new Agora (Map 4, p. 107) was laid out in the form of a triangle with its vertex resting on the Eridanus river, its base at the foot of the Areopagus and its two other sides bounded by the Panathenaean way and the Colonus Agoraeus. The roads from Eleusis and from the hinterland came together at the vertex of the triangle and formed the natural entrance to Athens. In 521-0 a grandson of Pisistratus erected an altar to the twelve gods on this spot which served as a point of reference for measuring distances from Athens. On the northwest side of this altar the Leochorium was built, marking the point from which the Panathenaean processions started.

Facing the Leochorium was a row of buildings which formed the western side of the Agora. At the northernmost end stood the sanctuary and altar of Zeus, followed by the temples of Apollo Patroos and of Cybele, the Bouleuterion, the Prytaneum (which served as a dining hall for members of the assembly) and, lastly, a marble stele marking the boundary of the Agora at its southwestern angle.

49. Neck of Proto-Attic amphora depicting the blinding of Polyphemus, *c. 675, height* 1 ft. 6¹/₂ in. *Eleusis Museum*

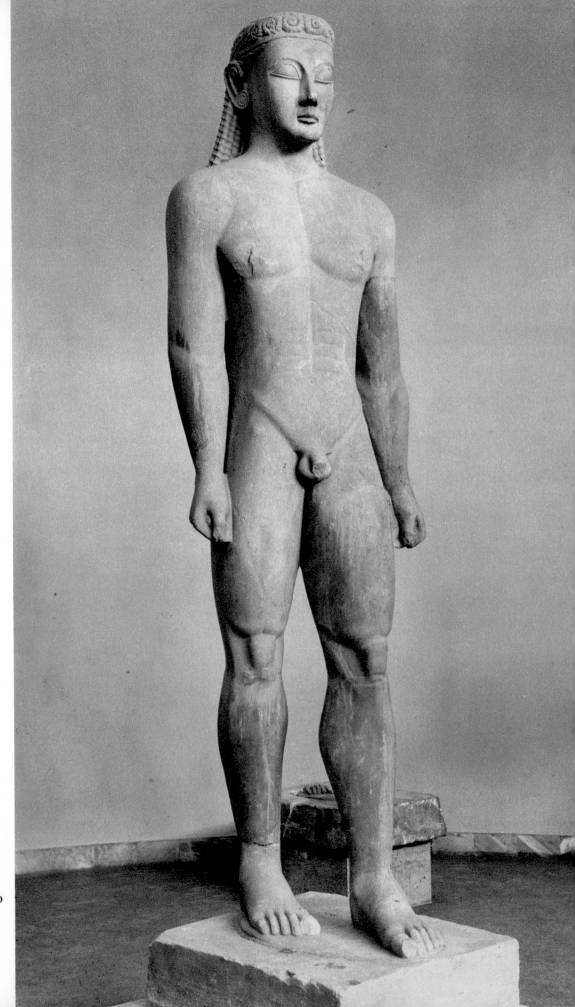

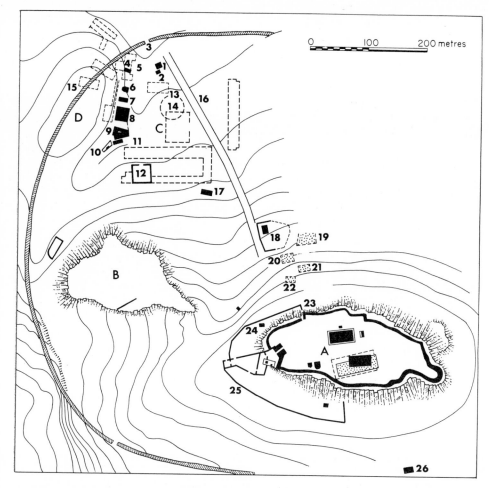

A	Acropolis
B	Areopagus
C	Agora
D	Colonus Agoraeus
1	Altar of the twelve gods
2	Temple of Ares
3	Leochorium
4	Temple of Zeus
5	Sanctuary of Zeus
6	Temple of Apollo
7	Metroum
8	Bouleterion
9	Dining Halls of the Prytaneum
10	Peribola of tombs
11	Limit of the Agora
12	Court of the Heliaea
13	Monument of the tyrannicides
14	Orchestra
15	Temple of Hephaestus
16	Panathenaean Way
17	Enneakrounos fountain
18	Eleusinium
19	Theseum
20	Prytaneum
21	Bucoleum
22	Thesmotheteum
23	Cave of Aglauros
24	Clepshydra
25	Enneapylon
26	Temple of Dionysus

Map 4. ACROPOLIS AND AGORA BEFORE THE PERSIAN INVASION (480-479)

Forming the southern side of the Agora were the court of the Heliaea, the temple of Demeter and Persephone (known as the Eleusinium) and, in the south-eastern corner, the Enneakrounos fountain which Thucydides describes: " The fountain is now called the Enneakrounos (nine spouts) since the tyrants made it so, but its old name was Callirhoe (fair stream) when the water came straight out of the ground. In those days it was used for all purposes but, according to present custom, it is reserved for ceremonies before marriage and other religious rites." Pausanias who also saw the Enneakrounos says that it was so called because Pisistratus made it with nine spouts. " Though there are wells throughout all the City, this is the only Spring. Above the fountain are temples: one of them is a temple of Demeter and the Maid (Kore), in the other is an image of Triptolemus." The Enneakrounos was an artificial fountain, built to augment the insufficient water supply. The subsoil contained no subterranean streams and the Athenians had been forced to bring water from Caesariani to the Agora by underground conduits which were laid deep in the rocky soil, often below the level of private wells, some of which went down to a depth of thirty or forty yards. The Enneakrounos was a Doric structure with columns and architraves. It was decorated with murals and below the nine spouts there were places for the women to rest their hydriae. A drainage system had also been installed to

50. Statue of a youth (kouros) set up as a dedication in front of an earlier temple to Poseidon at Sunium, c. 600. *National Museum, Athens*

carry off rain water from the western edge of the Agora to a large underground drain and thence into the Eridanus.[72]

A circular orchestra for musical and dramatic contests was built in the centre of the Agora. For perfomances, a semi-circular wooden stage and seating accommodation for the public were erected. It is possible that the stage of this wooden structure was mounted on wheels so that it could moved out of the way into a storage building when it was not needed. Excavations made at Sparta and Megalopolis in 1963 show that the stages of their theatres were movable.

The eastern boundary of the Agora was marked by the Panathenaean Way where the procession passed and which was used for athletic contests and horse races. Its total length from the altar of the twelve gods to the Eleusinium was approximately 400 yards. At either end stood sculptures depicting horse-racing.

With its public buildings, sanctuaries and temples, the Agora in the sixth century served as the business, religious, political and intellectual centre of Athens. Situated at the junction of the road system which led to the outlying demes of Attica, it was the natural place for merchants and farmers to congregate to display their wares and to transact their business affairs. The proximity of the cemetery reminded Athenians of the debt they owed to their forebears and created an atmosphere propitious to intellectual achievement and athletic contests. As a rule athletic contests in ancient Greece had their origins in funeral rites.

As well as the two temples built on the Acropolis under Pisistratus, building activity in the sixth century spread beyond the limits of the city towards the Ilissus river where the temple of Olympian Zeus is now situated. It was begun by Pisistratus, but was not completed until the second century A. D. by the Roman emperor Hadrian. In the same vicinity stood some of the finest temples of archaic Athens, including the Pytheum and the sanctuaries of Gaea, of Demeter and Persephone, of Artemis, of Aphrodite and of Heracles. Also outside the city limits were the three gymnasia of Athens: the Lyceum on the bank of the Cefissus, and the Academy and the Cynosarges by the Eridanus and the Ilissus, where the young men were encouraged to exercise their bodies and train their minds.

It is not certain whether there was a city wall round archaic Athens, although Thucydides refers to its destruction by the Persians. If it existed, it must have been nearly circular, for, according to Herodotus, the Pythian oracle called Athens the circular city. The probable circumference has been estimated at a mile and two-thirds and the whole city comprising the Acropolis, the Areopagus, the Agora of Theseus and the Agora of Solon covered an area of 5,380,000 square feet.[73]

Religion

Judging from the temples built in Athens during the archaic period, it is evident that the gods had already acquired their anthropomorphic forms, their names and their cults, their special habitations within the city. Herodotus credits Homer and Hesiod with having endowed the gods with human attributes, but the Linear B tablets make it abundantly clear that they had had already acquired these five hundred years earlier. The poets had not invented the gods. They had found a tradition whose roots went back into the Mycenaean age and beyond and which they had shaped and coloured to make more real, more easily apprehended. Around the gods they had created a social and political setting which reflected very closely that of Mycenaean monarchy. Olympus became a Mycenaean citadel with Zeus as supreme ruler surrounded by an assembly of peers. The gods held meetings and banquets, waged war on their enemies and rivals, made laws, held trials and took delight in meddling in the affairs of their subject mortals. The transition from monarchy to oligarchy and finally to democracy did not alter the structure of Mycenaean Olympus. As Martin Nilsson has put it: " Democracy flourished on earth, but monarchy held sway in the heavens." [74]

Greek religion in its official form was not a mystical but a political and ethical religion which demanded obedience to the law, respect for the gods, fulfilment of obligations, moderation in behaviour and a deep knowledge of one's limitations and of one's inability to rival the immortals. " Know thyself," inscribed on the temple of Apollo at Delphi and Plato's precept, " Nothing in excess," are typical canons of the Greek ethical code.

To transgress the boundaries of moderation constituted *hybris* of which it is easier to give examples than a translation. It means something like " overweening pride " and was to be the subject of many classical tragedies in which the hero aspires to a role which is proper only to the gods, for example Prometheus in Aeschylus' version of the story. *Hybris* incurred *nemesis* or retribution, for too much honour, power or wealth provoked the jealousy of the gods who were always ready to re-establish balance and order in the state. (We shall meet this idea again in human terms when we come to discuss the law of ostracism.) But the actions of the gods themselves were often incomprehensible and to account for this the concept of *moira* or blind destiny arose which readers of the *Iliad* will remember as the ultimate mover of divine as well as human events.

In Athens Apollo Patroos was the guardian and interpreter of divine law. The laws of the state were enacted on his oracular recommendation and obeyed because they had his sanction. Not only did Athenian art express itself in terms of geometry: religion also was built up in a similar manner. A rational system always tends to be static, because it strives to maintain the social group within stable and time-honoured forms. The official religion of archaic Athens, which sought to confine individual initiative within the austere limits of set ritual practices and a well-defined code of behaviour, was often restrictive and oppressive.

But official religion had to confront a powerful rival, a swirling current of religious revolt which aimed at dissolving the rational confines set by Apollo. The cult of Dionysus [75] attracted countless adherents because the state of inspired ecstasy which it induced brought them into close personal communion with their god. They derived a comfort and satisfaction from this immediate contact which the hieratic and authoritarian forms of Apollonian religion denied them.

The tone of this orgiastic worship was set by the wild bands of women, the Bacchae, who chanted the old Phrygian laments to Mother Earth and devoured raw meat, until they entered a state of divine trance. It had many of the characteristics of a return to the past, to the primitive world of matriarchy, totemism, fertility rites and communal ownership and allowed individuals of every class, even slaves, to participate on an equal footing. It conflicted with the efforts of cities to organize themselves on the basis of patriarchy, private ownership and the submission of slaves and many attempts were made to put it down.

The fullest description of the Dionysiac revolt is in Euripides' *Bacchae*, which recounts the legend of the implantation of the cult in Dionysus' native Thebes. This is vigorously opposed by the Theban king, Pentheus, whose efforts to prohibit it result in his being torn limb from limb by his own mother while she is in a state of ecstasy. Written in classical times, its theme takes us back to an earlier age. The Bacchae are depicted as living in the open air with loose locks of hair falling over their naked shoulders. Gaudy hides are thrown over their lithe bodies, their heads are crowned with wreaths of ivy and little wild animals cling to their breasts and suckle. With their Bacchic wands they strike rocks and springs gush forth; by scratching the soil they produce honey and milk; they plant fennel in the earth and fountains of sweet wine spring up, carrying them into the realms of divine ecstasy. They are women who have abandoned their husbands and their homes in the cities to live freely as the mystical brides of Dionysus among the mountains and the streams.

Dionysus was indifferent, even hostile, to the foundation of cities, to their laws and institutions, which were watched over by Apollo. Dionysus inspired and led the revolt against order. In the Euripidean tragedy, Pentheus who represents the state, patriarchy and the rule of reason, is destroyed by his mother and her sister Bacchae on a wild mountainside, driven on by Dionysus in the form of a bull. It is only when Pentheus' mother returns to the city that she is able to recognize that the head of a lion which she believes she has brought back is in reality the head of her son.

In Homer, Dionysus is not numbered among the Olympian gods and his role is insignificant. It is with the establishment of the first city-states that his cult gained importance, as the expression of revolt against the new order and as an outlet for forces which civilization could not easily accommodate.

The appearance of Dionysus in Attica is very ancient. Before he was worshipped in Athens, his cult was already established in Marathon. It is possible that it arrived from Crete, for some evidence exists of its practice there in Minoan times. As cities spread and grew, the Greeks had somehow to reconcile the conflict between Dionysus and Apollo, to find a compromise between the popular religion of revolt and the state religion of the oligarchs. One solution was found by combining them in the same religious form, the drama, in which the orgiastic bands of Dionysus were gradually made at home in the form of a chorus which commented on the actions and sufferings of the ill-fated heroes of aristocratic Greece. Sculpture and painting took the same path, for they attempted to domesticate Dionysus by endowing him with human attributes. From a tree, a formless fetish of the forest and a phallus, he became a god, a brother of Apollo and the son of Zeus.

Later he shared Apollo's shrine at Delphi. His prophetesses and seers were also those of Apollo and his primitive ties with the matriarchal earth-goddesses were recognized and accepted. In the classical period, the centre of the earth (the navel) was located in the adytum of the Delphic temple of Apollo which also contained the tomb of Dionysus. When Apollo emigrated for the three winter months, Dionysus was fêted at Delphi with orgiastic rituals. The sculptures on the eastern pediment represented Apollo, Artemis, Leto and the Muses, but the western pediment was devoted to Dionysus and his maenads. Thus the temple at Delphi became the symbol of reconciliation between mysticism and rationalism, unbridled freedom and respect for the law, the passions of the individual heart and the order imposed by collective existence.[76]

To the Greeks of the classical age, the religious crisis of earlier times had transmitted an impulse of Dionysiac enthusiasm which enriched their quest for knowledge and artistic perfection by leaving a door in their minds half open to the dark world of the instincts. Through this half-open door, a woman of Mantinea, Diotima by name, was to show Socrates the mystery of erotic passion.

THE ARCHAIC TEMPLE

NONE OF THE TEMPLES erected during the archaic period survived the Persian invasion of Attica. They were to be rebuilt during the classical age and the only example of a Doric pre-classical temple building still standing today in the vicinity

51. Three-bodied *daemon*, perhaps Nereus, from a porous stone pediment from the ancient temple of Athena on the Acropolis. The original polychrome has survived. *c.* 580. *Acropolis Museum, Athens*

52. Archaic marble statue of a Kore. One of the Korai with the archaic smile, *c.* 510, *height* 4 ft. *Acropolis Museum, Athens*

of Athens is the temple of Aegina in the Saronic Gulf. There are, however, several examples in other cities of Greece and in the colonies which illustrate the architectural principles and the two main styles of archaic temple-building.

Where did the basic elements of Greek temple architecture come from? We have seen how the Olympian pantheon reflected the monarchic structure of Mycenaean monarchy. In much the same way, the Mycenaean megaron—or palace—provided the basic groundplan for the abode of the gods on earth.[77]

The ancient Mycenaean megaron consisted of one *cella* and a single entrance (Plan 1, p. 42). In the archaic temple, two columns *in antis* replaced the entrance between the extension of the two side walls and the hearth in the centre of the cella became the wooden statue or palladium of the deity. The Treasuries of Delphi and Olympia are examples of this type of temple. To make the temple symmetrical, the prodomus or vestibule leading to the cella was duplicated at the back, the latter being known as the opisthodomus. In the earliest examples, the two-column stoa of the entrance (*in antis*) was repeated for the opisthodomus and this form of structure is known as amphiprostyle, expressing the regularity and symmetry of this type of building. An example of simple amphiprostyle is the small classical temple of Athena Nikê at the entrance to the Acropolis (Pls. 4 and 5). In more complex temples, there was a second chamber beyond the cella known as the adytum or inner sanctuary which served as a kind of store-room and housed the sacred idols. From an early date, the bare and solid surfaces of the outside walls were surrounded with a peristyle or colonnade. Temples of this type, to which the Parthenon and the temple of Hephaestus belong, are known as peripteral. The cornices and the pediments of the peristyle were decorated with bas-reliefs depicting scenes from mythology and the temple became an open book recording the traditions of the community and instructing the citizens in political cohesion.

The two styles or orders of temple architecture, Ionic and Doric, which dominated Greek religious building throughout its history and which attained their most perfect expression in the classical Parthenon and Propylaea, were created during the archaic period. The earliest monuments in Ionic style are in Aeolia (at Neandreia and Lesbos) and in Ionia (the Artemeseum at Ephesus, the Heraeum on Samos and the sanctuary of Apollo on Delos). In continental Greece, the Ionic style made its appearance during the sixth century at Delphi with the dedicatory column of the Naxians and the treasuries of the Cnidians and Siphnians. It was not used in Athens until the fifth century.

The earliest examples of Doric temple-building are the temple of Hera at Olympia and the temple of Apollo at Corinth, both in the Peloponnese. In western Greece, the ruins of two Doric temples of Apollo survive at Delphi and Thermae.

The two styles can be distinguished most easily by their columns and capitals. The Ionic column stands on a pedestal, while the Doric column rests directly on the stylobate or floor of the peristyle. The Ionic column is tall and slim and its capital is formed by two volutes, which have been compared to a crown decorated with leaves or the pigtails of a girl's coiffure. The Doric column tapers from base to top and is altogether shorter and squatter than the Ionic. Its capital is plain and severe, consisting simply of an echinus and a quadrangular abacus or plinth. In both orders the capitals carry an architrave or band supporting the roof structure. Above this comes the frieze. The Ionic frieze is decorated with continuous motifs which run round all four sides of the building, whereas the Doric frieze is divided into metopes separated from one another by sets of three perpendicular grooves known as triglyphs. The restricted space offered by the Doric metope forced the sculptor to treat his themes tersely and pungently, to give, as it were, a laconic answer, whereas the Ionic running frieze allowed

53. Archaic marble statue of a Kore, known as the Peplophoros, attributed to the sculptor Phaedimus, *c.* 540, *height* approx. 4 ft. *Acropolis Museum, Athens*

54. Detail of the Aegina marbles, *c.* 480. *Glyptothek, Munich*

him to develop his subject at length like Homer. In general the Doric style is simple, compact and forceful in keeping with the austere masculinity of the Dorians (Pl. 14) while the Ionic style with its wealth of decorative detail reflects the opulence and sensuality of the Ionians (Pl. 10). Vitruvius compared the Ionic column to a marble maiden and the Doric to a stone warrior.

Although the temples built on the Acropolis during the seventh and sixth centuries were destroyed by the Persians, many fragments of pediments made of porous stone have survived and are on display in the Acropolis Museum.[78] The earliest—late seventh century—is a pediment depicting the fight between Heracles and the Lernean Hydra, a nine-headed sea-monster resembling an octopus. Iolaos, Heracles' charioteer, stands with one foot on his chariot and his face turned to watch the struggling hero. On the left, a gigantic crab is coming to the rescue of the Hydra. The figures stand out against the triangular wall (the tympanum) at the back of the pediment and the scene is decorated with marine motifs which recall those of ancient Aegean pottery.

In another fragment, somewhat better preserved, Heracles is struggling with Triton, the son of Poseidon. The composition consists of two parts: on the left, Heracles has seized Triton's head and is clutching it in his powerful arms; on the right, a three-headed monster is looking on with an air of benevolence. This is probably Nereus who has the power to change into fire, water and wind and here appears in his triple state of being (Pl. 51). The three heads still retain traces of their original colour: the hair, moustache and beard are blue-grey, the skin ochre, the lips red and the pupils of the eyes outlined in black.

A marble pediment representing Athena staying the giant Encelados is interesting in that it inaugurates a new cycle in Attic temple sculpture. The Dorian hero Heracles ceases to be the central figure and yields his place to Athena and to Theseus. There is no difference of material or technique between the two cycles, but the new iconographic programme reflects the growing political consciousness of Athenians. Although they had never been conquered by the Dorians, they fell under their influence artistically. The religion of the Dorians had developed on anthropomorphic lines and they did not believe in sacred animals as the Minoans and Mycenaeans had done. For the latter, animals represented totemic and tribal deities and they considered it sacrilegious to depict a sacred animal being killed by a hero. But Dorian influence prevailed, even in places like Athens which had escaped their rule. The Dorian hero Heracles was adopted and venerated and his appearance on the archaic pediments of the Acropolis marks the progress of the Dorians. It is significant that he is always depicted in his role of slayer of monsters, for these monsters symbolize the old divinities of Mycenae and their death at the hands of Heracles celebrates the victory of the Dorians over the Mycenaeans. But as Athens developed politically and economically, her sculptors felt the need of themes which would express more directly her growing self-confidence.

KOUROI AND KORAE

IN THE ARCHAIC reliefs which I have described above Heracles is shown nude as as is the giant Encelados. The representation of the male nude is closely linked with the Greek view of the universe. Man is "the image and the measure of all things." Natural phenomena, as symbolized by mythology or interpreted by religion, were expressed in terms of man and anthropomorphic explanations of natural and supernatural forces are the most characteristic contribution of the poetry of Homer and Hesiod to Greek thought.

This "anthropocentric" attitude of the Greeks is revealed in the two basic types of religious sculpture: the *kouros* and the *Kore*. The kouros is usually identified with Apollo and examples have been found in countless sacred precincts such as the Acropolis and the temple of Poseidon at Sunium. But it also had a social and civic function when it was used to represent Olympic victors. Pausanias often comments on kouroi of this type erected in the agoras of Greek cities which he visited.

The enormous kouros of Sunium (Pl. 50), one of a group of kouroi which Gisela Richter [79] has called "the Sunium group," belongs to the religious type. Its imposing rigidity betrays the influence of Egyptian temple sculpture—but the arrangement of the hair in spirals and the decorative treatment of anatomical detail suggest the presence of Mesopotamian influence as well. (During the period to which it belongs, 615-590, the Greeks were sending colonists to the valleys of both the Nile and the Euphrates.)

In the group as a whole we can discern the successive and continuous efforts of the sculptors to liberate their figures from an architectural context and from the rigidity of hard stone. In the kouros, they were seeking to create a statue which could stand by itself in the open, representing, in an ideal and impersonal way, the civic aspirations or the religious feelings of a society of individuals. The kouros does not depict a king or a general or a high state official in the manner of Egyptian statues. It is a humanized god or a deified athlete standing naked and free as did all citizens exercising in the gymanasia or taking part in athletic contests.

Until the middle of the sixth century, the posture of the kouroi was standardized. The left foot is projected slightly forward, but the knee is not bent. From the nose to the feet a vertical plane can be traced, dividing the body into two equal segments. This law of symmetry and the equal distribution of the body's weight on both legs constitute what is known as the canon of frontality. The faces of the earliest kouroi are expressionless and serene; later they are enlivened by a faint smile, like that of the Calf-Bearer (Pl. 58).

The rigidity of the kouros is due to the sculptor's doubt as to whether it was possible to erect large, free-standing, unsupported figures. In reliefs, the movements of the body could be treated with much greater freedom and the artist could arrange rhythmic compositions more confidently: the running hoplite in the Archaeological Museum (Pl. 47) is an example of how freely archaic sculptors were prepared to treat movement when they were working in relief. But they would not have attempted it in free-standing statuary. The immobility of the kouros is also due to the fact that early sculpture, particularly free-standing sculpture, was dominated by the canons of architecture and the kouros is in a sense an architectural structure in sculptural form.

The nearer we approach the end of the sixth century, the more the dimensions of the kouros approach life-size. The bronze kouros found in July 1959 at Piraeus and now in the Athens Museum (Pl. 66) is only slightly over six feet in height. Its sculptor has freed himself from the uncertainty and restraints of the past and has released the hands of the kouros from its sides. Instead of projecting the left foot slightly forward, this one advances its right foot and all the muscles of the legs are taut and ready for movement in an attitude full of vitality and vigour. There is something tense, too, in the extended lower lip of the half-open mouth and the forceful triangular nose. The gaze of the large, wide-set eyes is firm and resolute and the short, sturdy neck is rooted firmly on the shoulders. The chest seems to breathe and the back unfolds into a broad expanse. The powerful arms, bent at the elbows, rise upwards and display the hands, one holding the fragment of a bow and the other all that remains of a vase. It is a masterpiece of archaic art.

After the Doric kouros, the archaic sculptor of Ionia created its sister. The Kore comes to us dressed in a *chiton* or robe drawn in at the waist, with its hair falling abundantly over its breasts and shoulders. The Kore was originally cylindrical in form like the Hera of Samos and it is reminiscent of the Assyrian statuary Assurnazirpal. Some Korae, like the Artemis of Nicandros, resemble a wooden palladium, others have their legs bound together, like the ivory statuettes found in the Dipylum (Pl. 43).

The Kore with the Doric shawl in the Acropolis Museum (Pl. 53) dates from 540. It is made of Parian marble and is about four feet tall. A Doric shawl, slit below the shoulders, is thrown over its woollen robe. The legs are bound, but the arms are free, the left arm bent at the elbow and the right, now missing, probably holding a pomegranate. The wavy hair, bound by a black headband, falls in plaits over the breasts and shoulders. The protruding almond-shaped eyes—characteristic of archaic sculpture—are painted in red ochre. The lips curve upwards in a faintly mocking smile which betrays its Ionian origin. The work is attributed to Phaedimus, who created the first equestrian statue in Athens whose head is now in the Louvre while the torso is in the Acropolis Museum (Fig. 17). In both museums the missing part has been replaced by a cast.

Towards 530 the Kore begins to change, more rapidly and more radically than the kouros. It starts to be decked out with earrings and bracelets and the hair is decorated with gold pins. Instead of the clinging chiton and the plain Doric shawl, it wears a fuller garment which falls in many folds almost down to the ankles. The sleeves stop short at the elbows and an elaborate kind of shawl is draped over one shoulder (Pls. 52 and 56). These Korae brought the oriental luxury of Ionia to the austere city of Pisistratus and in the Acropolis Museum they still continue to radiate charm with their seductive faces and their graceful bodies (Fig. 18, p. 119).

The emancipation of the Kore did not stop here. Freeing itself from the vertical position, its knees bent and its arm raised, it began to resemble a soaring Nike or Victory. Movement was first treated in Greek statuary in the winged Victories attributed to Archermos (Fig. 15, p. 93), but in vase painting, the flying movement had already appeared, as we have seen, with the Gorgons.

Another change of a different kind had occurred earlier, in funerary steles, where the Kore took on the form of a winged sphinx with the body of a lioness [80] (Pl. 59). It was set on the capital of a type of stele which developed in Attica towards the end of the seventh century (Pl. 59). The theme of the sphinx has certain peculiar features. It is present in the sculptures of Egyptian Memphis, but there it is male, [81] whereas in Attica it is female. Long before its appearance in sculpture, the sphinx had played its enigmatic role in the legend of Oedipus, and its presence on the capitals of funerary steles suggests that it had no evil connotations, but symbolized the soul inquiring into the secrets of the after-life. It lacks the charm and grace of the Korae of Ionia, its features express determination and the foot which rests on the base of the stele like a column, has an air of unshakeable certainty.

The Ionians taught the Athenians the use of Cycladic marble, particularly that of Paros in preference to the yellow porous limestone of Piraeus and Aegina which was widely used in archaic times until the middle of the sixth century. Its grain was finer in quality than the stone of Hymettus and it was easier to work. Moreover, Parian marble has warm natural tones that give a life-like quality to the surface of sculpture. Athens also learnt from Ionia the use of a sharp saw to cut the deep and delicate folds of drapery, and how to carve the head, hands and hair separately and to join the parts together. This meant that a statue need not

Fig. 17. Horseman by (?) Phaedimus, *c.* 560, *Acropolis Museum, Athens*

55. Detail of the Aegina marbles, *c.* 480. *Glyptothek, Munich*

56. Archaic marble statue of a Kore dressed in Ionian style. The left hand was originally raising the skirt slightly. One of the Korai from the courtyard of the ancient temple, dedicated to Athena, *c.* 530, *height* 1 ft. 10 in. *Acropolis Museum, Athens*

57. Marble gravestone fo Aristion, *c.* 510, *height* 6 ft. *National Museum, Athens*

118

be made from so large a piece of marble as would otherwise have been necessary. This new technique was applied for the most part to Korae.

Attic sculpture produced Korae and kouroi towards the end of the sixth century as the result of a long period of development. But the sculptor of the female statuettes of the Dipylum (P. 43) was still unable to dominate his material: his modelling was stylized and his figures rigid and motionless, ruled by the canon of frontality. The sphinx of the Kerameikos (Pl. 59) retains traces of frontality only in the head, for the body is turned sideways. But in the Running Hoplite (Pl. 47) the head is seen from the side, with the almond eyes shown full face, while the chest is depicted in all its breadth. The legs, seen in profile, heighten the effect of movement. Although the various part of the body are shown from different angles, nevertheless they are combined by the artist into a unified whole.

Another trait of archaic sculpture in Athens is the conventional smile. The artist raised the ends of the mouth and cut its angles deeply in an attempt to give expression and life to the face. The Ionians adopted this technique for all their statuary and the Dorians imitated them. The kouroi, Korae and warriors of the sixth century, even as they lie dying, wear this smile on their lips.

The triangular head, the large, almond eyes, the rounded cheeks, the flat ear, the thorax muscles at the armpits, the stylized treatment of the stomach and the conventional bone structure are characteristic features of archaic sculpture, by which works, whether in stone or terra-cotta, may be dated (Pl. 60).

The transition from archaic to early classical sculpture may be said to take place when the faces of the Korae and the kouroi begin to express character and emotion, as in the Kore of Euthydicos. Archaic sculpture made no attempt to explore the psychological possibilities of stone, whereas in classical times this became one of sculpture's main preoccupations.

THE TEMPLE OF AEGINA

THE ONLY ARCHAIC temple in Attica which survives today together with most of the sculptures of its pediments is the temple of Aphaea in Aegina (Pl. 20). The Persians, after they had destroyed all the temples in Athens and in the surrounding countryside, did not attempt to capture the island of Aegina in the Saronic Gulf. Thus the temple of Aphaea was spared. Most of the sculptures of the pediments are now in the Munich Glyptothek but some parts of an older version of the eastern pediment, dug up by Furtwängler in his excavations of 1911, are in the Archaeological Museum of Athens. The two Ionic Korae which decorated the western side of the temple—now at Munich—belong to the age of archaic sculpture (525-19) and are contemporary with the Korae of the Treasury of the Siphnians at Delphi and with the Korae of the Acropolis of Athens. The Korae of the temple of Aphaea must have been placed on the roof soon after it was completed before the actual decoration of the tympanum of the pediments. The western pediment dates from about 510; the eastern one, replacing the older version, displays all the characteristics of early classical style and must have been made about 490. According to Jean Charbonneaux,[82] the difference between the new eastern pediment of Aphaea and the earlier ones is due to the influence of Athenian sculpture.

An inscription on a broken slab, found by Furtwängler [83] in the foundations of the temple in 1901, says that the temple of Aegina, the ivory statue of the goddess and the peribolus were built in the time of the priest Cleoeta and that the temple was dedicated to Aphaea. Pausanias, who visited the temple, gives this account of the myth of Aphaea in Book II of his *Description of Greece:*

Fig. 18. Kore, *c.* 500, *Acropolis Museum, Athens*

58. Archaic marble statue known as the Calf-Bearer, *c.* 570. *Acropolis Museum, Athens*

59. Marble sphinx, *c.* 570, *height* 2 ft. 2¹/₂ in. *Kerameikos Museum, Athens*

" In Aegina, on the way to the mountain of Panhellenian Zeus, there is a sanctuary of Aphaea, about whom Pindar composed a song for the Aeginetans. The Cretans say (for her legend is native to Crete) that Carmanor, who purified Apollo for the slaughter of the python, had a son Eubulus, whose daughter Carme became the mother of Britomartis by Zeus. Britomartis delighted in running and hunting, and she was very dear to Artemis. But Minos fell in love with her, and she, flying from him, flung herself into some nets that were let down to catch fish. Artemis made her a goddess, and she is worshipped not only by the Cretans, but also by the Aeginetans, who say that Britomartis appears to them in their island. Her surname is Aphaea in Aegina, and Dictynna ('she of the nets') in Crete."

This myth is Minoan in origin and spread from Crete to the islands of the Aegean and the Saronic Gulf and along the Mediterranean coast as far as Marseilles. Britomartis became the virgin goddess of the moon. She was the patron of fishermen and sailors and the symbol of motherhood. The Mycenaean idol found at her temple in Aegina depicts her holding a new-born child. She travelled over the waves to show the way to sailors and fishermen. At sunrise, she would slip through the nets and disappear into the sea.

Her temple at Aegina was built in the late sixth century of yellow Aeginetan porous limestone. The two sculptured pediments, the cornices and the roof were of Parian marble. Its proportions (Pl. 3) are similar to those of the temple of Demeter at Paestum built about 524. Both temples are peripteral hexastyles, the Aegina temple having twelve columns on each long side whereas that of Demeter has thirteen. The resemblance between these two temples is not accidental, for the temple of Aphaea was already in existence when the naval battle of Cydonia took place in 519. Herodotus describes how the fleets of Aegina and Crete jointly attacked the Samian vessels, captured their crews and reduced to slavery the colonists of Cydonia who, though they hailed from Samos, were descended from old settlers from Aegina and Epidaurus who had fled during the Dorian conquest. He adds that the Aeginetans cut off the figureheads of the Samian vessels, which were sculpted in the shape of boars, to dedicate them to the temple of Aegina.

There is no doubt that the temple mentioned by Herodotus is the same as that which Pausanias describes, for no other temple was ever built on this spot, and Herodotus' assertion that the temple dated from 519 is borne out by the archaic style of its architecture as well as by the techniques which characterize the two Ionic Koae and the sculptures on the western pediment.

Plan 3. TEMPLE OF APHAEA AT AEGINA

1 Temple
2 Prodomus with columns *in antis*
3 South terrace
4 West terrace
5 North terrace
6 Ramp
7 Altar
8 Cistern
9 Propylaeum
10 Terrace and residence of the priests

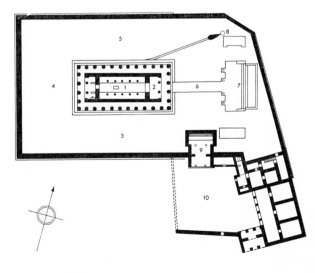

The temple of Aphaea stands on top of a hill in the eastern part of Aegina above the bay of Ayia Marina. Facing it, at the eastern entrance of the Saronic Gulf, stands Cape Sunium with its Doric temple (Pl. 19) of Poseidon, built about 440. These two temples of the Saronic Gulf, together with the Parthenon, form an imaginary isosceles triangle with Sunium as its vertex.

The temple of Aphaea rises in the centre of a terrace (Plan 3). The peribolus which surrounds it has three sides parallel to the sides of the sanctuary. The propylaeum of the peribolus is placed in the southern side. The eastern side deviates to include the residences of the priests. The cistern was situated in the north-east corner. The altar and the beginning of a ramp which led to the pronaos were placed on the central eastern axis of the temple.

The structure of the temple rests on a foundation of worked limestone slabs. On top of this lies the base consisting of three tiers, of which the uppermost (called the stylobate) supports the columns and the walls of the temple. The columns are approximately seventeen feet high including their capitals. They taper from a diameter of thirty-eight and a half inches at the bottom to twenty-seven and a half inches at the top.

The goddess Athena is represented in the centre of both pediments; in the eastern she is presiding over a scene from the Heracles myth and in the western over the exploits of Agamemnon. The Trojan War had a special place in the national pride of the Aeginetans for several of the heroes who took part in it came from Aegina. In the older western pediment, there are six warriors on either side of Athena. They are arranged in groups of three and one warrior is wounded in each group. On the eastern pediment only two warriors are shown as wounded and are placed one in either angle of the composition. Battle scenes of this type were a favourite theme of archaic bas-reliefs.

We can trace the development in sculpture from archaic to early classical by comparing the two pediments of the temple. The geometric arrangement into sharply defined planes of the warriors in the western pediment gives way to the studied but more relaxed treatment of the warriors' anatomy in the eastern pediment. At the same time their movements are bolder. The beardless warrior falling wounded in the right corner of the eastern pediment (Pl. 54) is no longer smiling like the wounded hoplites of the western pediment: his expression is grave and melancholy. Care and solicitude mark the face of the naked warrior (Pl. 55) who, on the same pediment, hurries to help a wounded comrade. The faces and attitudes of the warriors are stamped with an individual touch such as we find in the heroes of classical painting and poetry. They are allowed to show their pain openly, contorting their bodies as they die. The proportions of the figures become finer and their movements more fluid. The treatment of the eastern pediment is altogether more realistic than that of the western one.

The statues of the two pediments of Aphaea were discovered by a group of German, British and Danish archaeologists in 1811 during excavations near the temple. Greece was still under the rule of the Turks who allowed the findings to be sold to Ludwig I of Bavaria. They were eventually placed in the Munich Glyptothek. We do not know the names of the artists who were responsible for the masterpieces of Aegina; their works have survived with the temple they embellished, though the original colours have vanished and the warriors no longer hold the bronze weapons which once glinted in the sunlight. We can see them in the Munich Glyptothek, at closer range than if they were in their original positions, and we can feel the religious significance which these epic heroes must have had for the sculptors of Aegina, who worked so patiently and carefully, even on the figures at the sides of the temple which were not meant to be seen by visitors.

Fig. 19. Handle of the François crater (Fig. 8), depicting Ajax and Patroclus, *Archaeological Museum, Florence*

AFTER A SHORT period in which Corinth dominated the scene, Athenian potters recaptured their former supremacy which they were not to lose until the very end of the Athenian city-state.

This third artistic flowering of the Athenian school [85] was not only due to the general political development of Athens resulting from the reforms of Solon in the early sixth century, but also to the ability of Athenian potters to adapt their style to the demands of the Mediterranean markets. The Athenian ceramic workshops were compelled to renew their technical equipment and their manufacturing methods in order to compete with the easily transported vases of the Corinthian type, which were pleasing to the eye and practical for everyday use. Athenian potters borrowed the small dimensions of the Corinthian vase, but their choice of decorative motifs was all their own. They concentrated on the human form, seeking to define its natural and moral character and to make it the essential aesthetic and intellectual expression of their art. The feature that distinguishes the Attic vase from all others was, in the last analysis, intellectual.

In the first quarter of the sixth century, the vase painter who decorated a small crater with a scene of a funerary horse-race held in honour of Patroclus and bearing the legend " Sophilos made me " (Pl. 67), started to work in Athens. The crater, which was discovered at Pharsala and is now in the Archaeological Museum of Athens, shows a gallery full of spectators on either side of the track, absorbed in watching the race. The same artist's signature appears on two other pieces, a goblet from the Acropolis and a potsherd from Menidi. The first depicts the wedding of Peleus and Thetis in the presence of the gods of Olympus. Sophilos' work differs from the stylized decorative themes of his Corinthian contemporaries by the individuality and animation of his figures which seem to have been sketched from life. It represents a final break with eastern influences in vase painting and, in it, man takes the centre of the stage.

The themes used by Sophilos recur in the second and third friezes of the famous François crater in the Florence Museum (570), which bears the signatures of two miniaturists of the Athenian school, Clitias and Ergotimos (Fig. 8, p. 59). But along with these traditional themes, they also depicted the struggle of Theseus with the Minotaur and with the Centaurs, Ajax bearing the dead Achilles on his shoulders (on the handle of the vase) (Fig. 19) and others. In the François crater, the painters depict scenes crowded with gods, heroes, horses and monsters, but by placing the various scenes at different levels in the friezes, they manage not to sacrifice the unity of the composition. Episodes from mythology, the epic struggles of heroes and scenes of everyday life were their favourite subjects.

In these examples of Attic vase-painting of the sixth century, we can already discern the basic elements of Athenian black-figure style. Its repertoire of themes is drawn from heroic tradition, from the poetry of Homer and Hesiod, and later from scenes of daily life. It developed from the techniques of the geometric style, some of which it retains, for example the contrasts of light and shade on the bright surface and the clarity with which anatomical details and drapery are defined.

Clitias and Ergotimos are more disciplined than Sophilos; their drawing is distinguished by precision and purity of line. The style of Nearchos, a contemporary of Clitias and Ergotimos, is marked by its fine and delicate outlines which convey an air of dramatic seriousness and refinement. But it is with Execias that black-figure painting in Athens attains its greatest heights. His paintings are all the more expressive for their monumental simplification of line and in his restrained treatment of his themes he achieves a harmonious style of truly classical charm (Pl. 76 and Fig. 20).

60. Terracotta oil flask in the form of a kneeling athlete binding his hair with a victory fillet (540-30). *Agora Museum, Athens*

126

With Sophilos, Clitias, Ergotimos, Nearchos and Execias, Athens raised its vase industry to the level of a refined art form. Black-figure style, with its mastery of the incised line which enabled it to handle light and shade and to pick out the anatomy of the figures in subtle curves which give the impression of solidity and depth, made Athenian vases supreme on the international market, bringing the city wealth which its barren soil could not produce. The challenge of nature was answered by artistic inventiveness.

This artistic renaissance was due to seven centuries of peace under the Dorians. From the twelfth to the fifth centuries, Athens remained aloof from military adventures such as the invasion of Messenia by Sparta. The appeal of the Alcmaeonidae to Sparta to overthrow the tyranny of Hippias in 510 was a recognition of the military hegemony of Sparta and of her right to intervene, as arbitrator, in the internal affairs of other Greek cities. By her intervention, Sparta had expelled the tyrants of Corinth, Sicyon, Samos and Aegina. Her alliance with Croesus, king of Lydia, in 545, against the threat of Persia, shows that her power was also recognized beyond the limits of continental Greece.

The emergence of Sparta as the foremost military power had advantages for Athens. It assured her internal peace and stability and enabled her to devote her energies to the pursuit of art and letters, to which the Spartans were indifferent. But the growing intellectual dominance of the Athenians awoke in them a consciousness of their aptitude for political leadership in Greece and the events of the Persian Wars led them eventually to challenge the hegemony of Sparta.

Fig. 20. A black--figure amphora by Execias: Achilles and Ajax playing dice, *Museo Etrusco Gregoriano, Vatican*

CLEISTHENES AND THE REORGANIZATION OF THE STATE

AFTER THE OVERTHROW of the tyranny in 510, the two other parties, the oligarchs (plains-people) and the democrats (coast-people), struggled for power. The former was led by Isagoras, whilst Cleisthenes, a member of the Alcmaeonidae family, was the leader of the democrats. At first Isagoras who had won over the former supporters of the tyranny [86] was able to gain control. But Cleisthenes, appealing for popular support with the slogan " All power to the people," threatened to oust Isagoras. The latter immediately called upon the Spartan king Cleomenes, who was still in Athens where he had been invited to overthrow Hippias, to arrest and exile 700 democratic families on the plea that their fathers had been implicated in the Cylon episode. When Cleomenes tried to intervene, the citizens of Athens reacted violently. Cleomenes and Isagoras were beseiged in the Acropolis and had to surrender two days later. Cleisthenes and his friends returned from exile and the supporters of the tyranny and the oligarchy could no longer prevent the democrats from taking over the government.

Cleisthenes began his rule by a radical reorganization of the state. His first target was the clan system which had formed the bulwark of aristocratic power. He re-divided Attica into thirty administrative regions, or demes, which replaced the older patriarchal organizations. The area immediately round Athens, the coastal areas of Attica and the inland plains were divided into ten demes each. The clans were spread throughout the demes and members of the same clan found themselves belonging to different demes. By losing its last vestiges of political and administrative unity, the clan degenerated into little more than a loose religious association.

Each deme had an elected archon, or mayor, whose duty it was to keep the public records, to organize the collection of public funds and to supervise their expenditure. The deme took its name from its geographical location, which was used as a surname by its citizens, so that those who had recently acquired political rights could no longer be distinguished by their family names from those who had inherited them from their fathers.

The assemblies of the demes became schools of politics where citizens learned to debate public affairs and to prepare themselves for greater civic responsibilities in the central administration of the city-state.

These administrative districts were grouped into ten tribes, each consisting of three demes. The composition of the tribes was decided by lot, so that neighbouring demes might easily belong to different tribes. Each tribal assembly had to select fifty members to represent them in the Assembly of Five Hundred (the Boulê) which had grown out of the older Assembly of Four Hundred.

More numerous than the Assembly was the Ecclesia, which comprised all the citizens of Athens, and may have numbered as many as 30,000 in the early fifth century, if we can accept the estimate of Herodotus. Without its approval the Assembly of Five Hundred could not impose the death penalty, sign treaties with other states or declare war.

Cleisthenes also instituted the council of the ten *strategoi*, or generals, elected by the ten tribes and presided over by the polemarch. The limitation of the polemarch's powers, which was one of the purposes of the new council, reflected how bitterly Athenian democrats felt about Pisistratus, who had been able to seize power as soon as he had secured control of an armed force.

To avoid any possible abuse of power by holders of public office, Cleisthenes introduced the institution of ostracism, originally in order to exile Pisistratus' relatives. Every political leader who had supported the tyranny was exiled by this method for a period of three years. Later the period of exile was extended to ten years. The Ecclesia, with all members present, convened in the Agora under the presidency of the archon and voted by inscribing the name of the accused on a sherd. Sherds bearing, among others, the names of Cimon, Aristides, Themistocles and Pericles were found in the Agora recently during excavations carried out by the American School of Archaeology and are now on display in the Agora Museum. When the name of a citizen was inscribed on a minimum of 6,000 sherds, he had to leave Athens within ten days. This exile did not entail any other moral or economic sanctions and the person thus ostracized could freely select his own place of exile.

Ostracism was not a punishment, but a safety measure. It was designed to curb the power of ambitions citizens who had overstepped the normal bounds of democratic equality and to some extent protected Athens from the possible excesses of a democratic system. A story told by Plutarch about the ostracism of Aristides illustrates how the system worked. When sherds were being collected, an illiterate peasant, on his way to the Agora, stopped Aristides and, unaware that he was addressing the statesman himself, asked him to inscribe his name on the sherd. Aristides was rather surprised and asked the peasant whether he knew the man in question and whether he had done him any harm. The peasant replied that he did not know him, but that he was sick and tired of hearing him referred to as the Just. Aristides thereupon inscribed his name on the sherd and returned it to the peasant.

Cleisthenes retained the old court of the Heliaea which met in a building of the same name, on the southern edge of the Agora, but converted it into a court of first instance. Though the Areopagus remained the stronghold of aristocrats and tended to be hostile to democratic reforms, Cleisthenes did not tamper with its former functions.

The new regime was thus far more democratic than that of Solon. But although Cleisthenes' laws greatly increased popular participation in the administration of the state, democracy was far from secure. The aristocratic power of the Areopagus, the division of Athenians into social classes with unequal rights, the offices of the archons which were only open to wealthier citizens, none of these had yet been abolished and continued to constitute a threat to democratic rule. The thetes were to remain in a position of subjection until the age of Themistocles when they served as free citizens on the ships, and played their part in winning for Athens her command of the seas.

But for the moment it was Aegina who was still the dominant naval power and when Athens wanted to make war on her she was compelled to borrow triremes from Corinth. On the eve of the Peloponnesian War, the Corinthian envoy was to remind the Ecclesia of this. "When you were short of war vessels," he said, "in the war you waged against the Aeginetans, you received twenty ships from the Corinthians."

The first clash between Athens and Aegina had occurred when Solon abandoned the Aeginetan monetary unit, which had hitherto been used in Attica, in favour of the Euboean-Corinthian unit: the *mna* made up of 100 drachmas. The new currency thus became equivalent to that of the great trading cities of Chalcis and Corinth and its adoption by Athens indicated that she had every intention of extending her commercial activities into areas as far away as the Danube basin and the plains of Scythia,[87] whence the Aeginetans carried wheat at great profit to Mediterranean ports. Another of Solon's economic measures which had antagonized the Aeginetans was his prohibition on the export of foodstuffs from Attica on which Aegina depended. These differences became less acute during the rule of Pisistratus, when Athens imported large quantities of building stone from Aegina for construction work on the Acropolis, the Agora and the city. But the overthrow of Hippias and the return to democratic rule caused serious anxiety to the oligarchs of Aegina, for a democratic movement had begun to grow on their own island.

HERODOTUS

How AND WHY did the Persians confront the Athenians at Marathon, so far from their own country? Perhaps the same question moved Herodotus, in the fifth century, to write the first history which has come down to us from antiquity. The nine books into which his work is divided bear the titles of the nine Muses and, as well as dealing with Greece, they cover peoples well beyond, particularly in the east, such as Lydians, Persians, Egyptians, Phoenicians, Assyrians and Scythians. He describes their customs and manners, their beliefs and their political evolution. Herodotus had travelled widely throughout the places he describes and had gathered much of his information at first hand. Though he prided himself on being a Greek—he was born in Halicarnassus in 485 and died in Athens in 424—and called all non-Greeks barbarians, he nevertheless writes about foreigners objectively and without prejudice. He does not possess the analytical mind or scientific rigour of Thucydides. His work can be described as a kind of prose epic told by an intelligent and observant traveller whose curiosity is insatiable and who is also a gifted writer of narrative. Certain reservations have to be made about parts of his work, but in the main Herodotus' account of the Persian Wars can be read with profit, certainly with pleasure.

In his view the conflict began when Croesus, king of Lydia in Asia Minor, learnt that Cyrus had seized the throne of Persia from Astyages in 550 and decided to march against the usurper. Thales, the Greek philosopher of Miletus, constructed a bridge over the Alys river so that Croesus' army could capture the fortified city of Pteria in Capadocia. Cyrus appealed to the Ionian cities, wealthy but divided amongst themselves, for assistance, but they turned a deaf ear. But Croesus' allies also failed him and he was forced to retreat within the walls of his capital, Sardis. After a siege which lasted fourteen days, Sardis fell to Cyrus' armies and Croesus was captured. He was condemned to be burnt alive and when he was tied to his funeral pyre, waiting for the executioner to set it on fire, Cyrus asked him as a final jibe if he knew of anyone happier than himself. As an answer, Croesus called out the name of Solon. Cyrus asked what the Greek name signified and Croesus told him that Solon was an Athenian and that when he had visited Sardis and seen the wealth and the palaces of Croesus, he remained unimpressed, saying that he could not call any man happy so long as his future was unknown. Cyrus spared Croesus for this moral lesson and retained him as a counsellor.

Despite their refusal to fight for him, Cyrus did not at once attack the Greek colonies of Ionia as he was preparing an expedition against Bactria. His first direct contact with Greeks from the mainland occurred when the Spartans sent an ambassador to warn him that they would go to war if he disturbed the Greeks of Ionia. Cyrus sought to learn more about a people who first refused to help him and now threatened him with war. He was informed that they differed from the Persians in that they had market-places for the storage and the disposal of merchandize and that they swore false oaths amongst themselves. The Greek threat did not alarm Cyrus and he turned his attention again to campaigns in the east which kept the Persians occupied until the reign of Darius (522-486).

The first Greek possession to fall into the hands of the Persians was Samos which they conquered in 517. Once they had established a foothold in the islands of the Aegean, they were able to neutralize the Ionians who were now surrounded on all sides and had little hope of resisting. In the spring of 512 Darius moved his troops across from Chalcedon to Byzantium by means of a bridge across the Bosphorus built by a Greek engineer from Samos. He then advanced into Scythia, supported by Ionian ships which passed through the Euxine Sea on their way to the mouth of the Danube. At this point an Athenian general, who was also tyrant of the Chersonese, appeared in the narrows of the Hellespont and urged the Ionians to cut the Persian bridges and to revolt. It was Miltiades who twenty years later was to defeat the Persians at Marathon.

THE IONIAN REVOLT AGAINST THE PERSIANS

THE PERSIAN occupation of Byzantium was a permanent one and when Darius returned to Asia, he left a garrison of 80,000 troops under Artabazus to complete the subjugation of the Hellespont and Thrace. These conquests were a fatal blow to Ionian trade which throve on carrying wheat from the Euxine to Egypt and to other parts of the Mediterranean. The Ionians decided to revolt and the tyrant of Miletus visited Sparta and Athens to seek aid. Cleomenes refused, but the Athenians sent twenty ships which were followed by five from Eretria. Miletus, then, rose against Darius, and set fire to Sardis, destroying the temple of Cybele, In retaliation the Persians resolved to demolish the temples of all Greek cities which fell into their hands. After the capture of Sardis, the Ionians sailed to the Hellespont and freed the straits of the Persian garrisons. The revolt then spread from the Bosphorus to Salamis in Cyprus.

Darius struck back, using Phoenician ships to carry his armies. In 494 he captured Miletus and razed it to the ground, massacring the male population and sending the women and children to the slave markets at the mouth of the Tigris. When he had reduced all the colonists of Ionia and Aeolia to submission,

65. Black-figure amphora showing a shoemaker's workshop, c. 580. *Ashmolean Museum, Oxford*

132

he started to make preparations for a punitive expedition against Athens and Eretria who had sent aid to the Ionians.

In 491 Aegina was confronted by a challenge which decided her destiny. Darius requested earth and water, symbols of submission, from her and she had to choose between Asiatic despotism and Greek freedom. In 487 a revolt against the oligarchy had set up a democratic regime which the oligarchs of Aegina harshly suppressed. In her response to both these crises Aegina showed that she was not capable of assuming the leadership of the Greek states in defence of their national and civil liberty.

It was Athens which possessed the vision and the capacity to lead Greek resistance against the Persians and against oppression. When the Athenians learnt that the Persians had destroyed Miletus, they understood the fate which awaited them and were determined to resist it by every available means. Phrynichus wrote a tragedy about the fall of Miletus which so moved the public that he was fined a thousand drachmas by the city leaders and further productions were forbidden.

The Aeginetans reacted differently. They did not have a renegade like Hippias in the camp of Darius, ready to be restored to power by Persian arms and thirsting for revenge on the democratic regime which kept him in exile. As a Persian satrapy, its submissive ruling oligarchy would not have suffered; indeed it would have been maintained in power. The destruction of Miletus and the suppression of the Ionian revolt offered Aegina the chance to corner trade with the east, for the Persians had not learnt the art of seafaring and relied on the Phoenicians for their fleet. The Aeginetans well knew how vast were the resources of Darius' empire which stretched from the Indus to Thrace and from the Nile to the Danube, covering more than 1,350,000 square miles. They knew that Darius had despatched 600 ships and 700,000 troops to the Hellespont to suppress the other Greek cities. How could the Aeginetans ply their trade between the Euxine and Egypt if they were not on friendly terms with Darius? And what benefit had the Ionians derived from their revolt?

When the Athenians learnt of Aegina's attitude, they suspected that Darius would want to use the island as a base for operations in the Saronic Gulf. They sent envoys to Sparta to try and induce her to take preventive measures. Cleomenes had recently brought a war against the Argives to a successful conclusion and his reputation was at its peak. But his colleague in kingship, Demaratus, was in league with Darius and he was able to thwart the Athenians' plans. Cleomenes agreed to intervene in Aegina. He would seize ten hostages from amongst the " Medizing " oligarchs and deliver them up to the Athenians. But when he arrived, the oligarchs had already been forewarned by Demaratus. They refused to hand over hostages on the pretext that his co-ruler was not with him and Cleomenes was ejected from the island by force.

The incident did not end there, however. The Spartans discovered the secret contacts which Demaratus had made with the Persians and he was forced into exile. Cleomenes then returned to Aegina with his new co-ruler Leotychides, seized ten archons and handed them over to the Athenians. As a result Aegina made no move to support the Persians in the campaign.[88]

MILTIADES

WE HAVE ALREADY encountered Miltiades at the outset of the Ionian revolt. He was now destined to play a decisive role in Athenian history. A member of a noble Athenian family, the Philaidae, he was the nephew of another Miltiades who under Pisistratus had established a tyranny in the Thracian Chersonese. In

66. Bronze statue of Apollo. The left hand originally held a bow, the right a vase. The oldest known hollow-cast statue of large scale (slightly over 6 ft.). Found at Piraeus in 1959, c. 525. *National Museum, Athens*

524 or thereabouts, after the extinction of his uncle's heirs, he was sent by Hippias to annex the Chersonese on behalf of Athens, but instead he established his own rule. He married Hegesipyle, daughter of the king of Thrace, who bore him a son, Cimon. His earlier relations with Darius appear to have been somewhat ambiguous, but about 500 he liberated Lemnos from Persian rule. In 493 the Persians occupied the Chersonese and he fled to Athens. At first he faced a charge of having established an illegal " tyranny " in Thrace, but he survived to become a general in time for the Marathon campaign.

In the spring of 490 Darius placed his nephew Artaphernes and the Mede general Datis in command of an expedition against Eretria and Athens. The army was assembled in Cilicia and 600 triremes as well as transport-ships carrying infantry and cavalry set sail for Eretria which was swiftly captured and burnt and the Persians moved on towards Athens. The council of generals sent Phidippides to Sparta to ask for aid but Spartan customs did not allow an army to march before the full moon. From the whole of Greece, the only city which responded to the appeal of Athens was Plataea which sent a thousand men.

Meanwhile the generals were deliberating whether an attempt should be made to halt the Persian advance at Marathon. Five generals voted against, because the Persians outnumbered the Athenians, but Miltiades, Aristides, Themistocles and two other generals favoured an immediate attack. The polemarch, Callimachus, who presided over the council, had the casting vote. Miltiades put the following arguments to him; " It is now in your hands, Callimachus, either to enslave Athens or to make her free and to leave behind you for all future generations a memory more glorious than ever Harmodius and Aristogiton left. Never in the course of our long history have we Athenians been in such peril as now. If we submit to the Persian invader, Hippias will be restored to power in Athens—and there is little doubt what misery must then ensue; but if we fight and win, then this city of ours may well grow to pre-eminence amongst all the cities of Greece ". Callimachus was persuaded and cast his vote in favour of battle. The generals who supported Miltiades gave him their turn of command—each general had the right to command for one day—but Miltiades delayed operations, on the pretext that he was awaiting the day on which command fell to him by right, but in actual fact he still hoped that Spartan aid would arrive in time.

THE BATTLE OF MARATHON

THE COASTAL plain of Marathon was chosen by the Persians because it seemed to afford space for them to deploy their cavalry in which they were strong. The plain—approximately five miles by one and a half—stretches like a crescent along the coast. On the eastern side, it is bounded by the foothills of Parnes and Pentelicum, its centre is traversed by a ravine and its northern and western parts are marshy.

On 13 September 490, the day the battle began, the first autumn rains had already fallen, saturating the sides of the plain beneath the dense rushes and preventing the Persian cavalry from taking an effective part in the battle. The Persian army probably numbered some 60,000 troops, if one calculates that each of the 600 triremes in which they were transported carried 100 armed men. They were drawn up along the shore, near their ships. The Greek force numbered 10,000. Miltiades set up his camp on the heights of Heracleius and spread his troops thinly along the plain about a mile from the Persian array, to keep them well out of range of the Persian bowmen. He kept his centre weak with only three lines of troops in depth, but each wing was eight lines deep. The right wing was formed by the troops of the clan of Aiantis under the polemarch Callimachus, and the left wing was held by the Plataeans. The centre was formed by the remaining clans of Attica under Themistocles and Aristides.

The signal for the attack was given by Miltiades. The Athenians rushed towards the Persians who, seeing them advancing without cavalry or bowmen, believed they were being confronted by fools. But the Athenians continued their advance unperturbed beneath a shower of arrows and soon came to grips with the enemy whom they hacked with their short swords in close combat.

The Persian counter-attacked against the weak centre of Militiades, forcing the Athenians to retreat inland. Thus, while the two wings of the Greeks were moving forward, their centre was broken, leaving the road to Athens open. Realizing that the situation was critical, Miltiades sent messages to the commanders on the wings ordering them to turn and cut off the Persian advance in the centre. The troops of the centre rallied and attacked the Persians again. Datis attempted a diversionary attack on the flank. Miltiades allowed him to deploy his forces and then forced them back into the marshes. While they were temporarily out of action, he ordered the Athenians to attack the Persian ships and set them on fire. Panic at once swept the Persian ranks and the battle turned into a massacre. The Athenians burnt as many ships as they could and captured seven. Aeschylus' brother who took part in the battle was killed attempting to climb on to one of the Persian vessels. When his hands were cut off, he tried to hold on with his teeth. The Athenians lost only 192 men including Callimachus who was the first to fall, whereas Persian casualties totalled 6,400.

Miltiades then noticed that the Persian fleet was sailing round Sunium in the direction of Phaleron bay and, leaving Aristides with a small force to guard the booty, hastened with his army to the defence of Athens. A light reflected from a shield glinted on the summit of Pentelicum. This was a pre-arranged signal informing the Persians that the supporters of tyranny were ready to open the gates of Athens for Hippias. But Miltiades had already drawn up his troops along the coast of Phaleron. Datis and Artaphernes were reluctant to place much trust in the promises of Hippias and his supporters and they turned and sailed for home.

The following day, two thousand Spartans reached Athens from Laconia after a three-day march. There was nothing for them to do except visit the site of the battle, congratulate the Athenians and return to Sparta.[89]

The Athenians did not bring back their dead for burial in the public cemetery. Instead they buried them in a common tomb on the site of the battle to remind Greece eternally of their bravery. The stele of an Athenian hoplite,[90] Aristion, made by the sculptor Aristocles, discovered at the tumulus of Marathon, gives us an idea of the uniform worn by the Athenians. It is now in the Archaeological Museum of Athens (Pl. 57) and a copy has been placed at Marathon.

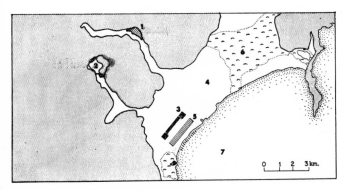

Map 5. THE BATTLE OF MARATHON

1 Marathon
2 Athenian camp
3 Greek lines
4 Persian camp
5 Persian lines
6 Marsh
7 Marathon Bay

Athenian Hegemony

THEMISTOCLES AND ARISTIDES

DURING THE YEARS between the first and the second Persian Wars, two parties were formed which, in turn, were in power or in opposition: the conservative party of Aristides and the radical party of Themistocles. The differences in character between the two leaders were typical of their political divergences. Aristides was cautious, undemonstrative, poor of his own free will, unswervingly virtuous and above personal passions. His honesty and soundness of judgment in the management of public affairs gave him great prestige in the eyes of Athenians who saw in him the ideal successor of Miltiades. Aristides hid neither his preference for the oligarchic regime of Sparta nor his opposition to fresh reforms. He strove continually to obstruct Themistocles, sometimes in a somewhat sterile manner. One day, particularly discouraged after a meeting of the Assembly, he was heard to mutter: " There is no salvation for Athens, unless the Athenians throw both myself and Themistocles over a precipice." Two years after the battle of Marathon, he was elected Commander-in-chief, but, in 483-2, Themistocles succeeded in having him ostracized.

The dynamic personality of Themistocles was more representative than the cautious Aristides of the Athens of his time. He was not of aristocratic origin and appears to have been the illegitimate son of a certain Neocles and a Thracian woman, known by the neuter name of Abrotonon, as was the custom among courtesans. But his undoubted ability more than made up for his humble origins.

" Themistocles, " writes Thucydides, "was a man who showed an unmistakable natural genius; in this respect he was quite exceptional, and beyond all others deserves our admiration. Without studying a subject in advance or deliberating over it later, but using simply the intelligence that was his by nature, he had the power to reach the right conclusion in matters that have to be settled on the spur of the moment and do not admit of long discussions, and in estimating what was likely to happen, his forecasts of the future were always more reliable than those of others. He could perfectly well explain any subject with which he was familiar, and even outside his own department he was still capable of giving an excellent opinion. He was particularly remarkable at looking into the future and seeing there the hidden possibilites for good or evil. To sum him up in a few words, it may be said that through force of genius and by rapidity of action this man was supreme at doing precisely the right thing at precisely the right moment."

Themistocles was able to predict the actions of his enemies with a remarkable degree of accuracy. He considered that the battle of Marathon was only the beginning of a greater struggle and he therefore prepared himself and the Athenians, both psychologically and militarily, for a prolonged defence of their country. As the danger of a Persian invasion was not yet pressing nor certain, Themistocles exploited the tension which war with the Aeginetans had caused to secure the adoption of a programme of ship-building. Three years after Marathon, Aegina

67. Fragment of an Athenian crater, signed by Sophilos, depicting a chariot race in a hippodrome, *c.* 575. *National Museum, Athens*

68. Detail of an Athenian red-figure calyx-crater, representing Theseus, Heracles and other heroes in the underworld, by the painter of the Niobids, 5th century. *Louvre, Paris*

69. Attic red-figure amphora by the Andocides painter. Singer with his guitar and two figures listening, *c.* 480. *Louvre, Paris*

138

67   68

69

had attacked the sacred vessel which the Athenians sent every five years to Sunium and captured the crew. This was an occasion for war, but, by this time, a democratic movement had started in Aegina which the Athenians decided to support. They bought ships from Corinth and built up a fleet of seventy ships altogether to proceed against Aegina. In the event, the Aeginetan democrats moved too soon and were suppressed before Athenian aid could reach them. A subsequent engagement resulted badly for Athens, but the war had served its purpose: Athens had taken a first step to enlarge her naval forces.

During this period rich deposits of silver were discovered near Laurium, producing a surplus in the public funds. Some citizens were in favour of distributing this money but Themistocles proposed that it should be used for building more ships. The Assembly voted in favour and a further 100 vessels were added to the Athenian fleet.

The construction of a powerful fleet marked the change from an agricultural to a mercantile economy. The salvation of Athens henceforth depended on her wooden walls and political power passed into the hands of the mercantile and maritime classes. It is significant that under the democratic regime the rostrum on the Pnyx where the Assembly met was set up facing the sea and that later, when the Thirty Tyrants overthrew the democratic regime, the tribune was turned again towards the hinterland, for they considered that naval power had favoured democracy, whereas citizens engaged in agriculture were more inclined to accept oligarchic rule.

THE INVASION OF XERXES

ON THE EASTERN shore of the Aegean, the Persian king Darius was preparing a second campaign against Greece. Death overtook him before his plans were ready and it fell to Xerxes, his son, to carry them out.

The mobilization of the Persian army was completed by the autumn of 481. Herodotus describes the uniforms and the equipment of the soldiers of the forty-six nations Xerxes had enrolled, " a monstrous mass of men " which according to Aeschylus in *The Persians* drained Asia of all its males. Xerxes' army which had assembled at Sardis crossed the Hellespont by two bridges. Supported by the fleet, it followed the coast of Thrace, Macedonia and Thessaly until it reached Thermopylae where it encountered the first resistance on the part of the Greeks. The Persian forces consisted of 1,207 ships manned by 518,000 men and carrying 1,400,000 infantrymen, 80,000 horsemen and 20,000 Arab stablemen and camel-drivers: a mass of more than two million Asiatics ready to descend like a cloud of locusts upon the soil of Greece.

Herodotus does not report the size of the Greek forces at the beginning of 480. But on the basis of the forces at Plataea and at Salamis, one may estimate them at 380 triremes (200 from Athens) and 75,000 hoplites. The fleet was manned by 25,000 oarsmen and 3,300 hoplites. Thus the Greek forces probably totalled about 105,000.

A first line of defence was established at the two extremities of the straits of Euripus. At Thermopylae, at the western end, a force commanded by Leonidas, king of Sparta, and consisting of 300 hand-picked Lacedaemonians, 1,000 *Periocei* from Laconia and 3,500 soldiers from other parts fortified the only pass leading from Thessaly into Phocis. At the eastern end at Artemisium the Athenian fleet under Themistocles was able to prevent the Persian fleet from entering the straits.

At Thermopylae, the Spartans fared less well. A traitor guided the Persians through the mountains to a position in the rear of the Greek forces. Leonidas,

70. Red-figure psykter (wine-cooler) by Douris, decorated with scenes of Satyrs at their revels, c. 480, *height* 9½ in. *British Museum, London*

141

realizing that the situation was hopeless, allowed those of his allies who wished to, to depart, but he and his Spartans remained in position and fought, shoulder to shoulder, to the last man.

The Persian army continued its advance through Phocis and Boeotia, unopposed. The Peloponnesian troops withdrew behind defensive positions on the Isthmus and the Athenians embarked their women and children on the ships which had returned from Artemisium to evacuate them to places of safety, while the men crossed to the island of Salamis. When they reached Athens, the Persian found the city deserted except for a few suppliants who had barricaded themselves in on the Acropolis: guardians of shrines and citizens too poor to escape. But the Persians had no difficulty in dislodging them and sacking the Acropolis, plundering the temples and destroying the statues.

SALAMIS

THE SITUATION of the Greeks in September 480 after the events of the summer campaign was as critical as it could well be. Thermopylae had added another heroic chapter to the epic of Greek history, but had served little practical purpose. The whole of northern Greece had submitted to the Persians and from their place of refuge on the island of Salamis, the Athenians could watch the invaders destroying their beloved city and laying waste the Attic countryside. The Peloponnesian troops had retired to the Isthmus and Eurybiades, the Spartan admiral-in-chief, was in favour of withdrawing the Greek fleet, now sheltering in the bay of Salamis, to support them. Only one factor offered any encouragement: in the naval engagements off Cape Artemisium, although they had not been decisive, the Greek ships had shown that they were quite capable of holding their own with the larger vessels of the Persian fleet and in the eyes of Themistocles this was of such importance that it outweighed all other considerations. He was convinced that by forcing the Persian fleet to fight in the narrow waters off Salamis, the situation could be retrieved and Greece saved.

But he was faced with two problems: he had to convince Eurybiades and the commanders of the other allies that this was so and he had to make sure that the Persians attacked. The way in which he succeeded offers a good example of his energetic and ingenious character at work. It is also in many ways typical of the Athenian approach in general, for in spite of their rationalism and the care with which they were discussed, Athenian policies were sometimes opportunistic.

The conference at which Themistocles persuaded his colleagues is one of the most dramatic scenes in Herodotus. It took place at night on board Eurybiades' ship and was marked by heated exchanges between Themistocles and the commander of the Corinthinian contingent who said that since Themistocles was stateless—Athens being in Persians hands—, he had no right to speak. Let Themistocles, he cried, provide himself with a country before he offered advice. In fact, Themistocles replied, that is exactly what the Athenians would do: if the allied fleet did not fight at Salamis, the Athenian contingent would sail away to Italy and leave the others to their fate.

Eurybiades himself was convinced by this threat, but in case he was outvoted by the others, Themistocles decided to force the issue. He sent a messenger in stealth to the Persians saying that the Greeks were completely demoralized and were planning to flee. If the Persians prevented them, they would be certain of success, because the Greeks would start fighting amongst themselves. The ruse worked and the Persian moved up their fleet to blockade the two entrances to the Gulf.

At this moment Aristides arrived. He had sailed over from his place of exile at Aegina and slipped through the Persian fleet under cover of darkness. He sought out his old enemy Themistocles who was still in conference and announced that he had come to offer his services. " At this moment ", he said, " more than ever before, you and I should be rivals, and the object of our rivalry should be to see which of us can do most good to our country." He then told Themistocles that the Greeks were surrounded and must prepare to withstand an attack. Good, was Themistocles' reaction, but *you* must tell my colleagues: if I told them, they would think I had made it up.

The outcome of the battle confirmed Themistocles' appreciation to an extent that must have come as a surprise even to him. In the confined space of the Gulf of Salamis, the larger ships of the Persian fleet proved difficult to manoeuvre and were no match for the Greeks. The events of the day are magnificently described by Herodotus and a reader with a taste for battle-pieces will scarcely find a better one in the whole of European literature. In spite of occasional inconsistencies of detail and chronology—Herodotus was writing after all to be read aloud, not to be cross-examined in the printed page—his narrative captures the colour and atmosphere of a great naval engagement, as well as the enthusiasm and sense of purpose of the Greeks.

For in addition to being a military defeat for the Persians, Salamis was also— and more importantly—a moral one. In terms of material and numbers their losses probably did not justify a complete retreat, but the impetus of their invasion had spent itself. Morale is always easier to sustain in defence than in attack. For an aggressor, patriotism is nothing like enough: he needs the stimulus of success. And throughont the campaign this had conspicuously eluded the Persians. The rout at Salamis was the *coup de grâce*. Pretending that they were about to mount a military attack on the island, the Persians sailed secretly away under cover of darkness.

The Greeks now faced the task of liberating their homeland from the army of occupation which Xerxes left behind in Thessaly under the command of Mardonius.

THE BATTLE OF PLATAEA

THE DOMINANT part played by Athens in the victory at Salamis was universally recognized as the amusing story from Herodotus of the reward of the generals testifies: " When the plunder had been distributed, the Greeks sailed to the Isthmus, where a prize of valour was to be awarded to the man who was judged best to deserve it by his conduct throughout the campaign. The commanders met at the altar of Poseidon to cast their votes for first and second place; and, as they all thought that they had fought more bravely than anybody else, every one of them put his own name at the top—though the majority agreed in putting Themistocles second. Consequently nobody got more than one vote for first place, while Themistocles easily headed the poll for the second." But in clearing the mainland of Mardonius' army, it was the turn of the Spartans to play the leading part.

A confederate army was assembled in the isthmus to which Athens sent 8,000 hoplites under Aristides. The total force commanded by the Spartan general Pausanias numbered some 110,000 men. Moving north towards Thebes where Mardonius had established his headquarters, the Greeks first offered battle on the slopes of Mount Cithaeron, near Erythrae. They wanted if possible to avoid the plains of Boeotia, which they feared would be favourable to the Persian cavalry, but they were finally forced to descend into the plain through lack of water.

Mardonius moved his own forces to confront them, but the two camps remained inactive, facing each other for ten days because on both sides the omens were not favorable. In the end, Mardonius took it upon himself to interpret the oracle and it sheds an interesting light upon the role of Delphi in the Persian Wars. The prophets of Apollo consistently took an adverse view of democratic institutions and just as later they favoured Sparta against Athens in the Peloponnesian War, so they tended to back Persian despotism against Greek freedom. Here is Herodotus' account of the scene:

" He (Mardonius) then sent for his company commanders and the Greek officers who were serving under him, and asked if they knew of any prophecy which foretold the destruction of Persian troops in Greece. Nobody said a word: perhaps some of them were unaware of the prophecies, while others, who knew them well enough, felt it was safer not to mention them. Mardonius accordingly said ' Either you know of no such prophecy, or are afraid to speak of it. Well, I *do* know of one, and I will tell it to you. It says that the Persians will come to Greece, sack the temple at Delphi, and then perish to a man. Very well then: knowing that, we will keep away from the temple and make no attempt to plunder it—and thus avoid destruction. All of you, therefore, who wish your country well, may rejoice at this, and be very sure that we shall defeat the Greeks., Thereupon he issued his orders to prepare for battle on the following day."

In spite of uninspired generalship, the day was won by the steadiness and discipline of the Spartan troops who fought their way doggedly through a bitter and protracted struggle to victory, unperturbed by the tactical disadvantage at which they were at one moment placed. When Mardonius himself fell, the Persian army broke and fled.

Herodotus qualifies Plataea as " the most splendid victory which history records " and his view seems to have been shared by Callicrates, the architect responsible for the temple of Athena Nikê, who devoted the frieze to scenes from the battle. Normally in temple sculpture, as in tragedy, the iconography was drawn from mythology. But already Phrynichus and Aeschylus had departed from this rule in their plays and Phidias in portraying the Panathenaean festival on the Parthenon was to follow suit. These lapses from the strictest canons of art may perhaps be taken as symbolizing the mounting self-confidence of Athenian democracy which judged that its own contemporany achievements were worthy to take their place beside the exploits of Theseus or Achilles.

THE FOUNDATION OF THE ATHENIAN EMPIRE

THE BATTLE OF PLATAEA virtually marks the end of the Persian wars on the soil of continental Greece, but the struggle continued elsewhere. And gradually the alliance against Persia which Athens created among the cities which she liberated turned into a maritime empire covering most of the Aegean (*see* Map 1, p. 14).

Even while war was raging in Greece, the Greek colonies in other parts had not been inactive. In the same year as Salamis, the Carthaginians, at the instigation of Xerxes, had launched an attack on Sicily and the victory won by Gelon, the Syracusan commander, at Himera was as important for the Sicilian Greeks as Salamis. On the very day on which Plataea took place, a Greek fleet defeated the Persians off the Ionian promontory of Mycale, seizing the Persian fortress and burning 300 triremes. The victory of Mycale freed the western coast of Asia Minor, the Greek colonies of Ionia rose up again in revolt, this time with greater success than before, and Samos, Chios and Mitylene joined Athens in an alliance against Persia. But the most important result from the Athenian

71. Epinetron or onos by the painter of Eretria. On the sides, scenes of the women's quarters taken from the myth of Alcestis. Above, the struggle of Peleus and Thetis, *c.* 430, *length* 11 in. *National Museum, Athens*

72. Red-figure vase in the form of a knuckle-bone depicting girls dancing, *c.* 400, *height* 6½ in. *British Museum, London*

point of view was the capture of the Hellespont. The Spartans did not care to venture so far afield and the Athenians, alone, laid siege to the strongest city of the Chersonese, Sestus, which was still in Persian hands. In the autumn of 478, the city capitulated. The Athenians now had the keys to the Propontis and the Euxine in their hands and Mycale and Sestus became the first bases of an Athenian empire in the Aegean.

The relative ease with which the Persians had been expelled from both coasts of the Aegean showed that a new power was rising to take the place of Xerxes. From Byzantium to Cyprus and from Egypt to Ionia, the Persian satraps were overthrown by the seamen of Salamis and the hoplites of Plataea, and the day had come for a new Mycenaean empire in the Mediterranean.

The first step towards this goal was the establishment of the Delian League in 479. This was a confederacy of cities, on the model of the Peloponnesian League, accepting the leadership of the most powerful member and entered into as an act of " collective security." Its one novelty was the establishment of a common treasury, situated until 454 at Delos, to which all members contributed. Aristides was appointed by Athens to fix the amounts to be levied and he deserves his title of " just "—if for no other reason—by the fact that his assessments were never challenged by any of the allies. Theoretically, the league, which eventually numbered as many as 200 states, operated democratically and was governed by an assembly of delegates which met at Delos and at which Athens, like each of the other members, had one vote. But in fact the overwhelming might of the Athenian navy gave her vote enormous weight. In 454 Pericles raised the level of contributions which began to look more and more like taxation and moved the treasury to the Acropolis. Thenceforth meetings of the League took place at Athens and disputes between members were heard by Athenian courts. The confederacy had become an empire in all but name.

The Spartans had lost the opportunity offered to them after Plataea to extend their hegemony, although they had at their disposal the most powerful land forces in Greece. The narrow and conservative character of their regime rooted their minds in the past and they were afraid of new ventures which might recoil on their own internal organization. Their foreign policy, betraying all the defects of a rigidly hieratic social structure, was governed more by fear of a revolt at home on the part of the helots than by ambition to increase their power and wealth abroad. But this very conservatism was to bring them into conflict with Athens. So long as the Delian League remained what it purported to be, they were quite prepared to accept it. But as soon as it developed into an instrument of Athenian expansion, they felt obliged to combat it, not because they wished themselves to expand, but because they feared for the *status quo*.

CIMON

SO LONG AS THE internal affairs of the League were managed by Aristides and its foreign policy by Cimon, the Spartans had no need to be alarmed. Cimon appears to have been the type of the *grand seigneur*. His family background was brilliant: his grandfather was an Olympic champion and both an uncle and a brother were tyrants in the Chersonese. He was the son of Miltiades, the victor of Marathon, and had himself fought at Salamis. He was connected with the wealthy Alcmaeonidae family by his marriage with a grand-neice of Cleisthenes. All the great sums he amassed during his periods of military command were put at the disposal of his fellow citizens. Foreign visitors were always welcome at his table and his gardens were unfenced. His courtesy and urbane manner won

73. Black-figure lekythos depicting women working wool. Found in Attica.
c. 540-30, *height* 6³/₄ *in.*
Metropolitan Museum, New York

74. Black-figure amphora depicting men weighing merchandize, by Taleides the Potter. Reputedly found in Argento
c. 560-30.
Metropolitan Museum, New York

75. Black-figure Attic skythos representing an oil press.
Boston Museum of Fine Arts

76. Fragment of black-figure amphora by Execias representing Theseus, *c.* 540.
University of Lund

the friendship of all those who sought his patronage. But the qualities of an aristocrat are not necessarily the most useful political assets in a democracy. He was not endowed with the gifts necessary to rule the Assembly: he was no orator, he tended to be intolerant and he lacked the rapidity of intellect and the psychological insight to succeed in public debate. But his courage, disinterestedness and practical good sense made him the natural successor to Aristides as leader of the conservative party.

Cimon's great successes were won in foreign policy and in battle. He completed the expulsion of the Persians from Thrace and reduced Thasos which had tried to secede from the Delian League. His greatest military achievement was the Eurymedon campaign in 468 in which the Persian fleet was utterly destroyed and further Greek cities joined the League.

This brought in its train the conclusion of a peace treaty between the Greeks and the Persians, according to which the Persians were obliged to keep as far as a horse could gallop from the Greek shores and, under no circumstances, to sail a warship equipped with a bronze battering-ram into the straits of the Chersonese. The spoils collected at the battle of Eurymedon were used to build the southern wall of the Acropolis.

Cimon's fall occurred in 461. In the preceding year, he had been invited by the Spartans to help them put down an insurrection of their helots. When he arrived, however, the Spartans, either suspecting that his cooperation was not wholehearted or fearing that the absence from Athens of the entire hoplite force might open the way for further democratic reforms, invited Cimon somewhat brusquely to go home. During his absence Ephialtes and Pericles had seized the opportunity to curtail the powers of the Areopagus. Cimon was ill-advised enough to try and get them restored, but the tide had flowed too far and he was ostracized.

PERICLES AND THE REVOLUTION OF 462

THE SUCCESSIVE REFORMS of Solon and Cleisthenes had left the enormous power of the Areopagus intact. Solon had confined membership of it to citizens of the two richest classes and Cleisthenes had refrained from tampering with Solon's legislation. Over the years the Areopagus had grown more and more powerful and had become the instrument by which conservative interests were able to frustrate the full working of democratic institutions. In the years preceding the fall of Cimon, the radicals had led prolonged agitation to transfer the privileges it had usurped to democratically constituted bodies and to confine it to its original function as a court of homicide. The failure of Cimon provided the opportunity which the radicals had been waiting for.

Their leader, Ephialtes, had won general respect for himself by his honesty and incorruptibility. He first brought charges of corruption against several important Areopagites and when he had secured court decisions for their dismissal, he introduced measures to deprive the Areopagus of all its privileges, which were transferred to the Assembly, the Council of Five Hundred and to the Tribunals. The Areopagus was, henceforth, dispossessed of its powers of supervising the affairs of the state and all public offices were thrown open to members of the *zeugitai*, the third category of Solon's class system. Shortly afterwards Ephialtes was assassinated by the aristocrats but after his death a zeugite became archon for the first time.

Democracy, which the reforms of Solon, Cleisthenes, Themistocles and Ephialtes had, little by little, established in Athens, was perfected by Pericles. For the first time in the history of the world, the rights of the individual citizen, whatever

class he belonged to, were officially recognized and protected. In the Athens of Pericles, he was able to participate in the direction of public affairs while, at the same time, he was free to lead his own life as he wished, unimpeded by state control or suspicion. The only restriction placed on his personal freedom was his obligation to respect the law and the personal freedom of others.

Athens had become the meeting-place of philosophers, poets and artists from all parts of the Hellenic world. Merchants freely imported products from foreign countries and foreigners were welcome in Athens. No one was forbidden to follow the debates on public affairs, to attend religious ceremonies or to watch athletic events or artistic performances. Foreign policy was debated openly and nothing was kept secret, even from foreigners. The self-confidence of Athenians was unbounded: it was reflected in their system of public education, in their spirit of enterprise and in their sense of public duty.

The personality of Pericles dominated democratic Athens. Thucydides who knew him personally represents him as a moderate ruler, prudent and disinterested, capable of excercising his authority over the Assembly without resorting to mystification or violence, but by appealing to reason.

Under Pericles, the Athenians achieved prosperity, security and grandeur, though at the price of surrendering some of their democratic rights to the first citizen who ruled personally. The eloquence of Pericles was never marred by vulgarity and he never allowed himself to appeal to the passions of his audience. His voice as he spoke is said to have been so calm and even that it sounded like a musical instrument His personal habits and his ideas were in keeping with the dignity of his utterances. He was a disciple of Anaxagoras whom he quoted frequently in his speeches. With his rhetorical gifts, his wisdom and the power of his intellect, he was, as a speaker, unrivalled. He was the " Olympian " and Plutarch tells us that he owed this epithet to his eloquence.

Political motives prompted him, as they had Pisistratus, to decorate Athens with monuments which continue to astonish the world today. He wanted Athenians to participate in the reconstruction of their city and to be rewarded, both materially and spiritually, for their labours. " Our city," he said, " must be embellished and support itself by its own means." When he put his building programme before the Assembly, he explained that it would permit everyone to take a fuller part in public life; artists and craftsmen would serve their *polis* as the soldiers and seamen did, and like them, would be rewarded from public funds.

In Plutarch's account, he outlined a plan which today we would call a type of " State Socialism ": " For building we shall need stone, bronze, ivory, gold, ebony and cypress wood and to fashion them, carpenters, masons, dyers, goldsmiths, ivory-carvers, painters, and sculptors. Our shipwrights and seamen will work to bring the materials we need from overseas and our wagonners will find employment hauling materials from the hinterland. Every auxiliary craft will be stimulated, from metallurgy to cobbling and every trade will be organized under a chief, becoming part and parcel of the services of the state. In a word, all the different needs will be carefully planned and catered for and prosperity will spread to every citizen of whatever age and trade. "

Pericles entrusted the overall direction of his programme to Phidias.

PHIDIAS

ATHENIAN ART REACHED its maturity in the middle of the fifth century. From its beginnings with the idols of the Dipylum ivory (Pl. 43), after two centuries of experiment, it attained its final form in the classical school. Perhaps the Kouros

80. Detail of the Dexileos stele showing a man on a horse c. 390, *height* 2 ft. 1 in. *Kerameikos Museum, Athens*

151

Aristodikos in the National Museum of Athens[91] may be considered as one of the earliest products of the new school. After the anonymous Kore of Euthydicos and the last archaic youth of the Acropolis standing on its one remaining leg, Athenian art at the beginning of the fifth century is represented by Calamis, Pythagoras and Myron. But Phidias soon became the dominant personality. He was born in Athens about 490 and, like Myron and Polycletus, was a pupil of Hegias. His first work was the gold-encrusted statue of Athena Areius, with feet and hands in Pentelic marble, for the temple at Plataea which was built with the proceeds of the battle of Marathon. It was a huge statue measuring about twenty-five feet in height, only slightly shorter than his great bronze Athena on the Acropolis which faced the Propylaea. On the walls of the temple at Plataea, Polygnotus painted a scene of Odysseus slaying the suitors of Penelope in which it is possible that Phidias may also have had a hand.[92]

The thirteen statues, set up by the Athenians at Delphi to honour their gods and heroes and including a portrait of Miltiades, should be numbered among the earlier works of Phidias.[93] This series was commissioned some time after 470, in the age of Cimon who wanted to rehabilitate the memory of his father Miltiades.

According to Plutarch, Phidias carved a portrait of himself as well as of Pericles on the shield of the Athena Parthenos, in a composition depicting the battle against the Amazons. A copy is preserved in the British Museum, known as the Strangford Shield and on it Phidias has depicted himself in the nude, fighting the enemy, axe in hand (Fig. 21).

81. The head of the " Blond boy."
Marble. *c.* 470, *height* 9 in.
Acropolis Museum, Athens

Fig. 21. The Strangford Shield *British Museum, London*

152

82

83

Archaeologists today agree that the Eleusinian relief [94] of Demeter, Persephone and Triptolemus, now in the National Archaeological Museum of Athens, should be attributed to Phidias (Pl. 96). It is perhaps the most beautiful relief surviving from antiquity. The impression the viewer gets from a photograph is quite different from that which the sculpture itself makes when it is studied at close quarters. In photographs the legs, arms and parts of the chest away from the camera, appear to merge into the background of the relief; but they are in actual fact on the same plane as the other parts of the body. The arrangement of the figures disregards the canon of pyramidal arrangement, for, occupying the centre, Triptolemus is not as tall as the figure to either side of him, as in the ivory Trio of Mycenae (Fig. 4, p. 40). But the space above the head of the youth is somewhat reduced by the sceptre of Demeter which appears to beckon the newly converted Triptolemus to spiritual exaltation. Behind him, the staff of Persephone slants at a slight angle towards his unbent left leg to form with it a kind of lever as though to raise the young man's body. It is a device in plastic terms designed to suggest the spiritual exaltation or lifting of Triptolemus. Demeter entrusts him with the first ripe ear of grain, symbol of the resurrection of nature and of the immortality of the soul, and with this gift Triptolemus will begin teaching mankind the elements of civilization. Persephone, who has just emerged from the underworld, full of youth and beauty, crowns the young man with a wreath. The composition expresses the essence of the Eleusinian myth according to which the human race was civilized by Demeter. But, at the same time, it is the first synthesis of Doric and Ionic style, of archaism with the realism, introduced by Phidias into Attic art. This can be seen in the contrasts in the garments of the two deities. Demeter wears a woollen Doric *chiton* whose heavy folds fall like the fluting of a Doric column. Her daughter is clad in an Ionic tunic whose soft folds stress the curves of her body. The head of Demeter still shows the stylized archaic manner, whereas Persephone's face is treated more freely.

The relief was probably made sometime after the ostracism of Cimon (461) when Pericles had put Ictinus in charge of completing the Telesterion at Eleusis. Ictinus later collaborated with Phidias on the Parthenon and, like him, was a friend of Pericles. It seems more than likely, therefore, that needing a relief to decorate the interior of the Telesterion he should have commissioned the work from Athens' greatest sculptor.

Phidias also made an ivory and gold statue of Zeus for the temple at Olympia. If we accept Pliny's statement that Phidias reached the peak of his creative life with the building of the temple of Zeus, dedicated during the LXXXIII Olympiad, we have to conclude that his greatest work was done in about 448 when he was forty-two years of age and before he undertook the projects on the Acropolis. Thus the period when Phidias' reputation was at its highest coincides with the formulation of Pericles' plans to undertake the great monuments of the Acropolis. In commissioning Phidias to supervise the decoration of the Parthenon, Pericles was giving public expression to the esteem in which his work was held.

But although the statue of Zeus is regarded as Phidias' masterpiece, it nevertheless appears to have suffered from a defect which was not present in the statue of Athena Parthenos. It was much too big for the temple in which it stood. Strabo observed that if it had risen from its throne, it would have gone through the roof. It was conceived after the completion of the temple which had to be modified slightly to accommodate it. A taste for the colossal in art was a relic of the age of Pisistratus who, in the manner of an oriental despot, felt the need of concrete expressions of his power. Had Phidias executed this work later in his career, he would surely have given Zeus the classical proportions he gave to the statuary and reliefs of the Parthenon. [95]

82. Relief of Athena,
height 1 ft. 9½ in.
Acropolis Museum, Athens

83. Ampharete's stele,
height 2 ft. 5 in.
Kerameikos Museum, Athens

With the experience acquired at Olympia, Phidias was able to achieve an exquisite balance between architecture and sculpture in his work for the Parthenon. The temple was given more comfortable dimensions while the façade was extended to include eight Doric columns rather than six as at Olympia. The large figure did not occupy the entire width of the sanctuary for Ictinus had provided space around the statue so that it could be well lit and seen from all angles. The height of the statue was about thirty-six feet, and its pedestal nine feet across.

Neither the Zeus nor the Athena has survived. But copies enable us to know what they were like. A miniature of the Athena (measuring just over three feet in height) from the second century A. D. was discovered in the Varvakeion excavations in 1880 and is now in the Archaeological Museum of Athens (Fig. 22). Another statuette found twenty years earlier on the Pnyx, also in the same Museum, resembles an unfinished model of the Athena, without helmet and holding a Victory in its hand like the Varvakeion figure, This version is interesting because the decoration of the shield resembles so closely that of the Strangford Shield. The Olympian Zeus is known to us only by the coins of Elis which circulated during the reign of Hadrian. It is said to have been moved from Olympia to Constantinople in 475 A. D. before the temple of Zeus was burned down, only to be destroyed by fire itself a century later. But it is difficult to take this tradition seriously because chryselephantine statues are notoriously fragile and cannot be transported over great distances.

We know from Pausanias that Phidias worked on his Zeus in a "studio" outside the precinct of the Altis, with the help of two assistants, the painter Panaenos who was either his brother or his nephew and the famous goldsmith Colotis. The workshop of Phidias was located by French scholars in 1829 in a Byzantine church of the Altis. Its dimensions are approximately the same as the cella of the temple for which the statue of Zeus was made and a circular stone basin was found beneath the floor which had been used to keep his materials damp so that they could be worked more easily.

Recent excavations by the German Archaeological Institute [96] have added fresh evidence that this was indeed the workshop of Phidias, for on the site clay moulds of the Zeus were found, together with fragments of worked ivory for the flesh of the statue (face, chest, arms and legs). The excavations also unearthed a small hammer, scrapers and other tools, pieces of glass for rubbing and polishing, coloured pencils and potsherds of reddish Attic vases dating from the middle of the fifth century.

Fig. 22. Marble copy of the Athena Parthenos, found at Varvakeion, *National Museum, Athens*

CLASSICAL ART

CLASSICAL ART in Athens reached its peak with Phidias. But what precisely do we mean by classical art? The description of the Eleusis relief may help us to define it as the synthesis of three conflicting elements: rationalism, archaism and realism [97]. Rationalism, in ancient Athens, expressed the self-confidence of the individual in his ability to explore the natural world and, with logic as his guide, to discover its properties and laws. In the field of art, rationalism is reflected in the plastic arrangement of the figures in a logical manner, so that the parts fit into the whole by the simplest means (Pl. 81). The classical artist tries to create human figures which are at once universal eternal and in his quest for the ideal his forms become almost abstract. The elements which are purely descriptive or circumstantial tend to be removed.

The second feature of classical art is its respect for archaic themes and methods.

The poems of Homer and Hesiod and the heroic legends of the Mycenaean age continue to inspire the decoration of classical temples. The canon of frontality continues to be observed, although statuary has escaped from all that is constrictive in the conventions of the past and treats the human form in motion with freedom and confidence. Myron's Discus-Thrower for example is dynamic in the extreme, yet the archaic canon of frontality is strictly respected in the treatment of the chest. In the reliefs of the Parthenon, archaic forms exist side by side with realism, and the frontal representation of the chest which we observed in Myron is apparent in most classical reliefs. The same is true, and in a higher degree, in the Sunium relief representing a youth holding a bronze wreathe which has been placed on his head after an athletic triumph. The head is shown in profile and the eyes frontally, while the body is set in a three-quarter view.

Realism is the third feature of classical art. Movement of bodies, expression of the faces and folds of the draperies acquire freedom and ease, without being carried to excess. In the classical period the artist has at last learnt to dominate his materials and his plastic space is given new life by the presence of figures full of movement. He has discovered the full possibilities of the free standing figure and is no longer afraid to place it on one leg and to support the other with projections and bends. The bodies are turned sideways and are no longer disposed like soldiers in a row on the parade ground. The garments are lighter and softer, falling into gentle folds. The facial expression is capable of reflecting a wealth of psychological and emotional subtleties. Classical artists, in their treatment of anatomical detail use gentle curves and seek by means of real forms to express an ideal beauty, in which every part is in harmony with the whole (Pl. 89).

Reserve and dignity in facial expression is typical of gods, heroes and free men whereas monsters such as the Centaurs who represent the world of unbridled instincts are allowed to show it (Pl. 99). Classical art did not ignore the passions; it subdued them, just as in the relief by Praxiteles in the Archaeological Museum of Athens Apollo, having defeated the satyr Marsyas in a musical contest, proceeds to flay him alive.

In their greater works, classical artists did not depict commonplace characters; they were searching for ideal figures whose serene faces, athletic bodies and graceful movements would express man's possibilities and console him if he could not attain them. But classicism also produced a popular school which showed men at play or at work in lively scenes of everyday life and vase painters and sculptors of the popular school did not hesitate to portray passion in all its forms in the faces of their figures.

The official classical school drew first and foremost on mythology and religion for its themes. Sculpture was preoccupied with the immortals, just as painting retold the legendary adventures of gods and heroes or described religious processions and sacrifices. Artists of the popular school, though they did not neglect mythology (even here they preferred Dionysus and his Maenads to more conventional subjects), turned to more congenial themes: symposia and dances, athletic contests and burial ceremonies; above all, they delighted in the events of everyday life, recording scenes from the daily round of miners, craftsmen, farmers, merchants and shepherds.

But as well as seeking to stir the imagination of their fellow citizens—and this is also true of classical poets—classical artists also tried to educate and instruct them. Classical art in Athens was religious, hence its moderation. Artists could not disturb faith which provided one of the most effective cohesive forces of society. The tragedies of Aeschylus and Sophocles, no less than the sculpture and reliefs of Phidias on the Parthenon, had a didactic purpose. They aimed to enlarge man's understanding of his universe and to make him feel more at home in it.

Classical art could not therefore be merely a funerary art as geometric art had been. It drew its themes from life in all its forms. For example, artists regularly visited the palaestra and gymnasia to study the naked bodies of the athletes who spent their days there (Pls. 87-8) wrestling, running, throwing the discus and the javelin. The nude body became the main vehicle of expression in art, just as Athenians took part naked in athletic contests and religious processions.

Physical training however was not the sole preoccupation of the Athenian youths as it was in Sparta. They strove with the same zeal to cultivate their minds. " We succeed in being lovers of the beautiful " Pericles said, " without straying from simplicity, and we cultivate our minds without ignoring the hardening of our bodies."

Changes in art technique came about slowly. The artist strove to imitate rather than innovate. He was not obsessed by originality. He wanted only to express the ideals of his society with vigour and accuracy and only when the techniques he had inherited proved inadequate to do so did he think of finding new ones. This combination of progressiveness with tradition ensured that classical art in Athens developed, as it were, organically.

The classical school of Athens was not limited to the handful of artists whose names have become household words to us or to the masterpieces which, though we may not actually have seen them, are as familiar to us through reproduction as the members of our own families. A whole army of artists whose names we shall never know were at work on the monuments of the Acropolis and the Agora and on the sanctuaries of Attica outside Athens, at Eleusis, Sunium and elsewhere. Many works of art created during the classical age are known to us only from literary sources such as Pausanias. Some have been destroyed by war or natural disasters; others have been scattered to every corner of the earth in museums and private collections and in the land which they once adorned survive only as a memory.

THE PARTHENON

THE FIRST GREAT achievement of Athenian democracy, after the tyranny had been overthrown, was to lay the foundations of a new temple to Athena made of porous stone. This first Parthenon was started under Cleisthenes on its present site but only the base had been laid by the outbreak of the first Persian War.

After Marathon, work was resumed. The new temple was slightly smaller than the earlier one (*see* Plan 2, p. 52) and was made entirely of marble. Narrower by two and a half yards and longer by four than the present temple, it had nearly the same groundplan. It was a peripteral with prodomus and opisthodomus and had the conventional divisions within. But work was interrupted a second time by the renewal of the Persian War. When the Persians occupied the Acropolis, they razed the building to the ground together with five other smaller sanctuaries—those of Brauronian Artemis, Pandrosos, Cecrops, Aglauros and the old Erechtheum.

When the Persians were finally defeated, the Athenians rebuilt the wall on the northern slope of the Acropolis as well as a new wall round Athens and Piraeus, using the supports, architraves, triglyphs, cornices and other fragments from their gutted temples as building materials. The south-western slope was levelled with fragments of statues which the Persians had desecrated. The excavations of Cavadeas in 1885 brought many of these fragments to light and they are now on display in the Acropolis Museum.

In 456 Pericles summoned a congress of the Delian league to decide upon the rebuilding of the sanctuaries. In spite of Spartan opposition, the congress approved

84. Detail of an archaic quadriga, *c.* 570, *length* (of head) 8 in. *Acropolis Museum, Athens*

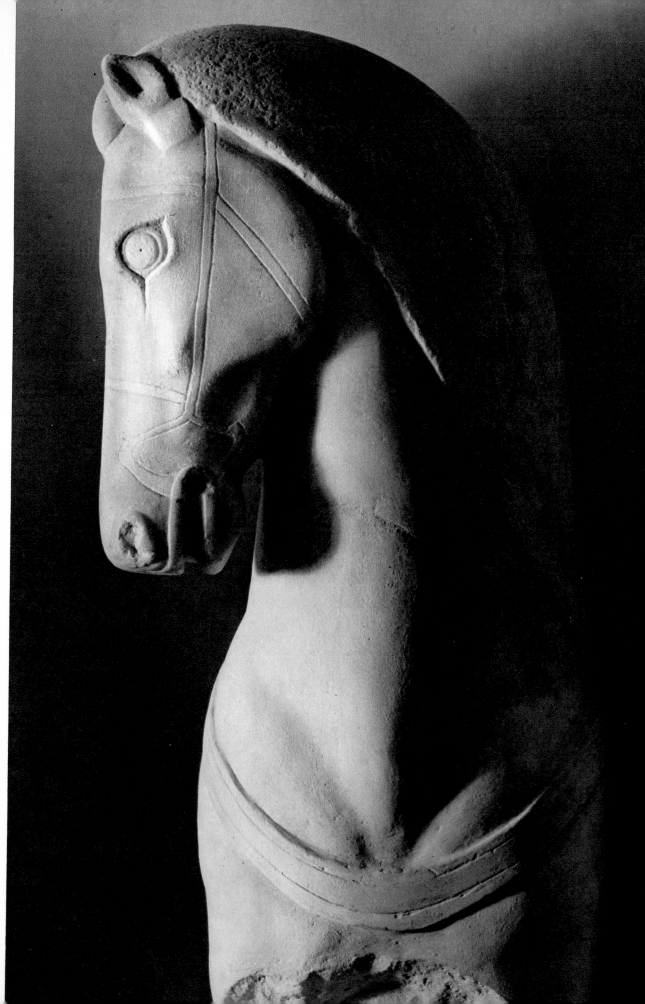

85

86

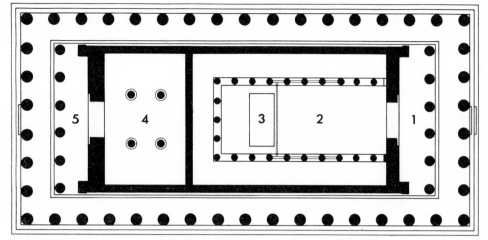

Plan 4. PARTHENON

1 Prodomus with columns prostyle
2 Cella
3 Base of statue of Athena Parthenos
4 Adytum with four Ionic columns
5 Opisthodomus

the proposals put before it and in 454 the treasury of the allies which had originally been intended to finance the war against the Persians was moved from Delos to Athens. Thus it was possible for Pericles' building programme to be carried out without undue economic strain to Athens.

The first work to be undertaken was the Parthenon, begun in 447 and completed nine year later. Pericles appointed Ictinus who had worked on the Telesterion at Eleusis as chief architect, Callicrates who had designed the temple of Athena Nikê as his assistant, and Phidias as general supervisor.

The style of the columns, the cornices and the peristyle was Doric. But the columns were not short and squat as in older Doric temples, nor was the peripteral composed of six columns. The height of the columns, the eight-columned peristasis, the amphiprostyle form, the friezes on the four outer walls of the enclosure, the columns which supported the ceiling of the adytum, and, lastly, the joints of the cornice were all borrowed by Ictinus from Ionic architecture. He thus brought together the severity and the strength of the Doric order with the refinement and grace of the Ionic. The Doric and Ionic elements lost their individuality in the architectural composition of the Parthenon and fused into a new unity which possessed special aesthetic qualities of its own.

The Parthenon seems to move upward. This is due to the convergence of the vertical axes towards the centre of the building—which resembles the shape of the frustum of a pyramid rather than a solid rectangle—due to an imperceptible inward inclination of the end columns and to the tapering of the trunks of the columns which increases as it gets nearer the top. A sense of movement is also achieved by a slight curvature applied to the trunk of the column above the lower third. This treatment of the column is known technically as "entasis." Moreover, all the horizontal lines, both visible and invisible, such as those in the architraves, the stylobate and the foundations, appear straight, although in fact they too are curved to strengthen the illusion of upward movement.[98]

The new temple (Plan 4) was made wider than its predecessors by two and a half yards and the old foundation on the north side was proportionately increased. But the western side was drawn in to make it shorter by four yards. Thus the stylobate on which the temple was set measures 30.88 metres in width and 69.51 metres in length. The floor consists of three layers of marble and at each end central steps lead up to the colonnade. The latter consists of seventeen columns on its long sides and eight at either end. Each column measures 10.45

85. Relief from Brauron showing Zeus, Leto, Apollo and Artemis, *c.* 400, *height* 2 ft. 8 in. *National Museum, Athens*

86. Brauron: Relief of Artemis, *c.* 400, *length* 1 ft. 8 in.

161

metres in height, or 5.5 times the diameter, and possesses twenty flutings. The trunk is separated from the capital by four incisions round the column and terminates with an echinus and an abacus supporting the cornice. The inner divisions consist of the prodomus, the cella, the adytum and the opisthodomus. The prodomus and opisthodomus are six-columned peristyles, but without supports or jambs. The cella was originally known as the hecatompedon because it measured exactly 100 Attic feet in length. A naos enclosed the chryselephantine statue of Athena by Phidias on three sides, separated from the walls by an aisle. The position of the statue is known because the foundation of porous stone is exposed at the point on which it rested. Elsewhere it is covered with slabs of marble.

Behind the shrine was a rectangular chamber with four Ionic columns which supported the roofing. It was separated from the shrine by a wall and communicated with the opisthodomus by means of a gateway. This area was known as the " Parthenon " or Virgin's chamber, for here the goddess was served by Athenian maidens during the Panathenaean festival. In the fourth century this name started to be applied to the entire temple. This " Parthenon " served as the treasury of the temple until the middle of the fifth century when it became the public treasury. The entire temple was roofed with thin marble slabs and Pentelic marble was used throughout. Red, black, ochre and blue paint did not cover it completely as it did the Temple of Zeus at Olympia, but was restricted to the reliefs, joints, metopes and other decorative details.

The sculptural decoration of the Parthenon for which Phidias was responsible occupied the two pediments, the ninety-two metopes (each measuring 1.34 by 1.27 metres) above the colonnade, the frieze (measuring 159.41 by 1.06 metres) on the wall of the temple itself. Co-ordinator and inspirer of the whole project, as well as author of the cult-statue, Phidias devoted most of his efforts to the decorative programme, laying down the style in which it was to be carried out. The actual sculptures were made by anonymous artists, the only evidence of whose presence is the variation in quality and technique in the six-hundred or so figures decorating the building.

The eastern pediment had as its theme the birth of Athena who springs in full armour from the head of Zeus and is received by a Nikê. Behind Zeus' throne stands Hephaestus who has cleft open his head with an axe. The birth takes place on Olympus before the gods and goddesses, some of whom are seated like Demeter, Persephone and Aphrodite, others reclining like Dionysus (Pl. 101) and others standing like Artemis. In the right hand corner, Selene (the moon) descends in her four-horsed chariot (Pl. 103) into the Ocean, while on the left Helios (the sun) mounts into the heavens. The figures from this pediment, together with most of the surviving sculptures of the Parthenon, were " abducted " by Lord Elgin and have been in the British Museum since 1826.

The western pediment, now no longer in existence, depicted the struggle between Athena and Poseidon over the possession of Athens. The two deities occupied the centre of the pediment with the symbols of their power — Athena with her spear and Poseidon with his trident. To their right and left were their war chariots attended by their charioteers, ᐟNikê and Amphitrite, escorted respectively by Hermes and Iris. A figure who is either Erechtheus or Cecrops watched the divine rivals, while in the corners of the pediment reclined the two rivers of Athens, the Ilissus and the Cefissus. The triangular pediments measure 26.35 metres across, while the height at the centre is 3.45 metres. Neither pediment exists today, but we have a good idea of them from drawings which Jacques Carrey made in 1674 when he visited the Acropolis in the company of the Marquis de Nointel, French Ambassador to Constantinople, and which came into the possession of the Bibliothèque Nationale in 1770.

87. Base of a kouros decorated with reliefs of wrestlers, c. 510, 2 ft. 6 in. by 11½ in. *National Museum, Athens*

88. Base of a kouros found in Athens, depicting scenes of the palaestra, 510. *National Museum, Athens*

89

90

The decorative programme continued in the metopes. There were fourteen on each of the two ends and thirty-two on each of the two sides, all depicting battle scenes: the gods against the giants on the eastern frieze (Pl. 8); the Greeks against the Amazons on the western frieze; the Lapiths against the Centaurs on the southern frieze (Pl. 99); and the fall of Troy on the northern frieze. The style and technique of these metopes appear to have been somewhat archaic, suggesting that they were the first part of the decorative programme to be executed. Most of the metopes were destroyed in the seventh century when the Parthenon was converted into a Christian church. The southern frieze survived because it was not visible from the road leading up to the Acropolis. And it is again thanks to Carrey that we know what it was like, for on 27 September 1687 the temple was destroyed during a bombardment ordered by the Venetian admiral, Morosini. The Turks were using it as a powder magazine and a stray shell caused an explosion. Of the original ninety-two metopes, one only survives *in situ* on the corner of the southern frieze depicting a Centaur and a Lapith.

On the two sides of the building and on the architraves of the prodomus and opisthodomus—that is to say on the four walls of the temple itself inside the colonnade—the sculptures depicted in a continuous band the great Panathenaean procession which took place every four years in honour of the patron goddess. The procession starts from the western end with horsemen preparing or calming their steeds. It then moved along the two long sides (Pls. 100 and 102) and ends at the eastern end with the acceptance by the high priest and his assistant of a *peplos* or veil woven by Athenian maidens. The twelve gods of Olympus watch the procession seated on their thrones. In the three stages of the procession, there were 400 divine and human figures and 200 animals. Only one section has survived on the western side.[98]

In creating this great decorative programme, Phidias composed a tragedy in stone of which Athena is the heroine. It recounts her birth, her quarrel with Poseidon, her descent from Olympus into Attica to give battle at Theseus' side against the giants, the Amazons and the Centaurs for the freedom of the city. This is the plot of the tragedy and the Panathenaean procession led gradually to the " catharsis " of the drama which was completed with the help of the gods.

Phidias' tragedy contains all the elements regarded by Aristotle in his *Poetics* as essential in the theatre. The myth in the two pediments is divine, in the metopes it is heroic and in the frieze, human. The action begins in the eastern pediment with a scene of the goddess's birth and continues in the western one with her struggle for supremacy. In the metopes, Athena, with her companion Theseus, matches her strength against the giants, the Centaurs and the Amazons. The city is freed and the foundations of the first kingdom are laid. The chorus of the Panathenaean procession proclaims the triumph of the goddess. After the fear and compassion caused by the events have ended, peace reigns and the heroine is vindicated.

Following closely the story of the legends, the tragedy presents the character and the passions of the *dramatis personae*. Thus the Centaurs are bestial (Fig. 23), the Amazons frenzied and the giants brazen. Their expressions are wild and agitated and their movements violent. The treatment of these figures aims at the utmost realism in its representation of the passions. In contrast, those taking part in the procession are dignified and composed, their movements are calm and their expressions noble. The idealization of the characters finds its loftiest expression in the figures of the Olympian gods which are serene and beautiful.

The Panathenaean procession was immortalized in the sculptured frieze. The old men with their olive branches, the musicians playing flutes and harps, the maidens with their pitchers and baskets, the horsemen, the drivers of the sacri-

Fig. 23. A Centaur's head from on of the Parthenon metopes, *Acropolis Museum, Athens*

89. Bronze statue of a god (Hermes), probably by Praxiteles, dredged up from the sea in the bay of Marathon in 1925. *National Museum, Athens*

90. Bronze head of Nikê, *height* 7¹/₂ *in.* *Agora Museum, Athens*

ficial beasts, all the characters taking part represented members of Athenian society in a heightened and idealized version of their everyday life. The tragic poets always sought to express real issues in their plays, even when they were not doing so as directly as Aeschylus in *The Persians*. Once again in this stone tragedy, classical art demonstrates its composite nature, its ability to reconcile harmoniously archaic legend with historical truth.

The construction of the Parthenon began in 447 and the inauguration ceremony took place during the Panathenaean festival of 438 when Phidias' chryselephantine statue of Athena Parthenos was dedicated. The pediments were not completely finished until 432. It is evidence of the vitality of Athenian society that the most important masterpiece of ancient Greece required only fifteen years to build. It was the work of a single generation guided by a single inspiration.

The Temple of Athena Nikê

On the southwest side of the sacred rock there was an ancient tower with an altar and sanctuary dedicated to Athena. Pericles decided to convert it into a pedestal for an elegant Ionic edifice. Callicrates, who collaborated with Ictinus on the Parthenon, drew up the plans in 450 but work did not start on the project until the beginning of the Peloponnesian War (427). The temple of Athena Nikê expressed the desire of Athenians for victory in their new martial venture, just as they had obtained victory over the Persians in the past. They wished to show once again that their patron goddess was the goddess of victory.

The temple of Athena Nikê (Pls. 4 and 5) is four-columned, with Ionic colonnades at the front and back but not at the sides. The columns are made from single blocks and taper only slightly. Its cella is small (4.19 by 3.78 metres) and at either side of the entrance two openings allow the light of the east to enter. Entirely of Pentelic marble, the only sculptural adornment is its Ionic frieze which has survived in fragmentary form in its original place. It is probable that the walls were painted. The theme of the frieze on the eastern façade is the assembly of the gods, whilst those on the other sides depict scenes from the victory of Plataea in which Athenian hoplites give battle in the nude. The whole composition is charged with vigour and movement.

In about 408, the Athenians built a small protective parapet round the narrow veranda on three sides to prevent the temple being damaged. It was composed of slabs of marble and had an overall length of thirty-five yards. It was decorated with beautiful reliefs on all three sides depicting Athena seated, surrounded by winged Victories bringing her shields, helmets and quivers to decorate her trophies or preparing animals to sacrifice to her. A Victory, with a graceful movement, lifts her left foot to tie her sandal which had come unfastened while she plays (Pl. 104). Though the sculptor of these Victories was a pupil of Phidias, it nevertheless seems as though a breath of the spring air of Attica had inspired him with love for the feminine body of Nikê. His Victory is sketched in with fluid curves, like the waves which wrinkle the waters of the Saronic Gulf when a sea breeze touches them lightly. It is as though the sensuality of Praxiteles is making its first tentative appearance (Pls. 97-8).

The Propylaea

With the Parthenon completed and so many projects about to be realized, Pericles could not leave the Acropolis with the Propylaea which had been built

91. Red-figure stamnos with Odysseus and the sirens, early 5th century, *height* 1 ft. 1³/₄ in. *British Museum, London*

92. Red-figure Panathenaean amphora depicting Athena. *British Museum, London*

93. Red-figure amphora by Mycon, depicting Croesus at the stake. *Louvre, Paris*

94. Red-figure pelike by the Pan-painter, depicting Heracles in Egypt killing the attendants of King Bousiris who wish to sacrifice him, *c.* 470. *National Museum, Athens*

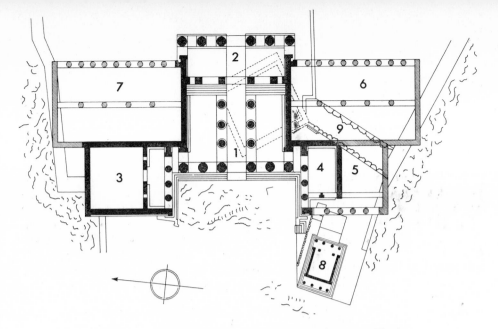

1 Central porch (west)
2 Eastern porch
3 Pinakotheke
4 South wing
5 Room corresponding
   with Pinakotheke
   (never built)
6 South-east interior
   porch (never built)
7 North-east interior
   porch (never built)
8 Temple of Athena
   Nikê
9 Part of the cyclopean
   wall

under Pisistratus. He wanted to provide the new sanctuaries with a monumental entrance which would be worthy of them. Mnesicles drafted the architectural plans and undertook its construction in 437. But work ceased after five years and with the outbreak of the Peloponnesian War was never resumed. Religious disputes also prevented the southern wing from being completed, because it came into conflict with the sanctuary of Brauronian Artemis.

The Propylaea extended over the entire western face of the Acropolis (Pls. 2-3) and consisted of three distinct sections (Plan 5): the imposing central gateway with a wing on either side. Both the eastern façade facing the interior of the Acropolis and the western façade facing the city had a Doric hexastyle portico surmounted with a pediment. The visitor approaching the Acropolis passed in through the western portico and after climbing six steps reached the five entrances into the eastern portico. In both porticos the two columns in the middle were more widely spaced than the others so that the central passage could be used by vehicles and processions. It is thus not paved and has no threshold or steps, but is lined with Ionic columns, three on either side, which also supported the roof. Of the two wings, only the northern was completed and is today the best preserved part of the whole building. It has a three-columned Doric prodomus *in antis* and a square cella behind, lit by two windows at the back of the prodomus. The interior chamber was called the Pinakotheke or Picture Gallery.

Of Mnesicles' original plan three sections were never completed, the southern wing of the western façade and both wings of the eastern façade. It was the last work of Pericles who died in 429.

The Erechtheum

It is likely that the Erechtheum was also one of Pericles' projects, but he did not live to see it realized. He had been dead for eight years when work started on it during the peace of Nicias. It was interrupted briefly during the Sicilian expedition (415-3) and was not finally completed until 405. The architects were Philocles and Archilochus. Built to replace the ancient sanctuary destroyed by the Persians, it was the abode of many gods and the architects achieved an astonishing *tour de force* in adapting the needs of all their cults to an irregular ter-

95. Statue of running girl
from a pediment at Eleusis,
early 5th century, *height* 2 ft. 2¹/₂ in.
Eleusis Museum

rain which tradition did not permit to be levelled. Retaining elements of the old Mycenaean plan (*see* Plan 2, p. 52), which we have described in connection with the myth and worship of Erichthonius and making subtle and ingenious play with the differences of level, they produced one of the most original buildings of the classical age (Pls. 9-10 and 12-13).

The Ionic frieze of the Erechtheum was completed at about the same time as the sculptures on the protecting wall of the temple of Nikê (408). To judge by the few fragments which have survived, it dealt with the myth of Erichthonius. The sculptor of the Erechtheum used the grey marble of Eleusis as a background upon which he attached figures carved out of white Pentelic marble. The figures were smaller and more highly finished than those on the Parthenon. The fascia which encircles the inner façades of the Erechtheum beneath the frieze was cared with the same skill. Together with the inlaid decoration of the northern doorway, the fascia is among the most beautiful stone patterns of the Acropolis. The Korae or Caryatides in the southern portico which stands on the traditional site of Cecrops' grave are very well preserved (Pl. 16). Of the six maidens, five only are original, the sixth being a replica of one which is now in the British Museum. The function of these statues is static only, for they act as columns supporting the roof, and they have therefore been treated in the archaic style like the Korae which form the entrance to the treasury of the Siphnians at Delphi. Three of the maidens support the weight of their bodies on their left leg and the other three on their right leg. This is the only variation in their movement. They are all garbed in Doric tunics which are tucked above the waist to break the monotony of the folds. Their hair falls richly over their neck and shoulders, giving greater volume to the slenderest part of the human column. They carry baskets on their heads which transfer the weight of the entablature to their bodies as the capital does to the columns. The projection forward of one leg gives movement to the figures as do the variations in the folds in their tunics. The maidens are tall and slender, robust and noble without, for that, losing their feminine grace.

The Erechtheum is deliberately less imposing than the Parthenon whose northern flank the Caryatides face. One of the problems which confronted the architects was that of producing a fitting monument for the important cult which it was to house without at the same time distracting the eye from the Parthenon. They solved it by contrast. The Erechtheum with its tall, slender, widely spaced Ionic columns, its asymmetrical structure and its air of Ionian delicacy and brilliance is the perfect complement to the massive grandeur and dignity of the Doric Parthenon.

THE ACROPOLIS IN CLASSICAL TIMES

THE ACROPOLIS today gives the visitor an impression which is very different from the one he would have received in classical times (Plan 6). The high outer walls which surrounded it on all sides have disappeared and, within, the successive terraces with their retaining walls no longer divide it into a series of separate sanctuaries surrounding each of the buildings (Fig. 24).

The great marble stairway leading up to the Propylaea is a Roman addition, dating perhaps from the reign of Claudius (41-54 A.D.). In classical times, the Acropolis was reached by a road which passes now below the pyrgos of the temple of Athena Nikê and winds its way up to the Propylaea. In front of the entrance, there was a space enclosed on three sides by the western portico of the Propylaea and its two annexes, the Pinakotheke and the Stoa.

96. A votive relief found at Eleusis. It represents the goddess Demeter giving Triptolemus an ear of corn. To the right her daughter Persephone seems to crown the youth. Attributed to Phidias. *National Museum, Athens*

97. Draped figure of a Nikê from the balustrade or parapet of the Temple of Athena Nikê, 410, *height* 3 ft. *Acropolis Museum, Athens*

99

Fig. 24. The Stevens model of the Acropolis

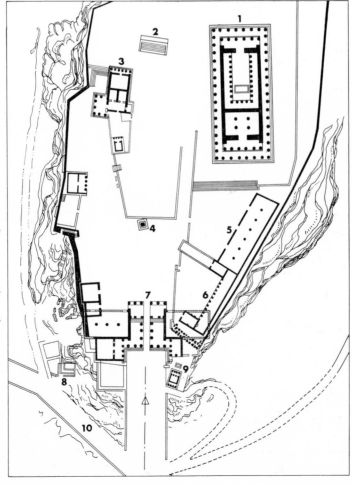

Plan 6. ACROPOLIS IN
CLASSICAL TIMES

1 Parthenon
2 Altar to Athena
3 Erechtheum
4 Statue of Athena
   Promachus
5 Chalcotheca
6 Sanctuary of
   Brauronian
   Artemis
7 Propylaea
8 Clepshydra
9 Temple of
   Athena Nikê
10 Panathenaean
   Way

98. Figure of a Nikê
from the balustrade of the Temple
of Athena Nikê, *height* 3 ft.
Acropolis Museum, Athens

99. Metope from the Parthenon:
a Lapith fighting a Centaur.
British Museum, London

175

Once the visitor had passed through the Propylaea and had penetrated into the Acropolis itself, he found himself in an open space. Directly before him, standing in front of the old Mycenaean wall, he could see the huge bronze statue of Athena Promachus (the Warrior) of which nothing remains but the marble plinth. From this first open space or square, two roads used to lead; one, to the right, led past the Stoa in the precinct of Artemis Brauronia and the small propylaea of the Chalcotheca (arsenal) to the western end of the Parthenon; the other, to the left, led towards the northern portico of the Erechtheum, beyond which stood an altar to Athena, the peribolus of the altar of Zeus Polieus and the sanctuary of Pandios. At the north-eastern corner of the Parthenon a small round Ionic temple was erected during the Roman period (14 A. D.) to the goddess Roma and the emperor Augustus.

All these open spaces, terraces, walls and roads were decorated with a wealth of statues and votive offerings: today only four marble masterpieces, bereft of their paint and most of their decoration, remain to remind the visitor of the vitality and genius of classical Athens.

The Building and Defence Programme

The sacred buildings of the Acropolis were the first part of a general programme of reconstruction planned by Pericles, which also included public and private building.

The part of the programme dealing with religious building provided not only for the Acropolis, but for Piraeus, Eleusis, Rhamnus and Sunium. Pericles also planned to include the western side of the Agora, the summit of the Colonus Agoraeus over which the city wall used to pass, among the areas set aside for religious

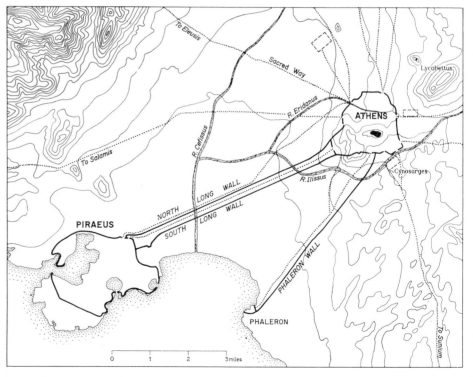

100. Detail of the Parthenon frieze depicting a youth and a boy. *British Museum, London*

Map 6. Athens, Piraeus and Phaleron at the time of Pericles

building. There the Doric peripteral temple of Hephaestus, popularly known as the Theseum, was built (449-4). It is the best preserved of all ancient temples (Pls. 14, 15 and 17).

It is surrounded by a colonnade, with six columns along the narrow ends and thirteen on the long sides The pediments contained reliefs as did the eighteen metopes On the eastern and western architraves, there are friezes which have survived in a mutilated state depicting an assembly of the gods and battles against the Titans and the Centaurs The metopes, which are very corroded, depict the labours of Heracles and Theseus. Two other temples in Attica, one at Sunium dedicated to Poseidon (Pl. 19) and another at Rhamnus dedicated to Nemesis, are both very similar in proportion and style.

The second part of Pericles' building programme covered defensive projects: two walls linking Athens with Piraeus (each 6,000 yards in length). a wall guarding communications with Phaleron (5,200 yards) and a strong wall encircling Athens (6,500 yards). The strongest and longest wall of all was that which surrounded Piraeus with its three harbours (9,000 yards) and which is described by Thucydides. The total length of these defensive walls amounted to 32,550 metres (Plan 7, p. 180).

Besides defence works, the plan also provided for buildings to house public services, most of them centred in the Agora. Existing buildings such as the Bouleuterion, the Court of the Heliaea and the Enneakrounos fountain were repaired or reconstructed. New buildings were also added. These have been studied by Homer Thompson [99] who directed the excavations carried out in the Agora by the American School (Plan 6, p. 175). and include the silver mint, the so-called south colonnade with its seven-couched chamber which was used for official banquets, the Metroum where public records were kept, the Tholos housing the official weights and measures, the dining halls of the Prytaneum and the army headquarters. The Poikile Stoa which contained paintings by Polygnotus of scenes from the siege of Troy has not been identified, since the ruins at the eastern end of the Agora have not yet been studied.

Throughout the length and breadth of the Agora, there were many statues by outstanding sculptors like Critias and Nesiotes, Phidias and (later) Praxiteles, as well as fountains to cool the atmosphere and plane trees planted by Cimon to provide shade. Pericles moved the theatre and the Odeion from the Agora to the southern slope of the Acropolis. The new theatre of Dionysus (Pl. 18) was built in stone, whereas the new Odeion, a square wooden structure with a conic roof to east of the theatre, has not survived.

The third part of the building programme included dwellings for private members of the community. It affected Piraeus more than Athens, for Athens was already densely populated and little could be done in the area along the slopes of the Pnyx, the Museum and the Hill of the Nymphs. Thus the residential quarters were not improved very much during the period which saw the construction of such impressive religious and public edifices. The Athenian cared more for the public splendour of his city than for his own personal comfort.

An Athenian house consisted of a series of rooms built round an inner courtyard. The construction was very simple; only the lower portion of the walls was made of small stones, the remainder being of crude brick. The floors were laid with green clay which in some instances was decorated with mosaics and the roofs were made of wood covered with clay tiles. Some houses had a second storey.

The streets were narrow and unplanned. Even the main street which passed by the Agora and led to the Acropolis was no more than about fourteen feet wide. The widest street was the Panathenaean Way, which was used for games,[100] and measured approximately thirty-six feet across.

101. Dionysus from the east pediment of the Parthenon. *British Museum, London*

179

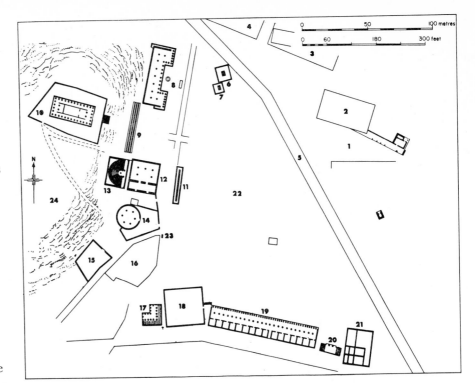

Plan 7. THE AGORA IN THE TIME OF PERICLES

More was done in Piraeus, because as a port, it received priority from a government whose policies were based on naval power. The three-fold programme of Pericles reflected the three fundamental aspects of city life; religious, political and private. The building of the private sector was based on principles conceived and formulated by Hippodamus, an Ionian refugee from Miletus, who at the request of Pericles undertook the planning of Piraeus.

Aristotle gives us a sketch of Hippodamus. His appearance was eccentric, with his rich locks of hair, his delight in jewelry and his robes of costly materials which he wore both summer and winter. He had gained a reputation as an architect, a meteorologist and a constitutional lawyer. He was the pioneer of town-planning on geometrical principles with the streets laid out at right angles like a checkerboard. Piraeus, Rhodes and Thurii are examples of his work.

Piraeus became the model of a commercial centre for the entire world.[101] It had walled communication with Athens and was divided into three sectors: the Agora was its religious and political centre; the three harbours with the naval arsenal of Zea constituted the defence zone; and finally the warehouses and wharves round the large Cantharus basin was the mercantile centre Round these three areas, defined residential zones were laid out in which the streets followed a grid system. The groundplan was not uniform for the entire city, but was applied individually to each quarter.[102]

The Athens of Pericles had two aspects, a peaceful and a military one, like its patron Athena who was at the same time goddess of war and goddess of handicrafts. She appeared on the Acropolis in both aspects: peaceful in the Parthenon statue and warlike in the bronze statue which faced the Propylaea. The walls protecting the city and its harbours were planned because war with Sparta and her Peloponnesian allies seemed inevitable. When it occured, the outlying countryside of Attica would be invaded and devastated before an attack could be

102. Detail of the Parthenon
frieze depicting
a horseman and horses.
British Museum, London

launched on Athens itself. The inhabitants would be forced to abandon their lands and pour into the city for safety. Thus accommodation and protection had to be provided for refugees.

The strategic principles of Pericles were based on naval rather than military power. His plan provided protection for the population of Attica within the walls of the city and left the fleet free to concentrate on offensive operations. The ships were to prevent the allies of Athens from revolting and withholding the tributes imposed on them. At the same time they were to harass the enemy by blockading or invading his coast-lines.

When the Peloponnesian War (431-404) broke out, Pericles told the Athenians not to be afraid of the final outcome of the conflict. Athens derived on average 600 talents a year from her allies in addition to other revenue coming from agriculture, mines and harbour dues. Moreover, a reserve 6,000 talents in silver coin was stored on the Acropolis. It was the balance left from the 9,700 talents amassed to finance the building of the sanctuaries. Besides these funds, there was ample gold and silver, either in the form of votive offerings and sacred utensils used for processions and games or of booty captured from the Persians. The total value of these was not less than 50 talents. In case of emergency, the 40 talents of pure gold on the statue of Athena was detachable and could be used without impairing the work of Phidias. The financial situation of Athens was secure and Pericles pointed out also that the army included 13,000 hoplites, 16,000 guards, 1,200 cavalry equipped with bows and arrows, 1,600 infantry bowmen and 300 warships.

Forty-eight years had passed between the destruction of Athens in 479 and the outbreak of the Peloponnesian War. During this period Athens had become the wealthiest, the most powerful and the most beautiful city of the ancient world.

POLITICAL OPPOSITION TO PERICLES AND HIS DEATH

THE POLICIES of Pericles aroused the criticism of his enemies—the aristocratic party—which had suffered a setback after the death of Cimon. They accused Pericles of ruling as a tyrant, of squandering the funds of the allies, which were intended for military defence, on embellishing Athens as though she were a pretty woman, with precious stones, statues and costly temples. To these criticisms, Pericles replied that the taxes collected from their allies belonged to the Athenians, for while the allies contributed only money, the Athenians gave their blood in the common struggle. Moreover, the city had ample resources to provide for the necessities of war and a surplus to spend on projects which would bring her immortal fame. He added that the citizens had every right to enjoy the fruits of their labours and to enliven their leisure with religious spectacles, processions, theatrical shows, games and works of art in their city.

But Pericles did not neglect military training. Every year 60 triremes manned by recruits and officers who were paid a salary went on manœuvres for a period of eight months. At the same time he prevented overpopulation by settling colonists in the Chersonese, Thrace, Naxos, Andros and Thurii in the Gulf of Tarentum.

His critics did not limit their attacks to the public activities of Pericles. They accused his mistress Aspasia, who originally came from Miletus, of attaining her position in society, not because of her culture and her exceptional abilities, to which Socrates and Plato both paid tribute, but because she used her charms to get political power. They compared her to another woman from Ionia, the

103. Horse's head from the quadriga of Selene from east pediment of the Parthenon. *British Museum, London*

beautiful and gifted Thargelea, who managed by the same means to ensnare the kings of Persia. They even accused Phidias of pilfering gold from the statue of Athena Parthenos. The clash between the two parties became so acute that the Athenians had to resort to ostracism to resolve the impasse. The leader of the opposition was ostracized and, after his exile, Pericles dissolved the aristocratic party.

When the war against Sparta started, Pericles tightened his control and became more and more indifferent to the protests of his opponents, to whom he refused to give an account of his actions. The Spartans reminded the Athenians that Pericles was descended from the Alcmaeonidae who had been stigmatized for their part in suppressing the conspiracy of Cylon and they helped to reorganize the aristocratic party which found a new leader in Nicias. Moreover, a third party had come into existence under the leadership of the demagogue Cleon, of whom Thucydides and Aristophanes have left vivid portraits as a vulgarian and rabble-rouser.

Pericles did not seek war with Sparta, but he had foreseen and prepared for it. With great lucidity he explained to his fellow citizens why they had come to hate him now that he was leading them to war and why the allies hated Athens now that she had become their master. " Do not imagine," he said, " that what we are fighting for is simply the question of freedom or slavery: there is also involved the loss of our empire and the dangers arising from the hatred which we have incurred in administering it. Nor is it any longer possible for you to give up this empire, though there may be some people who in a mood of sudden panic and in a spirit of political apathy actually think that this would be a fine and noble thing to do. In fact you hold your empire down by force: it may have been wrong to take it; it is certainly dangerous to let it go. And the kind of people who talk of doing so and persuade others to adopt their point of view would very soon bring a state to ruin and would still do so even if they lived by themselves in isolation. For those who are politically apathetic can only survive if they are supported by people who are capable of taking action. They are quite valueless in a city which controls an empire, though they would be safe slaves in a city that was controlled by others." With views like these, Pericles could scarcely exclude the waters of the Saronic Gulf from his defensive programme. He looked upon Aegina as a threat to Piraeus which had to be removed.

Twenty-seven years before the outbreak of the Peloponnesian War, the Athenians had, as a preventive measure, decided to destroy Aegina. In the winter of 457-6, the Athenian fleet struck, captured seventy ships complete with their crews, made a landing on the island and forced the beleaguered Aeginetans to surrender. The treaty was harsh: Aegina was compelled to demolish her walls, surrender her ships to the Athenians and to pay a heavy annual tribute of 30 talents. But her trials did not end there.

In the summer of 431, the people of Athens saw from the Acropolis smoke and flames rising in the plains as far away as Hymettus. The Peloponnesian army under Archidamus, king of Sparta, had made its first incursion into Attica and was ravaging the countryside. Athens retaliated immediately. 150 triremes set sail to harass the coasts of the Peloponnese. The ships also carried refugees from the plains of Attica who were to be settled in Aegina on lands confiscated from the Aeginetans. The Aeginetans who had been expelled from their homes fled with their wives and children to Thyrea (Cynouria) where lands had been offered them by their Lacedaemonian allies. But even there the Athenians gave them no respite, for, as Thucydides tells us, they burnt their new city, razed it to the ground, and carried the unfortunate Aeginetans back to Athens as prisoners.

104. Figure of a Nikê from the balustrade of the temple of Athena-Nikê. The slenderest Victory stoops to undo her sandal. *Acropolis Museum, Athens*

The Peloponnesian war was to result finally in the overthrow of Athenian democracy. But the role of Pericles ended long before disaster overtook his beloved city. When he fell victim to the plague which broke out in the third year of the war, in the summer of 429, the prospects for Athens still looked hopeful and if his successors had continued his policies, instead of indulging in reckless adventures, it is possible that the war might have had a different outcome. But it is in the monuments built before the outbreak of war that his memory survives. So long as the Parthenon stands, the achievement of Pericles and the democracy which he himself described so movingly in a funeral speech for Athenians who had fallen in the first year of the war, will continue to be remembered.

POLYGNOTUS

FROM THE DESCRIPTIONS of Pausanias, who visited Athens in the middle of the second century A. D., we know that most of the religious and public buildings were decorated with murals. During the reconstruction of Athens, the painter Polygnotus gained wide recognition for the part he took in this work.

On the walls of the Poikile Stoa in the Agora he painted four large compositions: the Athenians in battle array at Oinoe in Argolis; the fight of Theseus against the Amazons; the capture of Troy by the Achaeans and the enslavement of the Trojan women; and the battle of Marathon, with the Persians fleeing towards their ships. In the last the hero Marathon (after whom the plain was named), Theseus, Heracles and Athena are represented fighting at the side of Callimachus and Miltiades. Polygnotus had been commissioned to undertake this work by Cimon as part of the latter's efforts to rehabilitate the memory of his father who had died after his failure to conquer the island of Paros. Polygnotus was in close relationship with the family of Miltiades. Plutarch alludes to a love affair between the painter and Miltiades' daughter Elpinice and, as evidence of their attachement, says that he used her as the model for his painting of Laodicea, the beautiful daughter of Priam, whom the Achaeans took prisoner after the fall of Troy.

The decoration of the Poikile Stoa established Polygnotus' reputation in Athens. He came originally from the island of Thasos and both his father and his brother were also painters. When Thasos fell into the hands of the Persians, this artistic family settled in Athens where the young Polygnotus was brought up. He seems to have been a man of means, for he painted the Poikile Stoa at his own expense, without claiming a fee from the deme. In return, he received the unusual honour of Athenian citizenship. Naturally, it was Polygnotus whom Cimon chose to paint the walls of the Theseum, erected in 475-4 to house the bones of Theseus which had been brought from Scyros to Athens on the day that the young Sophocles first won the dramatic contest over the aging Aeschylus.

In the temple of Theseus, two walls were devoted to the hero's struggles with the Amazons and the Centaurs. A third painting, on which Micon collaborated, depicted the scene where Minos throws his ring into the sea to test the divine origin of Theseus and showed Theseus at the marine palace of his father Poseidon and Amphitrite. This composition provided vase painters with a favorite decorative motif, for example the crater in the Bologna Museum (Fig. 9, p. 61).

In the temple of the Dioscuri, Polygnotus painted the marriage of Castor and Polydeuces with the daughters of Leucippus, and Micon, the expedition of the Argonauts.

Pausanias visited the Pinakotheke attached to the Propylaea and describes the paintings he saw there. He attributes them to Polygnotus although in fact not

105. Statue from Cnidus by the sculptor Leochares, c. 330. *British Museum, London*

all were by him. One depicted Odysseus and Diomedes discovering Achilles at Scyros. Achilles is dressed in female attire among the king's daughters, clutching his sword at the sound of a trumpet; another showed Odysseus with Nausicaa and her maidens as they washed clothes and bathed in the river. Neither of these paintings has survived but they were copied by other painters and versions of them may be seen on murals found in the Campania, now in the Naples Museum.

But the greatest paintings of Polygnotus were those he made for the Lesche or meeting place of the Cnidians at Delphi. Pausanias describes them in great detail in the chapter on Phocis in his *Description of Greece*. The painting on the right of the building represented the capture of Troy and the departure of the Achaeans, and the painting on the left, the descent of Odysseus into the underworld. Both were crowded and animated compositions and Pausanias' description of the capture of Troy reminds one of Delacroix's *Massacre of Chios*: " Next to Helen," he writes, " sits the mother of Theseus, completely shaven. The captive Trojan women are weeping. Andromache is followed by her son yearning for her breast. A horse is rolling in the dust, close by the shore strewn with pebbles, with the sea appearing in the background, Pylis lies on his back, naked and dead; below, Eioneus and Admetus also lie dead with their armour still on... further up is Leocritus, son of Polydamas, whom Odysseus had slain... Glaucus stands higher still wearing his double armour; Eurymachus sits on a stone and Antenor is standing with his daughter Crino beside him, holding a baby in her arms. Their expressions show despair at the calamity which has befallen them."

In the descent of Odysseus into the underworld, Pausanias describes " Hector sitting grief-stricken, with his hands clasped round his knee... Sarpedon's face is buried in his hands... Penthesilea, whose face is turned towards Paris, gazes into the distance as if she is not looking at any thing in particular." And his description ends with the comment: " So varied and beautiful is the painting of the Thasian artist."

Similar praise had been bestowed on Polygnotus earlier by Aristotle and Plato. For Aristotle, he was the ideal teacher of art, as well as the painter best able to render the character and moral attitudes of heroes and he is mentioned by Plato in two of the dialogues.

But it was not only the depiction of psychology and emotion which Polygnotus introduced into Athenian painting; he also brought about a change in painting technique. Pausanias, in his description of his work, multiplies the expressions " above this one," " near that one," " below this one," " slightly higher than those already mentioned " and so on. This means that the heroes, in his composition, were not laid out in line as on the friezes, but set at different levels, either higher or lower, according to the method of isometric projection—called in French *perspective cavalière*—which Phidias was to use later to depict the fight with the Amazons on the shield of his Athena Parthenos (Fig. 21, p. 152). This method was not, in fact, invented by Polygnotus, for it is present in some of the older bas-reliefs and murals in the east. In Greek painting, however, it was a novelty to place the heroes at different levels of the composition, where to be " slightly higher " meant further away and " slightly lower," nearer. Although Polygnotus' works have not survived, his methods can be seen on the Orvieto crater in the Louvre (Pl. 68) which depicts, on one side, the slaying of the children of Niobe by Apollo and, on the other, Heracles, Theseus and Pirithous in the underworld [103]. The pose of Theseus reminds one of Pausanias' description of the melancholy Hector in Polygnotus' mural, sitting in the underworld holding his knee with both hands. The placing of the figures on different planes is also suggested by the painter by curved lines indicating hills and rocks. The disposition of the figures in echelons departs from the principles of Euclidian geometry, that is to say, from the system of linear perspective which was applied both during the Hellenistic period and the Italian Renaissance, for the human figures do not diminish as they recede into the distance, but maintain the same proportions as the figures in the foreground. Thus Heracles, on the Orvieto crater, although he is placed higher and hence further away, has the same proportions as Pirithous who is lower, therefore nearer. The same technique can be observed on the crater in the Bologna Museum (Fig. 9, p. 61) depicting Theseus in the palace of Poseidon.

The murals of Polygnotus and Micon were sketched and painted on a tectorium, specially prepared for the techniques of tempera painting. Vitruvius and Pliny have described the way the tectorium was treated and modern research on the murals at Pompeii suggests that it was first covered with two or three layers of limestone, mixed with sand and calcite. The background was then painted and allowed to dry before the figures were added. The colours were mixed with soapy limestone and some kind of size to make them adhere firmly and finally the composition was dressed with a compound of carbonic soap, wax and chalk to give it durability and brilliance.

None of the original murals of Polygnotus or Micon has survived and we know them only by description and by the copies which were made of them in the murals of the Campania and in vase-paintings.

RED-FIGURE STYLE

ATHENIAN VASE painting, besides the information it gives us about the work of the great mural painters, is an art in its own right. The Athenians did not make distinctions, as we are inclined to do today, between " major " and " minor " arts. Sculpture, base-relief, mural painting and vase painting, were all included under the common term of " art " (technai). Polygnotus was regarded as equal to Phidias, and Micon to Euphronius. Indeed, it is possible that it was the vase-painters who opened the way for the mural painters, when, leaving behind the techniques of black-figure style, they covered the surface of the vase with black on which they drew their compositions in light terracotta tones with delicate strokes of a brush. This new technique, called the red-figure style, freed line from the incised groove cut into the surface of the pot and made it possible to depict facial expression and movement with much greater subtlety.

From 530 to 480, red-figure style continued, however, to cling to the procedures of black-figure style and left unexploited all the possibilities which the change-over from chisel to brush had opened up. For example, Andocides, whose amphora now in the Louvre, representing a Homeric duel watched by Athena and Hermes, is one of the earliest examples of red-figure style, follows the traditions of the archaic school, although he makes use of new techniques. The faces are depicted in profile while the almond-shaped eyes are drawn front-wise, the geometrical contours, the exaggerated torsoes, the predominance of decorative themes drawn from the *Iliad*, all these are survivals of black-figure style, but already the main techniques of the red-figure style are apparent too. Another example of the combination of both styles is a second amphora of Andocides in the Louvre (Pl. 69), which depicts a musical performance.

The end of the fifth century witnessed an important step forward, when another red-figure painter, Euphronius, started to depict warriors and heroes no longer clad in armour, but nude. One of his Athenian craters, also in the Louvre, shows Heracles and Antaeus struggling, with their heads clasped in each other's powerful arms, the first kneeling and the second lying on the ground. Henceforth red-figure style is characterized by studies of the nude body, by a preoccupation with anatomical detail and, a little later, by attempts to represent movement in plastic terms. When we compare the portrait of Croesus at the stake (Pl. 93), on a red-figure amphora in the Louvre painted by Mycon during the first twenty years of the fifth century, with the comical episode of Heracles, in the kingdom of Bousiris in Egypt, hurling over his shoulder a Negro who wants to sacrifice him (Pl. 94), we understand how rapidly vase-painting has evolved from the early style of Andocides to the freer manner of Brygos and his pupils. By the end of the red-figure period, Douris had advanced still further in freeing drawing from the geometrical traditions of the archaic school. He was encouraged, no doubt, by the freedom with which comical scenes could be treated, as for example, on a psykter in the British Museum (Pl. 70).

With a hydria of the potter Midias, now in the British Museum, the red-figure school enters its final phase (425-390). The painter is no longer as interested in anatomy or in expressing sentiments as he is in rendering the richness of garments falling in light folds and the delicate movements of the dance; he is seeking to create a sensuous, even erotic, atmosphere in his sketches. Life in the gynaeceum inspired painters like Midias, Erginon, Aristophanes, Aisona and the unknown painter of Eretria whose study of a woman at her toilet on an Athenian vase (Pl. 71) displays all the subtlety of a miniaturist. The hydria of Midias treats the theme of the rape of the daughters of Leucippus by the Dioscuri. Polydeuces has seized Hilaeira and is holding her by the waist in his Chariot. Her sister, Phoebe, tries vainly to escape from the embrace of Castor whose charioteer is waiting nearby. Between the two chariots which face in opposite directions is the *xoano* of Aphrodite, showing that the abduction takes place in her sanctuary. The other side of the same amphora is decorated with the theme of Heracles in the garden of the Hesperides. Aphrodite is seated near the altar with the father of the Dioscuri, Zeus, in front of her. To the right, we see the escaping figure of Peitho, who disapproves of all this violence. On the other side, above the altar of Aphrodite, stands a tree laden with apples, round whose trunk a snake is coiled. Chrysothemis is stretching out her hand to pluck an apple while Asterope tries to dissuade her. Behind her Health is seated with Klytio in front of her. Opposite Chrysothemis, Lipara seems to be engaged in conversation with a beardless Heracles who is holding a club and sitting on a lion's skin. Behind him his son Iolaos is standing upright. With the hydria of Midias, dating from about 410, the history of Athenian vase-painting comes to an end and the erotic spirit which was to inspire the paintings of the Hellenistic period makes its first appearance.

THE ATTIC WHITE LEKYTHOS

RED-FIGURE style was preoccupied with light and it moved back the shadows from the figures themselves into the background. But this did not provide an answer to the problem of transparency, for the black background gives the impression that night is about to fall and blot out the whole composition. Classical sculpture sought to obtain effects of transparency by its treatment of the folds of the drapery which reveal the shape and movement of the body beneath. But the solution of Phidias and Praxiteles, depending as it did on their medium, was not possible for the painter.

His problem was to capture light and to enclose it, by means of line and colour, on the flat surface of his vase. The school of painting which explored this problem furthest is called the white style and it produced the Attic white lekythos, a form only used in funerary rites. The lekythos contained the oil or

106   107

108

myrrh with which the body was anointed before burial or which was poured over the funeral stele. When the ceremony was over the lekythos was either broken or buried with the body.

Darkness is banished completely from the Attic white lekythos and its place is taken by a whitish light which pervades the whole of the surface. With the most delicate touch, the fluid silhouette of a human form is sketched on light itself, acquiring a transparent quality akin to crystal, air or water. One may say that the figure on the lekythos exists without being. The space he occupies is metaphysical, for he belongs to the world of the spirit. He looks at us with melancholy tranquillity, prevented by invisible ties from uttering words, nor can we ever succeed in touching him. He is immaterial and speechless, like an apparition. The light which suffuses the surface of the lekythos and surrounds the figure possesses a sort of "untouchedness," for it is the light of Attica itself. The form of the dead man is enveloped in curves which run over the contours of the vase like a pale thread, undulating and nimble, reconciling him to his fate, easing aesthetically the pangs of death with the promise of spiritual immortality (Pls. 77-8). With the final period, Athenian vase painting has exhausted its creative energies, leaving to the great mural painters the responsibility of initiating changes, both in style and technique.[104]

COINS

ALTHOUGH THE ART of stamping coins had been practised in archaic Athens since the seventh century, hardly any changes took place in classical times in the themes and techniques used. Coinage is intimately connected with economic development and Athens did not want to alter her ancient coins for fear of impairing international confidence in their value. Thus, Athenian coins maintained into the classical period the archaic profile of Athena, on one face, with her helmet and big almond-shaped eye and, on the reverse, the figure of an owl with an olive branch, set within an incised quadrangular frame bearing the first three letters of the name of the city: (AΘE).[105] But the stability of the themes and of the technical methods used in stamping did not preclude variations in style and treatment by individual engravers at different periods.

According to their size, shape and the composition of the alloy, Athenian coins were struck in the following denominations: ten drachmas, four drachmas, two drachmas and the hemidrachmon or half drachma. The basic unit, the drachma, was rhomboid in shape and bore the head of Gorgo on one face and a bull on the reverse within an incised quadrangular frame. Under Solon and Pisistratus a scarab, a house and the spondyl, probably emblems of aristocratic families, were also sometimes used, with, on the reverse, an incised quadrilateral divided into triangles. The ten drachma piece, with the head of Athena on one side and the owl on the other, was struck for the first time at the Panathenaean festival of 556 and was never changed thereafter.[106] The stamping of coins was supervised by officials who were responsible for the composition of the alloy as well the shape and design of the coin. Athens' trade depended on her coinage and until her decline every effort was made to maintain its standard.

Towards the end of the fifth century, coins bearing the signature of the engraver started to appear in the cities of Greater Greece. Thus, after their victory over the Athenian army in 413, the Syracusans struck commemorative coins. The ten drachma piece bearing, on one side, a chariot advancing at full gallop while a winged Victory crowns the charioteer and, on the reverse, the head in profile of Arethusa (or Persephone) is the work of the sculptor Euainetos.

109. Head of a bronze statue of Athena found at Piraeus in 1959. *National Museum, Athens*

The Theatre

THE ARCHITECTURAL plan of the Greek theatre with its circular orchestra, its scene or stage and its auditorium corresponded to the three elements of the ancient tragedy: the chorus which represented the music, the hero who represented the word and, finally, the demos which represented the audience. In the definition of tragedy given by Aristotle in his *Poetics*, there are six elements: the first three: words, music and spectacle are the means of imitation; the other three: myth, character and emotion are the objects of imitation. He concludes his definition by saying that the purpose of tragedy was to purge the passions through the portrayal of pity and fear, calling this process *catharsis*.

The architecture of the theatre attained its final form under Lycurgus—340-30—when the theatre of Dionysus, on the slopes of the Acropolis, was rebuilt. It was further altered under the Romans who suppressed the circular form of the orchestra. All Greek theatres had circular orchestras or dancing-places as excavations carried out at Epidaurus, Eretria, Sicyon, Megalopolis, Amphiraeus and Delphi have shown without exception. When, during the Hellenistic and Roman periods, the chorus lost some of its importance, the shape of the orchestra was altered and the centre of interest was concentrated on the scene itself.

The decor of the Greek stage (*skenographia*) was influenced by the temple frieze. The proscenium was, as it were, a long screen on which the artist had drawn the heroes of the drama in clear-cut outlines and against which the masked actors appeared in their formal costumes like painted statues. The minute dimensions of the Greek stage circumscribed the movements of the actors but, on the other hand, threw them into greater prominence. Hence the importance of measured gestures and voice production in bringing the drama to its climax.

The acoustics of Greek theatres are too good to have been the result of accident. Professor B. Papathanassopoulos who has made a detailed study of this question [107] has been able to infer the principles on which the theatre architects worked and anyone who has attended a performance at Epidaurus can confirm how effective they were. The auditorium was usually built on the slope of a hill with its seats in tiers and was large enough to hold all the citizens of the city. The slope itself was covered with stone or marble revetments. The auditorium, unlike the orchestra, had three main centres and was more or less in the shape of an ellipse, the ends of which encompassed both the scene and the orchestra.

In the centre of the orchestra, stood an altar or *thymele* dedicated to Dionysus and at Epidaurus a circular plaque marks where it stood. Both orchestra and thymele are relics of the *thiasoi* or dancing troupes of the followers of Dionysus who sang and performed dithyrambic dances round the altar in honour of the god. The *thiasos* was the basic unit in the religious organization formed by the disciples of Dionysus or " rebels " as they called themselves. And the dance they performed was the expression of their revolt against the social and political order. Instead of banishing it as other cities had tried to do, the Athenians assimilated the thiasos and found a place for it within the framework of their society. The thiasos became the chorus of the tragedy and the drama evolved from the social revolt of the Dionysiac cult into one of the greatest archievements of Athenian social life.

Behind the orchestra the scene was used exclusively by the tragic actors. In the fourth century it was built on two floors; the lower, called the proscenium, had an entrance on either side linked with the ground by a ramp; the upper floor or hyposcenium was decorated with paintings and surrounded by columns. The whole scene was roofed and walled and had three gates like the façade of a palace or a temple. Most plays were set in a public square in front of a temple or

a palace, as though an important event in the life of the city were taking place before the spectators. The protagonist made his entrance through the royal gate in the centre of the decor. The gate on the right led to the guest-chamber and the gate on the left to the sanctuary or the gynaeceum. The two side-entrances had also their own conventional purposes; the entrance on the right led to the countryside and on the left to the city.

Tragedy or, more properly, dramatic form is usually ascribed to Thespis of Icaria who, in the years of Pisistratus, introduced the practice of letting the leader of the chorus assume various roles and enter into a dialogue with the chorus. Phrynichus in 522 stabilized the role of the actor, separating him completely from the chorus, and, in a sense, may be said to have created the Attic drama. Thenceforth, the dramatic and lyric elements in the tragedy became even more sharply differentiated.

The tragic hero emerged from the sacrificial altar of Dionysus. As a hero he bore the burden of tragic responsibility and endured the sufferings of the god himself whom he was supposed to replace in his role as saviour. The sacrificial altar originally symbolized the grave of Dionysus; later, it became the tomb of the hero who incarnated him. Thus Dionysus faded into the background and was replaced by the hero.

If the chorus sprang from popular cults, the protagonist may well have been of aristocratic origin. He entered tragedy from epic poetry as a symbol of the individualism of the aristocracy. He was set up in opposition to the anonymous social group represented by the chorus and, through his clashes with the chorus, created the dramatic episodes.

It was from the seats of the theatre of Dionysus (Pl. 18) that the citizens of Athens watched the comedies and the tragedies of their great poets. They participated in the action and felt themselves the emotions which the actors represented on the stage. The Aristotelian idea that the spectators at a drama purged themselves of passion by means of an aesthetic experience brings the theatre back to its origins, for this is very akin to the effect of a religious ceremony. But the drama had other purposes too. Like temple decoration, it aimed to instruct: from the masterpieces of Aeschylus, Sophocles and Euripides, the citizen derived a greater sense of democratic responsibility. They encouraged—and equipped— —him to participate more fully in public life and to offer an example of civic virtue to the rest of the world.

TRAGEDY AND COMEDY

THE HERITAGE of Athens was already rich in epic and lyric poetry. In the fifth century two new literary forms were added to it: tragedy and comedy. In Aristotle's view, the founder of drama was Homer. Homer, was not only a great poet, but also a great dramatist and in his poetry he had created a form of comedy in which humour was made dramatic.

The recognition of Homer as the forerunner of tragedy and comedy is due not only to the fact that the dramatic poets regarded the *Iliad* as primarily tragic and the *Odyssey* as comic, but also to Homer's concept of narrative. His stories proceed, as it were, dialectically, with his heroes discussing the events in which they are taking part. This method presupposes characters who can speak openly without reservations. It also requires the introduction of a third character or audience before whom the discussion takes place to act as moderator. In Homer, therefore, the basic elements of the drama are already present: heroes in conflict, listened to and commented upon by a chorus.

111. Fragment of a marble gravestone showing a woman, *c.* 350, *height* 2 ft. *National Museum, Athens*

197

Dialogue or debate passed from epic poetry not only into drama, but also into philosophy, history and rhetoric, to become, in the Athens of the fifth century, the accepted method of thought and expression. Aristotle regarded Zeno of Elea as the inventor of the dialectic method, but for Zeno the term had a narrow sense, meaning the art of rhetoric by which a speaker could defeat an opponent in argument, taking as a starting point principles which both accepted. But dialectics are more than the art of persuasion, they are the art of the dialogue in general. Socrates was to use the dialectical method to discover truths which were hidden in the consciousness of his interlocutor. Plato's inquiries into the nature of the " real " and " ideal " world proceed dialectically and Thucydides writes history dialectically, recording the opposing opinions which his characters express in their speeches. Thus dialogue became the basis of methodical thought in the history of Athenian *paideia*.

As we have seen earlier, drama also had its roots in the folk music of the Dionysian cult and in the dithyrambic songs which accompanied its celebration. We have already discussed this from the religious point of view. Here we are looking at the poetic origins of the drama. The dithyramb was essentially a group song, but it was always begun by one of the group known as the leader and was repeated by the chorus in the epode or the antistrophe. Thespis adapted this form to the needs of the stage: detaching the leader from the chorus and emphasizing his independent role by dressing him in a special costume, he turned him into an actor. He replaced his singing by the declamation of speeches which called for a new type of verse. Lyric song, based on dance rhythms, continued to be written for the chorus, but the actor was given dramatic verse to declaim. This was written in iambic metres which strove more and more to reproduce, in a heightened form, the rhythms of natural speech. At a later stage, one of the chorus, the coryphaeus, stepped out of the ranks and conversed with the actor, but returned to the chorus to take part with them in the musical and choric parts of the drama.

In the plays of Phrynichus, such as *The Phoenician Women* and *The Fall of Miletus* which caused such a stir, the single actor was allowed to play several roles, but it seems that he served more as a spectacle in the drama than as a means of carrying the action forward, for the chorus remained the prime mover. In Aristophanes' *The Frogs* Euripides is made to accuse Aeschylus as a disciple of Phrynichus of putting silent heroes on the stage, while the chorus sang and danced without interruption. This is true only in the case of *Prometheus Bound* and Aeschylus appears to have been aware of this weakness, for in other plays he added a second actor, just as Sophocles, somewhat later, added a third. But in spite of the increase in actors, for example, in *The Suppliant Women*, the principal part in developing the action continued to belong to the chorus, while the heroes remained preoccupied with their sufferings. A reversal of the roles did not occur until Euripides in whose tragedies the chorus plays a more passive role.

The same source from which tragedy sprang also produced comedy. It stemmed from another kind of popular song, also associated with Dionysiac cult, which consisted of improvisations on erotic themes often expressed in the coarsest language. It was known as the phallic song and derives its name from the large phallic symbols carried by intoxicated parties of singers during the Dionysiac festivals to symbolize the regenerative powers of the god.

Comedy resembled tragedy closely in form, but its content was very different. Its leading characters did not come from heroic legend but were ordinary people who, through their errors in dealing with everyday life or their inability to adapt themselves to their social surrounding, found themselves in situations that provoked laughter. It found its themes in contemporary political or literary events and in the changing currents of Athenian society. It was satirical, often polemical, seeking to teach what was good by ridiculing what was bad. It flourished with the decline of Athenian democracy and for this reason tended to be conservative in outlook. The past—particularly the period of the Persian Wars—is shown as a kind of golden age and new ideas and new forms of social behaviour are singled out for ridicule, sometimes somewhat indiscriminately.

Most of the ingredients of the drama were present in the work of the epic and lyric poets and it is possible that when certain scenes of Homer were recited publicly, they were accompanied by mime or by tableaux. But the dramatists, by concentrating on action, were able to achieve effects not possible to earlier poets. The heroes of Greek mythology were suddenly materialized, living, moving and speaking before everyday folk, who sat in the seats to watch and hear them. Never before had art attempted to confront life so directly, to compete with the real world on its own terms, to give such concrete expression to poetic imagination.

" Thespis was beginning to act tragedies " says Plutarch " and the novelty of the spectacle attracted the crowd, though they had not yet been thrown open to competition. Solon, who by nature liked to hear whatever was new in order to learn from it, and who in his old age was more given to leisure and amusement, and even, indeed, to music and wine, went to see Thespis, who, in the manner of the ancient poets, acted in his own plays. After the performance he questioned him, and asked if he was not ashamed to tell such gross lies to so many people. To which Thespis replied that he saw no great harm in speaking and acting in plays, as he did..."

As soon as he realized that imitation of action was the special function of the theatre, the dramatist concentrated on improving his methods of projecting it, knowing that the more successful he was, the more complete would be the fear and pity aroused by his work. Through stage action, he had to present and justify his theme, his characters and the ideas with which he endowed them. To create a satisfying play he had to concentrate his theme round a single event which had, as it were, to sum up the whole myth and to confine it within a single place and within given limits of time. It had also to have an inner continuity, so that the sufferings of his hero might be seen to have their deeper origins in the plot of the play. The drama had to be bound internally by a strong chain of cause and effect.

The critical point of the tragedy was the discovery of the cause which brought about the misfortune of the hero and here the poet had to offer his own interpretation of the mystery of life. Tragic fear [108], the basic psychological element of the drama, compelled the hero to reveal the cause of his suffering and his punishment.

Aeschylus looked for the roots of misfortune in the functioning of the divine law of retribution which punished *hybris*. Xerxes was destroyed in *The Persians* because he had built a bridge across the Hellespont to move his army from Asia into Europe, thus violating the natural order of things, and because he had burnt the temples, mutilated the statues and destroyed the altars of the gods of Athens. " For Zeus stands above, a stern judge who punishes overweening arrogance harshly", says the ghost of Darius and this declaration is typical of the instinctive awe of the Aeschylean hero for the retribution latent in the will of the gods who at any moment may strike the man who oversteps the norm and restore the balance of things.

Sophocles sees misfortune as stemming, not from a deliberate act on the part of the hero, but from the inescapable tragedy inherent in man's estate. If Oedipus had suffered justly for his overweening pride as had Xerxes, his fate would have satisfied the audience, but it would not have aroused fear in them, for in Sophocles' view they identify themselves less readily with a guilty person who deserves punishment than with an innocent victim. That is why Oedipus is a purer tragic hero than Xerxes. He is not evil, nor does he stand out above others by his virtues. His tragic responsibility is due to the fact that he exists, not because his actions are the result of good or evil motives. Oedipus murders his father and weds his mother unknowingly.

But in fact a violation of divine will had taken place earlier. For Laius, in begetting Oedipus, had not heeded Apollo's advice that he should remain childless if he wished to preserve his city. This paternal sin is the root cause of Oedipus' sufferings. When he does eventually discover—almost accidentally—what he has done, he tears out his eyes with his own hands. His sons, Eteocles and Polynices, were destined to fight and slay each other for the throne of Thebes, knowing that they were accursed because of their grandfather's sin. The death of Polynices, and his sister's violation of the edict concerning his burial gave Sophocles the theme of his most passionate tragedy, *Antigone*, just as the struggle between the sons of Oedipus provided Aeschylus with the theme for his *Seven Against Thebes*.

Oedipus does not fear divine retribution any more than he seeks to evade it. He accepts it as an irrevocable decision of Apollo, for by his very existence he has violated, however innocently, the natural and civil law, and he has the courage to impose punishment upon himself, for he no longer wishes to look upon the world.

> *Chorus*   Those eyes—how could you do what you have done?
> What evil power has driven you to this end?

> *Oedipus*   Apollo, friends, Apollo
> Has laid this agony upon me;
> Not by his hand; I did it.
> What should I do with eyes
> Where all is ugliness?

In this, Oedipus shows the nobility of his character. He rejects his fate by opposing to it an instinct for justice, by confronting it with a self-imposed punishment which destroys him physically but redeems him morally. More than anything else, Sophocles respects the individual conscience of his heroes which the laws of the state seek to bring under their control. Antigone, Electra, Philoctetes, Heracles and Ajax all are possessed of a strong individual sense of justice and in doing what they know to be right in spite of the inevitable consequences, they keep their own moral convictions free and uncompromised.

In the plays of Euripides the main cause of suffering is seen as the blind instincts or passions of man's nature. During the return of the Argonauts to Iolcus, Medea slays her brother and throws his body into the sea to delay her father who is pursuing the ship. But in Euripides' tragedy this terrible sin does not in fact play the decisive role that one would expect. Tragedy occurs because of the passionate actions of the characters, not because these actions are necessarily wicked. Jason abandons Medea at Corinth, even though she has borne him two children, to marry the daughter of the king of Corinth. The cause of the tragedy which ensues is the bitter humiliation of Medea at the hands of a man and her thirst for revenge. She destroys her rival and her rival's father, but to hurt Jason even more terribly, she murders their two children with her own hands. Above the will of the gods in Aeschylus, above fate in Sophocles, Euripides places the all-powerful passions of the human heart, in this case those of a woman whom he deliberately makes a barbarian and a sorceress so that her passions may seem all the more uncontrolled and uncontrollable.

112. Marble funerary urn. The custom of placing white lekythoi on the tomb stele or on the grave stops at the beginning of the 4th century. Thenceforth ceramic lekythoi were replaced by large marble urns decorated with reliefs. *Kerameikos Museum, Athens*

113. Terracotta figure of a woman, *c.* 330, *height* 6^1/$_2$ *in. National Museum, Athens*

12

13

There is no Greek woman who would dare commit such a crime,
Of all those women whom I thought worthy of my bed before
I espoused you, you my enemy and my ruin, a lioness and not a woman,
A woman with a nature more evil than the Scylla of Tyrrhene.

The forces that struggle in the heart of Medea make her alternately a tender
mother and vengeful monster. The situation changes from moment to moment
as the story proceeds and no one can predict how the tragedy will end. All that is
certain is that the final outcome will not be the one the spectator hopes for, for
endings like those of Aeschylus' *Eumenides* or Sophocles' *Oedipus at Colonus* are
rare in classical tragedy.

In the *Oresteia*, the only trilogy of Aeschylus which has survived, the spectator
feels the same uncertainty about the ending. In the first play *Agamemnon*, the
commander-in-chief of the expedition against Troy returns to Mycenae. His
wife Clytemnestra and her lover Aegisthus murder him. It is a mother's revenge
for the death of Iphigenia, sacrificed to enable the Achaean fleet to sail from Aulis.
Cassandra, a Trojan prisoner whom Agamemnon has brought back, foretells the
murder. The people do not accept such a crime without rebellion and the clash
between the rivals to the throne is one of the most dramatic scenes of the tragic theatre.

In the *Choephoroe*, the second part of the trilogy, Orestes, the son of Agamemnon
and Clytemnestra, returns to Mycenae in disguise to avenge his father's murder.
His sister Electra recognizes him from a lock of hair which he had deposited on
the tomb of his father. A recognition scene such as this occurs in many tragedies.
Sometimes it happens because of an object such as Orestes' lock of hair, sometimes by means of recollection and meditation, sometimes through the natural
course of events. Recognition turns ignorance into knowledge and enmity into
love, or love into hatred. After she has recognized him, Electra decides to help
her brother. But although Orestes, in punishing the guilty couple, is fulfilling
the will of Apollo, he will nevertheless taint his hand with the blood of matricide.

In *The Eumenides*, the final play, Orestes is pursued by the Furies who seek to
punish him for having violated the ancient unwritten laws of the matriarchal
system, more ancient than the Apollonian and patriarchal laws. The conflict
which takes place in *The Eumenides* is really the same as that which rages in the
heart of Medea, but in Aeschylus it is externalized, made objective. Orestes'
conscience is not the battleground here and he has no feelings of guilt about his
actions. It is a symbolic clash between matriarchal and patriarchal rights.

The Furies who pursue Orestes are depicted as terrifying daughters of the night.
They do not resemble any creature in heaven or on earth and neither man nor
god has ever set eyes upon them. Their eyes drip blood and they screech like
wild beasts round their prey. By representing them in this repulsive guise,
Olympian religion hoped to keep the Furies—and what they stood for—as far as
possible from human society. But the very strength with which this revulsion
from earlier social and religious practice was expressed shows how persistently
it had survived in the subconscious minds of man. The ugliness of the Furies
roused the hatred of the gods, for they had uttered threats of revenge against
Apollo and his laws. Their song shows this:

You gods, you new gods, you are violating and usurping my old laws.
And scorned and burdened as I am, poor wretch, in this land, beware,
For I will spread ruination and bitterness, and flood
The world so that I may unburden my soul. And bitterness
Will flow to the leaves and seeds and everywhere. Sweet revenge
Will I beget here on earth and where I have trod will there be death.

114. Figure of a girl from
the sanctuary
of Brauronian Artemis.
Marble, *c.* 360, *height* 3 ft. 8 in.
National Museum, Athens

Even Athena fears this threat and casts her vote in favour of Orestes when his case is heard before the Areopagus. An equal number of ballots are given to both parties and Athena justifies her vote as follows:

> With all my heart, I prefer the man, in everything else but marriage.
> Hence I support the father, and do not care one mite about the death
> Of a woman who slew her husband, the ruler of the house she lived in.

Then Athena turns to the Furies and proposes a pact of peace, that they should share Athens between them and receive honours in return for the good they do. The Furies accept and their shapes and names are changed. Henceforth they become respectable and are known as the Eumenides or goddesses of peace. The revolt of the old gods against the new thus ends with the peace of Athena at the Areopagus.

Forty-four years after the first production of the *Oresteia* (in the Spring of 458), Aristophanes staged his comedy *The Birds* which has a similar theme: the revolt of the old gods against the new. But this time the revolt is not made by anything so hideous as the Furies, but by birds.

Peisthetaeros and Euelpides, two Athenians, set out to find the haunts of a mythical king of Thrace, Tereus, who has been changed into a hoopoe and to beg the king to recommend an ideal city where they can live in peace. But since no such ideal city exists, Peisthetaeros suggests that the birds build one in the air somewhere between Olympus and the earth, erecting walls round it and making it independent of both men and gods.

At the assembly of birds, Peisthetaeros backs up his proposal by arguing that, in former times, people believed that birds were their leaders and gods, and that this belief has survived in the heraldic emblems of gods and kings, such as the cockerel of Darius, the owl of Athena and the hawk of Apollo, but that now the birds are living in misery and subjection. Peisthetaeros' speech rouses memories in the birds of their former glory and they decide to rebel and declare war on the gods of Olympus.

In a charming song, they describe their creation: how black-winged night embraced silent chaos to beget the first creature of the universe — the egg. From its shell emerged the first race of birds, long before the gods were even dreamt of. They describe how they taught human beings to make love, to sing and dance, to measure the hour and the seasons, to sail before a favourable wind and to predict the will of the gods.

> We are Ammon and Phoebus Apollo, we birds, and Delphi and Dodona
> All rolled into one; we cater to all your needs in life,
> In commerce and weddings, consult us first.

The city of the birds is called " Cloud-Cuckoo Land." Peisthetaeros makes sure that it will remain uncorrupt by barring it to all priests, diviners, city-planners, diplomats, sycophants, business men and profiteers; he even banishes Iris, the messenger of Zeus.

Prometheus, always the arch-foe of Zeus, comes secretly to Peisthetaeros to inform him that the siege of Olympus by the birds is succeeding, that the gods are on the verge of starvation and are prepared to sue for peace.

The revolt of the birds against the gods ends in reconciliation just as the rebellion of the Furies against Apollo did but if there are similarities in theme between the two plays, they belong to very different social and political climates. The *Oresteia* was presented in 458, four years after the democratic revolution of

Ephialtes and Pericles, and was primarily directed against those who wished to alter the aristocratic structure and political privileges of the Areopagus. Aeschylus, who had fought at Marathon and Salamis and took a keen interest in public affairs is writing in *The Eumenides* an eloquent tract in defence of the Areopagus.[109] In making Athena relate the glorious history of their city, he is trying to instil into his fellow citizens a proper respect for the Areopagus and to persuade them not to alter its constitution. Otherwise, he implies, they will bring despotism and anarchy upon their city. Sophocles, on the other hand, was not a conservative like Aeschylus; he was a friend of Pericles and a radical. But he had an equally strong sense of responsibility towards his *polis* and twice served as a general, taking part first under Pericles in the expedition against Samos and subsequently under Nicias. At 83, he offered his services to the committee of public safety set up to salvage what was left after the Athenian disaster in Sicily.

While Aeschylus was fighting at Salamis and Sophocles was dancing at the victory celebrations, Euripides was born. The lives of all three playwrights were in different ways bound up with the epic struggle against the Persians. But in Euripides, the memory was already beginning to fade and, with it, the urgency of political commitment. He never participated in public affairs and his works show more preoccupation with metaphysical speculation and feminine psychology than with any deep political conviction.

This evasion of responsibility is even more marked in *The Birds*. The ideal polity of the birds is, of course, a Utopia to which Aristophanes is comparing the actual city of Athens which, when the play was produced, was mourning the Sicilian disaster. But either because he could not face it himself or because he was afraid of outraging the sensibilities of his audience, he makes no allusion to an event which permanently affected the fate of Athens. Dramatic poetry spanned the period between two catastrophes, the destruction of Miletus and the defeat of the Sicilian expedition. The first was lamented eloquently by Phrynichus; the second was watched by Aristophanes in silence.

THUCYDIDES

HISTORY PROVIDED the dramatists with many of their themes, principally the history of the three great wars which had affected the whole of Greece, the Trojan, the Persian and the Peloponnesian wars. Thus episodes from the Trojan War formed the plots of Aeschylus' *Agamemnon*, Sophocles' *Philoctetes* and *Ajax* and Euripides' *Andromache, Hecuba, The Trojan Women* and *Iphigenia in Aulis*. The Persian Wars inspired Phrynichus' *The Fall of Miletus* and *The Phoenician Women* as well as Aeschylus' *The Persians*. Finally, the Peloponnesian War—or rather its social consequences—gave Aristophanes the theme of three of his comedies, *The Acharnians, Peace* and *Lysistrata*.

History on the stage was not, of course, portrayed with factual accuracy. The poet is not a chronicler: he seeks to interpret and to comment, to express what is significant about his subject. If in order to achieve this, he has to depart from facts, he does not hesitate, his justification being that he is aiming at a different, more profound, truth than the historian. This does not mean that his work is not interesting historically: what people think about their actions is as much a part of history as the actions themselves. But the dramatist, placing in the foreground the subjective and spiritual aspects of his theme cannot give us a reliable account of events.

Herodotus, as we have seen, for all that he has been called "the father of history," approaches his subject as an artist, rather than as a scientist. He has a story to tell and an audience to satisfy and one of the criteria by which he selects his material is its value as a source of entertainment.

But in the last quarter of the fifth century appeared the first Attic prose-writer to treat historical facts in what today we regard as a proper historical manner. Indeed few historians since have been as rigorous. Thucydides' subject was the Peloponnesian War which was to last twenty-seven years, from 431 until 404. " I lived through the whole of it " he writes, " being of an age to understand what was happening, and I put my mind to the subject so as to get an accurate view of it. It happened, too, that I was banished from my country for twenty years after my command at Amphipolis; I saw what was being done on both sides, particularly on the Peloponnesian side, because of my exile, and this leisure gave me rather exceptional facilities for looking into things."

We have little information about Thucydides' life. We know that he commanded an Athenian army in 424 and we may therefore conjecture that he was born at least thirty years earlier, that is to say, about 454. His father was called Olorus like the father-in-law of Miltiades and his tomb has been identified in the vault of Cimon's family. It seems likely therefore that Thucydides was related to Cimon and that his father, Olorus, was the grandson of Miltiades. In his account of his own role in the military operation at Amphipolis in Thrace against Brasidas, he tells us—as casually as if he were writing of a third person—that he owned gold mines in those parts and had influence on the local population. His failure to prevent so able a general as Brasidas from capturing Amphipolis (important to Athens as a source of wood for ship-building) does not mean that he was an incompetent soldier, but it cost him twenty years of exile, to the eternal benefit of history.

He returned to Athens in 404 when the Peloponnesian War was over, and died a few years later—murdered, according to Pausanias. The text of his *History* is incomplete, the narrative ending with a description of the events of the year 411. This last section is not written with the same care as the rest and, for this and other reasons, it is likely that he died before writing the closing chapters, rather than that these have been lost.

The work starts with a brief introductory survey of the whole history of the Hellenes from Pelasgian times to the breaking of the thirty years truce between Athens and Sparta, and then goes on to a detailed examination of the Peloponnesian War. Although Thucydides served as a general, he does not concentrate only on military history: he analyzes the character of the combatants and their social and political life and he gives us telling portraits of their leaders. Athens is always in the centre of the picture. He paints her audacity and her ruthlessness, her creative energy and her moments of despair. If Thucydides manages so well to understand and to describe the complex character of Athens, it is because he himself had benefited from the many-sided education which Athenians of the age received. Was he not at the same time politician, general, historian, man of letters, philosopher and sophist? But what distinguishes him from his contemporaries is that he applies the methods of the positive sciences to the examination of social phenomena.[110]

The heroes of Thucydides are no longer individuals as in the poets, but social groups as they are studied by modern sociology. When he makes the leaders state their policies in set speeches, he is treating them as the spokesmen of the groups they represent. His reluctance to go into the private lives of politicians or generals, as Herodotus and Plutarch were wont to do, is due to his scepticism about the importance, historically speaking, of the individual and to the universal character of his scientific synthesis. His subject is the behaviour of the principal social groups within the Hellenic people, at a period when the Athenians were

115. Double relief, the hero Echelos carrying off the nymph Basile in his chariot, *c.* 420, *height* 1 ft. 4¹/₂ in. *National Museum, Athens*

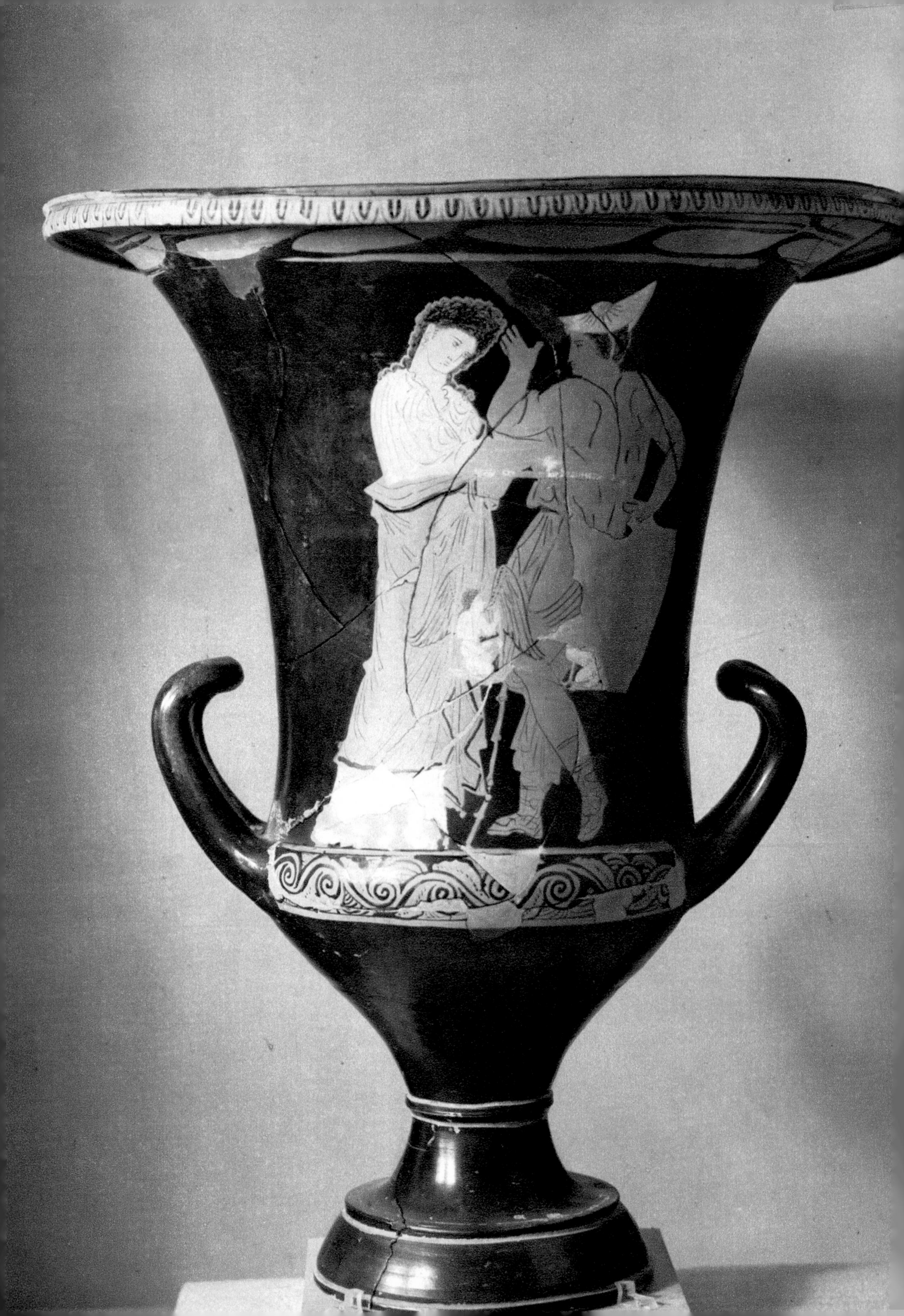

trying to expand their hegemony geographically and the Spartans were trying to contain them.

Thucydides has put on record his method of " objective observation " in a passage in which, though he does not mention him by name, he is having a dig at Herodotus: " With regard to my factual reporting of the events of the war I have made it a principle not to write down the first story that came my way, and not even to be guided by my own general impressions; either I was present myself at the events which I have described or else I heard of them from eye-witnesses whose report I have checked with as much thoroughness as possible. Not that even so the truth was easy to discover: different eye-witnesses give different accounts of the same events, speaking out of partiality for one side or the other or else from imperfect memories. And it may well be that my history will seem less easy to read because of the absence in it of a romantic element. It will be enough for me, however, if these words of mine are judged useful by those who want to understand clearly the events which happened in the past and which (human nature being what it is) will, at some time or other and in much the same ways, be repeated in the future. My work is not a piece of writing designed to meet the taste of an immediate public, but was done to last for ever."

Having thus gathered his material, Thucydides cast it in a chronological framework, dividing his narrative into periods of eight months during which war was being waged and periods of four winter months during which hostilities ceased. His careful attitude towards chronology is another way in which Thucydides is a better historian than Herodotus.

But most important is his total rejection of the supernatural as an explanation of historical phenomena. In his work, neither gods not even destiny have any effect on men's actions. For him social change occurs because of economic reasons: cities act aggressively because they are afraid of losing what they have or because they are anxious to get more. This does not mean, as some have maintained, that Thucydides invented a rule-of-thumb economic theory which he applied *a priori* to every problem of history.[111] Each time he deals with a specific problem, he examines it in its own terms and, in his conclusions, he takes into account as fully as he can the interplay of forces and events as he has observed and analyzed them.

There are many examples of this method in the introductory chapter on the formation of the Hellenic world and its subsequent development down to his own age. For example, he regards the fertility of the soil in Thessaly and Boeotia as well as in most of the Peloponnese as the cause of the population changes which took place there and therefore of the insecurity and political backwardness of those regions. On the other hand, it was the barrenness of Attica which enabled the economic and social development of Athens to take place peacefully and uninterruptedly.

The pursuit of wealth brought men into closer contact with the sea and with foreign lands. Thus, the Minoans, in order to collect tribute from the islands of the Aegean, established a " thalassocracy " with the result that piracy was reduced and trade prospered. Or turning to the Trojan War, if Agamemnon was able to mobilize all his vassals for the expedition, it was not because they loved him, but because they feared him. The campaign dragged on for ten years through lack of funds and men. Most of the time, the Achaeans were engaged in cultivating the fields or plundering the land in order to keep themselves alive. Dispersed and undisciplined, they were unable to undertake a systematic siege which would have brought the war to an earlier conclusion. In discussing the rise of Corinth, he explains her power by her geographical situation on the Isthmus which enabled her to act as a market, a port and a meeting-point between the

116. Red-figure calyx-crater depicting Erotostasia and Aphrodite weighing two small figures of Eros, by the Erotostasia painter. Middle of the 4th century. *National Museum, Athens*

209

Peloponnese and the rest of Greece. Finally he reaches the causes of the Peloponnesian War and his introductory observations are so typical of his approach that they must be quoted textually:

"War began when the Athenians and the Peloponnesians broke the Thirty Years' Truce which had been made after the capture of Euboea. As to the reasons why they broke the truce, I propose first to give an account of the causes of complaint which they had against each other and of the specific instances where their interests clashed: this is in order that there should be no doubt in anyone's mind about what led to this great war falling upon the Hellenes. But the real reason for the war is, in my opinion, most likely to be disguised by such an argument. What made war inevitable was the growth of Athenian power and the fear which this caused in Sparta."

These examples show Thucydides' mind at work.[112] Having found out that social phenomena influence one other, he was able to understand the influence of environment on human character and vice versa. The Athenian, as a free citizen, was a member of a democracy which allowed—indeed expected—him to use all his talents to the full in the interests of his *polis*. Since policy was the responsibility of every citizen, decisions were only taken after the facts had been analyzed and all possible interpretations had been publicly debated. This enabled both the citizens and their leaders to anticipate events, to adopt appropriate measures and to carry them out with the energy and ingenuity which are always available when people know what they are doing and why.

Themistocles' view, after Marathon, that the Persians would return, convinced his fellow citizens: instead of distributing a surplus in the national funds, they built ships and the result was Salamis. Pericles also realized that war with the Peloponnesians was inevitable and saw to it that Athens was able to resist and retaliate. His plan which he expounded on countless occasions before the Assembly was to make the fleet the spearhead of any attack, while her land forces would defend Athens from within her walls. He advised the Athenians to avoid operations on land so that they could concentrate on developing their naval power, and to abstain from expanding their empire during the war itself, because imperialist adventures could imperil the very existence of the city. Pericles died two and a half years after the outbreak of war and his successors did just the opposite. Alcibiades incited the Athenians to embark on the Sicilian campaign which, according to Thucydides, was the greatest blunder they ever committed.

For Thucydides, historical events were the result of two kinds of causes: on the one hand, the impersonal forces of economic geography, mass psychology, the pursuit of wealth; on the other hand, on a more personal plane, the capacity of societies to choose freely between the possibilities open to them and to adapt their conduct energetically to the aims in view. This is a far cry from the unforeseeable and inescapable causes invoked by the poets to explain men's fortunes.

But perhaps Thucydides' most remarkable quality is his ability to master his own personal preferences and to leave facts to speak for themselves, even when they go against his own private interests. An aristocrat and a rich man, his political sympathies lay with the conservatives and when he is making a comment or reporting an opinion he allows his point of view to show, but he is scrupulously careful not to let it distort his presentation of fact. This is an attitude which can only be acquired in a democracy, for democracy rests on the assumption that if every individual is free to express his opinions the truth will emerge from the clash of opposites.

Irrationality and anarchy were abhorrent to the objective mind of Thucydides. In spite of his conservative sympathies, he thought highly of Pericles, whom he regarded as representing a kind of classical equilibrium in the turmoil of Athenian democracy. He admired the courage which enabled him, when it was necessary, to tell his fellow citizens unpalatable truths, however unpopular it made him, and he approved of his wisdom in not calling the Assembly too often during the war, so as to avoid decisions prompted by passion. He despised the obsequiousness of demagogues towards the crowd and their eagerness to catch votes by appeals to greed or cowardice. Of all the demagogues, it was Cleon (who, according to Marcellinus who wrote a life of Thucydides was the public prosecutor when he was tried for his conduct at Amphipolis) whom he regards with the most distaste and he blames him for the massacre of the Mytilenians who had rebelled against Athens. In reporting what Cleon says, he allows his ruthlessness and vulgarity to show and he cannot refrain from expressing his astonishment at Cleon's success at Sphacteria. Cleon's victory created very favourable terms for Athens to make peace with Sparta, but, as Thucydides reports with a touch of complacency, he let the occasion slip.

His hatred of anarchy and of passion is perhaps nowhere so forcefully expressed as in his account of the civil war in Corcyra, which has a sinister modern ring.

" In times of peace and prosperity cities and individuals alike follow higher standards, because they are not forced into a situation where they have do what they do not want to do. But war is a stern teacher; in depriving them of the power of easily satisfying their daily wants, it brings most people's minds down to the level of their actual circumstances...To fit in with the change of events, words, too, had to change their usual meanings. What used to be described as a thoughtless act of aggression was now regarded as the courage one would expect to find in a party member; to think of the future and wait was merely another way of saying one was a coward; any idea of moderation was just an attempt to disguise one's unmanly character; ability to understand a question from all sides meant that one was totally unfitted for action. Fanatical enthusiasm was the mark of a real man, and to plot against an enemy behind his back was perfectly legitimate self-defence. Anyone who held violent opinions could always be trusted, and anyone who objected to them became a suspect. To plot successfully was a sign of intelligence, but it was still cleverer to see that a plot was hatching. If one attempted to provide against having to do either, one was disrupting the unity of the party and acting out of fear of the opposition. In short, it was equally praise worthy to get one's blow in first against someone who was going to do wrong, and to denounce someone who had no intention of doing any wrong at all. Family relations were a weaker tie than party membership, since party members were more ready to go to any extreme for any reason whatever. These parties were not formed to enjoy the benefits of the established laws, but to acquire power by overthrowing the existing regime; and the members of these parties felt confidence in each other, not because of any fellowship in a religious communion, but because they were partners in crime."

Thucydides has been accused of coldness, of being a mere " seismograph " mechanically recording the social shocks and tremors of his time. But no one can read this account of Corcyra without appreciating the feeling with which it is written, all the more intense for being kept under control. It is, in its ironical and patrician way, a passionate plea for reason and moderation. But just as he knows that history cannot be written unless the historian is prepared to confront the facts, however contrary they may run to his own interests, he seems also to have believed that, morally and politically, man will not be able to organize himself intelligently until he is prepared to face the truth about his nature and his situation.

Thucydides lived at an ideal moment to study the social and psychological motives for men's action. His lifetime coincided with the most ruthless and vigorous phase of Athenian expansion. For the first time, a historian was able to watch the activities of a naval empire which made no attempt to conceal or dissemble its motives. Witness this dialogue which took place in 417 between the Athenian generals, Cleomedes and Tisias, and the envoys of Melos about the submission of the island to Athens.

"*Athenians:* We on our side will use no fine phrases saying, for example, that we have a right to our empire because we defeated the Persians, or that we have come against you now because of the injuries you have done us—a great mass of words that nobody would believe. And we ask you on your side not to imagine that you will influence us by saying that you, though a colony of Sparta, have not joined Sparta in the war, or that you have never done us any harm. Instead we recommend that you should try to get what it is possible for you to get, taking into consideration what we both really do think; since you know as well as we do that, when these matters are discussed by practical people, the standard of justice depends on the equality of power to compel and that in fact the strong do what they have the power to do and the weak accept what they have to accept... What we shall do now is to show you that it is for the good of our own empire that we are here and that it is for the preservation of your city that we shall say what we are going to say. We do not want any trouble in bringing you into our empire, and we want you to be spared for the good both of yourselves and of ourselves.

Melians: And how could it be just as good for us to be the slaves as for you to be the masters?

Athenians: You, by giving in, would save yourselves from disaster; we, by not destroying you, would be able to profit from you.

Melians: So you would not agree to our being neutral, friends instead of enemies, but allies of neither side?

Athenians: No, because it is not so much your hostility that injures us; it is rather the case that, if we were on friendly terms with you, our subjects would regard that as a sign of weakness in us, whereas your hatred is evidence of our power."

The arguments of course convinced no one. The Melians decided to defend their freedom and the Athenians besieged them. The next winter, the Melians capitulated and the Athenians put to death all the men of military age and sold their women and children into slavery. 500 settlers from Attica were sent to the island which became an Athenian colony.

PHILOSOPHY: ANAXAGORAS AND THE SOPHISTS

THE FIRST PHILOSOPHER to reside in Athens was Anaxagoras of Clazomenae in Asia Minor who came there in about 462. He taught Pericles philosophy and physics and remained his friend throughout his life. From Anaxagoras, Pericles acquired his lofty idea of politics, his aloof and dignified bearing, his eloquence and his command of philosophical problems. Indeed Anaxagoras' influence on him was so great that his political enemies said that he took himself for Anaxagoras' first principle and called him " The Mind."

Anaxagoras also taught him not to accept a supernatural explanation of any phenomenon simply because the natural explanation was unknown. One day, a ram with one horn was brought to Pericles from the countryside. The soothsayer Lampo immediately prophesied that the party of the owner of the field in which the ram was born would rule Athens. Anaxagoras gave a different explanation:

" Having cut open the ram's skull, he showed that the brain was not in its usual place, but was shaped like an egg and had slipped from the cranium to the spot whence the roots of the horn emerged."

Anaxagoras came to Athens when he was about thirty-eight and started teaching philosophy. Thirty years later he was prosecuted for impiety and Pericles, fearing for the life of his teacher, helped him to escape to Lampsacus where he founded a school. But his influence remained strong in the intellectual life of Athens. Socrates, in his *Apology* at his trial in 399, mentions that Athenians still bought his books from the orchestra of the theatre for one drachma or more, although thirty years had already elapsed since he had left Athens. The only work of Anaxagoras of which fragments have survived is his book *On Nature*.

The philosophy of Anaxagoras, although stemming from the materialism of the Ionian philosophers, nevertheless contains the germs of Platonic idealism. Aristotle who on the whole approves of Anaxagoras was to criticize him for using his concept of *Nous* a little too readily: Whenever he could not find the cause of a " necessity " he appealed to *Nous* as *deus ex machina* to explain it.

Although Anaxagoras' presence in the city did much to stimulate the intellectual life of Athens, especially as his ideas had the stamp of Pericles' approval, his philosophy did not deal with a subject in which Athenians, living under democratic institutions, were particularly interested: political science. This became the special field of the sophists. The sophists were teachers of considerable learning who opened fee-paying schools where Athenians were able to acquire the knowledge and techniques indispensable to success in political life.

The term " sophist " has lost its original meaning and is now used pejoratively to describe some one capable of proving by verbal quibbles that day is night and vice versa or who can deliver a convincing lecture on any subject under the sun. The discredit into which the sophists fell was due to the criticisms of Socrates and Plato, who accused them of doubting the existence of truth itself.

Before they fell into disrepute, the sophists were esteemed in Athens as teachers. Pericles is known to have held Protagoras in great respect. When the case of an athlete who had accidentally killed a man with a javelin came up for trial, Pericles spent the whole day discussing the finer points with Protagoras. He also commissioned Protagoras to draw up a code of laws for the new colony of Thurii which was founded in 445-4 and built to the plans of Hippodamus.

The ideas of another sophist, Gorgias of Leontini in Sicily, are perhaps the most typical of the kind of scepticism which Plato attacked. He believed that nothing exists; that if anything does exist, nothing can be known about it; and that if anything can be known, the knowledge cannot be communicated by language. He came to Athens in 427 at the head of a diplomatic mission to persuade the Assembly to send military aid to his city against the Syracusans. His speech made a deep impression on his audience and became the model for a new school of rhetoric in Athens. Plato regarded Gorgias' style of oratory as pernicious and insidious because it deceived by flattering and seducing the ear.

No work of the sophists has survived by which we can judge their ideas as they would have expressed them themselves and we are reduced to deducing what they thought from the highly controversial dialogues of Plato. But even as they are portrayed by Plato, the sophists appear to us in an attractive light, for they come very near to the doubts nurtured by our age about absolute truth and to our own tendencies towards relativism and pragmatism.

The sophists did not construct a systematic philosophy of nature as the Ionians had done, nor did they advance a new theory of knowledge like Socrates and Plato. Their ideas originated, however, in Ionian modes of thought. Thus the relativism of Protagoras is based on Heraclitus just as the dialectics of Gorgias are based on Zeno. The sophists reaped the fruit of the intellectual disarray which the physicists of Ionia had sown when they replaced the religious interpretation of the universe offered by Homer and Hesiod by a rational and materialist explanation. This crisis of conscience spread through the whole of Athenian society during the period following the Persian wars. In the past Athenians had been so sure of their values: now they began to doubt and their certainties about justice and beauty and wisdom no longer seemed satisfying. But the sophists were there to proclaim the value of rhetoric. By the persuasive power of their arguments and the charm of their language, the sophists managed to give expression to the political and social aspirations of a city where freedom of speech was the most treasured right, as well as the condition, of the democratic system.

For the sophists, truth was what led a man to success. And in Athens success, whether in athletics or in politics, entailed struggle and the citizen who wished to succeed on the track or on the tribune had perforce to undergo training. Intellectual training aimed at developing certain specific techniques: the logical organization of evidence and arguments, speed of intellect and repartee, urbanity of speech and manner, in a word, all the arts of rhetoric. It was these arts, called by Athenians political virtue, that the sophists taught to young men ambitious of success in the Assembly.

The influence of the sophists is apparent in the tragedies of Euripides and the comedies of Aristophanes as well as in Thucydides and Plato. Their doctrine differed radically from Ionian philosophy in that their interest was centred on man and no longer on nature. The much misunderstood dictum of Protagoras —" Man is the measure of all things "—expresses the emphasis they placed on human needs and their scepticism about the universal validity of science or ethics. For them the importance of everything was relative to man. Theories which helped man to control any of the factors which formed his environment were true, while those that did not were false. Their teaching was therefore directed towards useful action and practical advantage, particularly in the field of politics. They adopted, in short, a pragmatic approach which judged the value of each and every truth by its practical results and in this sense they must be regarded as the first humanists in the history of ideas.

The sophists did not cause, as it has often been maintained, the decline of the Athenian democracy. On the contrary, it was the decline of democracy which caused the discredit into which the sophists fell. The first attacks directed against them came from Socrates, who, apart from military service, refused systematically to assume the political responsibilities which are the duty of every citizen if democratic institutions are to survive and flourish. Socrates' attacks on the sophists like his political " agnosticism " reflect the ebb which was flowing in the fortunes and self-confidence of Athens. If Athenian democracy had not perished in the wreck of Athenian imperialism, the sophists would have continued to enjoy the esteem in which they were held by Pericles.

The Decline of Classical Athens

THE CLOSING YEARS of the Peloponnesian War were dominated on the Athenian side by the personality of Alcibiades. Flamboyant, unruly, passionate and dissolute, unstable politically but undoubtedly an able military and naval commander, an ardent admirer and disciple of Socrates (*see* p. 221), he is the type of the Shakspearian tragic hero and it seems surprising that Shakspeare who took so much from Plutarch can have overlooked the life of Alcibiades.

In 415 Athens allowed herself to be swayed by his eloquence to engage in an imperialist adventure which was to bring her struggle with Sparta to an ignominious conclusion. Diverting from the main theatre of operations the finest force ever put in the field by a Greek state, Athens chose to intervene in a dispute between two colonies in Magna Graecia, Syracuse and Segesta. Command was first vested in Alcibiades, but he was soon replaced by the conservative Nicias who had opposed the Sicilian campaign from the outset. Initial successes which the cautious and dilatory Nicias failed to follow up soon turned into disaster. In spite of large reinforcements the whole force, including 200 triremes, was completely annihilated. [113]

Although she at once set about rebuilding her fleet, Athens could not replace the trained and experienced mariners she had lost. Her naval supremacy upon which her whole strategy depended was virtually at an end and final defeat could only be a question of time. In the absence of the Athenian force in Sicily, Sparta had established a permanent stronghold at Decelia in Attica and was building up a fleet. In 406 the Athenians were able to win a Pyrrhic naval victory at Arginusae, but a year later allowed their fleet to be surprised in the mouth of the Aegospotami in the Hellespont and utterly destroyed. Nothing now prevented Sparta from blockading Piraeus and in April 404 Athens capitulated. Her walls were dismantled, like her empire, to the sound of Spartan flutes. [114]

At the beginning of the fourth century Athens was no longer the dominant power in the eastern Mediterranean. But in spite of the brief reign of terror of the Thirty Tyrants she had managed to preserve democratic institutions within the city so that her intellectual and cultural life was able to continue to develop. The end of her political hegemony coincides therefore with her spiritual expansion in the Ancient World. What her commanders had lost on land and sea was reconquered in men's minds by her poets, artists and philosophers. This curious phenomenon can be seen already at work during the Sicilian debacle. Here is Plutarch's account of the experience of Athenian prisoners:

"The majority of the Athenians perished in the quarry in which they had been confined from disease and malnutrition, for each day they were given as a ration no more than a pint of corn and half a pint of water. Many were sold as slaves, branded on the forehead like horses... But some were saved because of Euripides. For more than all other Greeks, the Sicilians admired the poetic genius of Euripides. When excerpts and copies of his verses reached Sicily, they circulated from hand to hand and aroused excitement. People claimed that many of those who finally returned to their country embraced Euripides, explaining to him that some of the prisoners had been freed for having taught their captors whatever they could remember of his verses and that others who had wandered far and wide after the disaster often obtained food and drink for having recited his poems."

Athens was later able to piece together something of her empire in the form of a much looser confederation or " commonwealth," but her power never attained the heights it had reached in the preceding century. The lesson of the Peloponnesian War had not been learnt either by Athens or by Sparta and the problem of Greek disunity was further exacerbated by the emergence of Thebes as the strongest military power in Greece.

Persia which had intervened in the last stages of Athens' struggle with Sparta continued to cast greedy eyes on Greece, but instead of joining together in common defence, they preferred to exhaust themselves in a shifting and inconclusive triangular war with Thebes.

Among Athenian political thinkers, only the orator Isocrates saw the solution to the problem which the rise of Macedonia under Philip II offered to the Hellenic world. But instead of uniting voluntarily under under his leadership as Isocrates would have wished, the Greek states preferred to have unity imposed on them by force of arms. In 338 at the battle of Chaeronea, Athens' importance as an independent political force was for all practical purposes at an end and Greece was ready to take part in a second epic in Asia under a new Agamemnon, Philip's son Alexander the Great.

In the Macedonian conquests in Asia and Africa which welded Egyptian, Persian and Greek civilizations into an immense empire—the first in history—the predominating cultural influence was Greek. And in a sense the massive export of Greek civilization begun by Alexander has been going on ever since.

SOCRATES

IN FEBRUARY of 399, Socrates, who was then seventy years of age, died in an Athenian prison, sentenced to drink hemlock. His trial on a charge of impiety has remained famous throughout the centuries, not because of the decision taken by the court, but because of Socrates' defence.

A few years earlier, Athens had lost the Peloponnesian War and, with it, her empire. The attempts of the Thirty to suppress democratic institutions met with only temporary success. Two of the protagonists in the last act of the drama of Athens, Alcibiades and Critias, were both disciples of Socrates and the harshness of the court's sentence was not unconnected with Critias' attack on the democrats. But Socrates could in no way be held responsible either for the defection of Alcibiades or the reign of terror initiated by Critias. When he was charged, he did not try to rebut the accusations brought against him; when he was sentenced to death by 281 votes against 275, he refused to escape in spite of his childhood friend, Criton, who urged him to do so. For Socrates had no wish to transgress the laws of the city where he had been born and reared; he preferred to take his revenge on his accusers by bequeathing them his death. Indeed, by his example, Socrates sought to show how a citizen should discharge his responsibilities towards his country, holding them above his duties to parents and family. It was a silent but eloqent condemnation of the attitude adopted in the past by Alcibiades, Hippias and the great Themistocles himself. Yet Socrates had the courage to

117. Detail from a relief of Apollo
by Praxiteles.
National Museum, Athens

118. The Acropolis from
the north-west

feel that his country was best served if the individual citizen insisted that its own laws were justly applied. He had refused to comply with an order of Critias to take part in the arrest of an innocent citizen, Leon of Salamis, proscribed by the Thirty. This could well have cost him his life, but Socrates chose deliberately to respect law and justice, as Sophocles' Antigone had done, regardless of the cost to himself. He had shown similar courage as president of the Council, after the disaster of Arginusae, when, alone, he had refused to pass sentence collectively on the generals. In spite of the clamours of the public, he had insisted that the law must be respected and that each general should be tried separately.

But Socrates was never remiss in serving his country when his duties were not in conflict with the laws. He served three times as a hoplite, taking part in the siege of Potidaea in 432, at the battle of Delium in 424 and at Amphipolis in 422. Apart from these campaigns, he only left Athens once to attend the Isthmian games. His father, the sculptor Sophroniscus, and his mother, the midwife Phaenarete, were both Athenians by birth. He started by pursuing his father's profession and married Xanthippe by whom he had three children. Later he devoted himself completely to philosophic enquiry and to teaching. He lived frugally and although many of his pupils were rich aristocrats he always refused to accept fees from them. Unlike the sophists, Socrates was disinterested and so remained poor.

Alcibiades, who served with him at Potidaea and at Delium, has left a vivid portrait of Socrates' character in Plato's *Symposium:* "Many are the wonders of Socrates which I might narrate in his praise; most of his ways might perhaps be paralleled in others, but the most astonishing thing of all is absolute unlikeness to any human being that is or ever has been. You may imagine Brasidas and others to have been like Achilles; or you may imagine Nestor and Antenor to have been like Pericles; and the same may be said of other famous men, but of this strange being you will never be able to find any likeness however remote, either among men who now are or who have been, except that which I have already suggested of Silenus and the satyrs; and this is an allegory not only of himself, but also of his works. For, although I forgot to mention this before, his words are ridiculous when you first hear them; he clothes himself in language as the skin of the wanton satyr—for his talk is of packasses and smiths and cobblers and curriers, and he is always repeating the same things in the same words, so that an ignorant man who did not know him might feel disposed to laugh at him; but he who pierces the mask and sees what is within will find that they are the only words which have a meaning in them, and also the most divine, abounding in fair examples of virtue, and of the largest discourse, or rather extending to the whole duty of a good and honourable man."

The same feelings were shared by Meno, a disciple of Gorgias, whom Socrates questioned on the nature of virtue till he proved to him that he knew nothing whatsoever about it.

"I used to be told," he said to Socrates, "before I knew you, that you are casting your spells over me, and I am simply getting bewitched and enchanted, and am at my wits' end. And if I may venture to make a jest upon you, you seem to me both in your appearance and in your power over others to be very like the flat torpedo fish, who torpifies those who come near him with the touch, as you have now torpified me, I think. For my soul and my tongue are really torpid, and I do not know how to answer you; and though I have been delivered of an infinite variety of speeches about virtue before now, and to many persons—and very good ones they were, as I thought—now I cannot even say what virtue is. And I think that you are very wise in not voyaging and going away from home, for if you did in other places as you do in Athens, you would be cast into prison as a magician."

119. Detail from a grave stele, found in the Ilissus, depicting a little slave and a dog at the feet of their dead master. School of Praxiteles and Scopas. *National Museum, Athens*

What was the quality which so impressed men as different as Alcibiades and Meno? Socrates himself explains it in the *Theaetetus*. He reminds Theaetetus that his mother Phaenarete was a midwife and that his method resembles hers.

" My art of midwifery is in most respects like theirs; but the difference lies in this—that I attend men and not women, and I practise on their souls when they are in labour, and not on their bodies; and the triumph of my art is in examining whether the thought which the mind of the young man is bringing to the birth is a false idol or a noble and true creation. And like the midwives, I am barren, and the reproach which is often made against me, that I ask questions of others and have not the wit to answer them myself, is very just; the reason is, that the god compels me to be a midwife, but forbids me to bring forth. And therefore I am not myself wise, nor have I anything which is the invention or offspring of my own soul, but the way is this—Some of those who converse with me, at first appear to be absolutely dull, yet afterwards, as our acquaintance ripens, if the god is gracious to them, they all of them make astonishing progress; and this not only in their own opinion but in that of others. There is clear proof that they have never learned anything of me, but they have acquired and discovered many noble things of themselves, although the god and I help to deliver them."

But was Socrates being altogether sincere when he insisted that he knew nothing or was his ignorance a ruse to force his interlocutor to become aware, through inductive dialogue, of knowledge which he already possessed? Aristotle claims that Socrates consciously diverted Greek thought from inquiries into the physical nature of things towards problems of ethics, that he was the first in this field to use the " inductive " method and to establish " universal definitions." By the term " inductive," Aristotle means the passage from particular observations of a similar nature to a general principle. For example, from observations that the water of many specific seas is salty is derived the principle that sea-water in general is salty. After having noted the peculiar characteristics of beautiful or virtuous people, Socrates arrived in the same way at universal definitions of beauty or virtue. Thus Socrates laid down a philosophical system based on these two dialectical forms of inquiry: induction and definition.

Where the sophists resorted to " rhetorical monologue " to expound a thesis, Socrates used dialogue to elicit one. The dialogue presupposes a small and select company gathered in a spirit of confidence and seriousness of purpose. The sophist's speech was designed to be delivered and soon degenerated into a demonstration of verbal dexterity. Rhetoric tends to appeal to people's passions rather than their intellect, whereas the Socratic method brings about a change which may be called a kind of " interior conversion."

To proceed from the particular to the general and to establish universal definitions from the factors which discussion has made available, logic must be accompanied by certain intuitive gifts. According to Socrates and also to Pythagoras, these originate from the immortality of the soul which, through successive incarnations, never loses what it has observed and learned. What is called knowledge is, in fact, memory. But previous experience cannot be evoked without help. The Socratic method is therefore in a sense a theory of knowledge for it rests on the assumption that knowledge derives from the liberation the soul from the burden of memory. But in his own soul Socrates was aware of a sort of divine counsel regulating his response to every circumstance. Socrates called this inner voice his *daemon*. In his *Apology*, he tried to explain it to his judges:

" You have often heard me speak of an oracle or sign which comes to me. This sign I have had ever since I was a child. The sign is a voice which comes to me and always forbids me to do anything, and this is what stands in the way of my being a politician. And rightly, as I think. For I am certain, O men of Athens, that if I had engaged in politics, I should have perished long ago, and done no good either to you or to myself."

And what was the good that Socrates did to Athens? This is how he saw it himself:

"If I may use such a ludicrous figure of speech, I am a sort of gadfly, given to the state by the god; and the state is like a great and noble steed who is tardy in his motions owing to his very size, and requires to be stirred into life. I am that gadfly which the god has given the state, and all day long and in all places am always fastening upon you, arousing and persuading and reproaching you."

With his ability to reveal the fund of knowledge hidden in the latent memory of the soul, Socrates drew attention, for the first time in the history of Greek philosophy, to the dark substrata of the individual mind which he urged his contemporaries to explore. The "Know Thyself" inscribed on the temple of Delphi meant, in his sense, the transference of philosophic enquiry from the exterior to the interior world. At a moment in her history when Athens was losing her real empire and was experiencing as a result a psychological need to replace it with an ideal empire which would prove more durable, Socrates showed that the only lasting values were moral ones and, to restore the crumbling confidence of his fellow citizens, he set about discovering the meaning contained in the basic concepts of wisdom, justice, truth, piety, courage, love and beauty which the scepticism of the sophists and the failure of democracy had brought into disrepute.

These concepts which Socrates detected buried deep in the soul of his interlocutors were, in fact, the social and moral "pre-experience" of the collective soul within each individual consciousness. This "pre-experience" appeared to Socrates supernatural and impersonal and constituted a spiritual heritage common to every human mind. In a sense Socrates may be said to have formulated, twenty-five centuries before Jung, a theory of the collective unconscious.

Socrates did not write anything. He regarded the written word as suitable only for the recording of fact, whereas his efforts were concentrated on re-awakening the memory of ideas. We know him therefore only through the writings of disciples such as Plato and Xenophon or of enemies like Aristophanes and Aristoxenus, as well as through those of Aristotle and of exponents of later philosophical schools: the Megarians, the Sceptics, the Cynics, the Stoics and the Epicurians. In common with the founders of religions, his personality became, even in the generation which succeeded his, at once historical and legendary.

Which was the real Socrates? The one described by his admirers or by his detractors? For Plato, he was divine, for Xenophon, an ordinary man, for Aristophanes, a sophist. Or perhaps he was as he describes himself in the *Apology:* a sage who, having become master of himself, tried to lead others to wisdom.

"When my sons are grown up, I would ask you, O my friends, to . . . trouble them, as I have troubled you, if they seem to care about riches, or anything, more than about virtue; or if they pretend to be something when they are really nothing,—then reprove them, as I have reproved you, for not caring about that for which they ought to care, and thinking that they are something when they are really nothing. And if you do this, I and my sons will have received justice at your hands."

PLATO

If we compare the ideas discussed between Socrates and Callicles in Plato's *Gorgias* as to whether it is better to do wrong to others than to be wronged by them with Thucydides' account of the arguments put by the Athenians to the

Melians (*see* p. 212), it is clear that Callicles is expressing the ruthless *realpolitik* of Athenian imperialism while Socrates represents the voice of conscience protesting against the violation of justice. The *Gorgias* provides an answer in ethical terms to the logic of politics as Thucydides recorded it in his *History*. And the man who undertook to give it was Socrates' disciple, Plato.

He was born into an aristocratic Athenian family in about 427. His father, Ariston, claimed descent from king Codrus and his mother belonged to the family of Solon. She was the sister of Charmides and a cousin of Critias who both played leading parts in the government of the Thirty. Plato's family owned large landed estates and he himself had property in two demes of Attica. Owing to the wealth of his family, Plato was able to take advantage of the best education that Athens had to offer. He studied philosophy under Cratylus, a follower of Heraclitus, who taught him that matter is not static and immutable but is in perpetual flux like a river. Plato never wholly abandoned the ideas of Cratylus and tried all his life to reconcile them with the Eleatic doctrine according to which the world or being is one, immobile, immutable, indivisible and absolute. His method of doing so was to postulate a division of phenomena into two kinds: those belonging to the world of ideas which is eternal and unalterable and those belonging to the world of objects which is transitory and corruptible. Objects may only be apprehended by the senses and ideas only by the mind.

Plato was about twenty-two years of age at the downfall of the Athenian empire. At first, he hoped that the accession to power of the oligarchic party would give new life to Athens which democracy and war had brought low. But he soon realized that the new regime was worse than the old and broke off all relations with the oligarchs before they were overthrown. But the bitterness of these years was redeemed by his meeting with Socrates. For Socrates understood that the crisis which was tearing Athens apart was a moral rather than a political one. Furthermore, he alone had the courage to proclaim publicly that it was the demagogues and the sophists and all the so-called " saviours of society " who were responsible for the disintegration of the state. The condemnation and death of Socrates, occurring while Plato was still in his twenties, was such a shock to him that he left Athens, going first to Megara and then travelling widley in the Mediterranean.

In the conservative and ancient lands of the Nile valley, Plato was able to study a regime which had remained impervious to the passage of time; where the social hierarchy was respected and where science had been since time immemorial the exclusive privilege of the priests, the real rulers of Egypt. This form of government by the wise impressed Plato who often alludes to it in the *Republic*, the *Timaeus* and the *Laws*. In 395 he moved on to Cyrene where he studied under the mathematician Theodorus who appears in the *Theaetetus*, returning to Athens in the following year. During this period, he wrote his first dialogues: the *Apology*, the *Lysis*, the *Charmides*, the *Laches*, the *Hippias II*, the *Protagoras*, the *Gorgias* and the *Meno*.

Then he proceeded to Southern Italy or Magna Graecia to study the ideas of the Pythagoreans and the result of their application to political and social problems in towns where the Pythagoreans had managed to seize power. After Cratylus and Socrates, the Pythagoreans were to be the third masters of Plato.

In 388, Plato visited Syracuse at the invitation of the elder Dionysius. At his court, he struck up friendship with Dionysius' brother-in-law, Dion. But Dionysius soon realized that Plato's social and political ideas were a threat to his tyranny. He had him arrested and handed him over to the Spartan envoy, Pollis, with an order either to kill him or to sell him into slavery. Plato was taken to Aegina where he was sold to the Cyrenean philosopher, Annikeris. In 387 he returned to Athens once more a free man. He had by now reached maturity and devoted his energies henforth to continuing the work of his master, Socrates. In 387, he founded a school at Colonus near a grove dedicated to the hero Academus. The Academy, as it was called, where Plato himself taught for forty years, was to be the cultural centre of Athens for nearly a thousand years. The greatest philosophers of antiquity studied there, among them Speusippus, Xenocrates, Aristotle and Eudoxos of Cnidus. It is at the beginning of this period that Plato wrote the *Phaedo*, the *Symposium* and the *Phaedrus*.

Although Plato was busy with his teaching in the Academy, he did not abandon his political aims. All his teachings and writings were aimed to exert an influence on the ethics of politics and the *Republic*, which he wrote while at the Academy, expresses his political preoccupations directly.

When Dionysius the younger ascended the throne of Syracuse, Plato and his friend Dion had hopes of convincing him to change the tyranny into a constitutional regime. He went to Sicily for the second time in 367, full of expectation. But tyrants are tyrants and, after the first enthusiasm had worn off, Plato was imprisoned while Dion was ruthlessly driven from the country. It was only when Dionysius had to leave Syracuse to wage war that he let Plato leave.

He came back to the Academy and resumed his teaching and his writing. The years between 367 and 361 saw the completion of the *Theaetetus*, the *Sophist*, the *Politician* and the *Parmenides*. They are no longer as poetic in style as the earlier dialogues and the theatrical mise-en-scène has been abandoned. The prose is dry and precise, in keeping with the critical examination of his metaphysical theory of ideas.

The extreme subtlety of Plato's thought has defied every attempt by historians of philosophy to assign him to a specific metaphysical school. Metaphysician though he certainly was, Plato, in the *Sophist*, goes far beyond metaphysics when he shows that the distinction between materialism and idealism is devoid of significance. And the same kind of surprise awaits the reader of the *Republic*, for in it Plato, the aristocrat, constructs a communistic society, without rich or poor and without families, in which unity is achieved by the common ownership of women, children and property.

Plato was back in Sicily in 361 for a third visit, when he was sixty-six years of age to reconcile Dionysius with his disciple, Dion. He failed and only avoided losing his life at the hands of the tyrant's body-guards by the intervention of Archytas of Tarentum. The shattering of his hopes and later the murder of Dion contributed to darken the last years of his life. He died in 347, pen in hand, at the age of eighty. The last work he wrote was the *Laws*.

Aristotle was the first to comment on the difference between the philosophy of Socrates and Plato:

" Socrates," he wrote, " did not consider that inductive causes and universal definition constituted entities distinct from the tangible world. Plato, on the other hand, separated these causes and definitions from tangible things to give them an independent and autonomous existence under the name of ' ideas.' To each object corresponds an ' idea ', bearing the same name as the object but having an existence of its own."

The separation of ideas from objects was the consequence of the application of the method of mathematical analysis to philosophy. The idea of the good, of the beautiful, of the great and so on, are treated as though they were similar to the mathematical symbols, geometrical figures or algebraic formulae used as " hypotheses " in mathematics.

" As the geometrician," wrote Plato in the *Meno*, " when asked whether a certain triangle is capable of being described in a certain circle, will reply: ' I cannot tell you as yet; but I will offer a hypothesis which may assist us in forming a conclusion: If the space be such that, when you have drawn along the line given by another figure, the original figure is reduced by a space equal to that which is added, then one consequence follows, and if this is impossible then some other; and therefore I wish to assume a hypothesis before I tell you whether this triangle is capable of being included in the circle:' — that is a geometrical hypothesis."

Instead of mathematical hypotheses, Plato had recourse to ideas. Each manifestation of the beautiful or the good was more or less beautiful or good in as much as it approximated to the idea of the beautiful or the good.

The development of the dialectic of Socrates into a method of mathematical analysis and the borrowing from mathematics of hypotheses transformed into ideas were the means by which the separation of the spiritual from the tangible world was effected. But this separation could not be bridged either by mathematical analysis or by hypothesis. Man could only be reunited with the divine, and the real with the ideal, by means of love. Plato's theory of love is the most enthralling part of his system and the dialogue in which it is discussed, the *Symposium*, is his masterpiece.

The *Symposium* is devoted to an analysis of the beautiful and of the nature of poetic creation. Socrates, who had accustomed his pupils to the rationalism of dialectics, appears now, according to Plato, to be reluctant to use the same method in investigating a problem which belongs not to logic but to the instinctive forces of life. Hence Socrates pretends to marvel at the words of a woman from Mantinea, Diotima, who has revealed to him the true nature of love and the role it plays in intellectual creation.

Diotima explains to Socrates that the laws of logic have no meaning in the realm of love. When Socrates inquires whether love is a beautiful god, Diotima answers that if it were divine, it would be happy and if it were beautiful, it would not need to seek beauty. Therefore, love is not a god for it cannot be happy, nor is it beautiful, because it is always seeking beauty to possess it.

Socrates is ready to accept that since love is not divine, it must be human and since it is not beautiful, it must be ugly. But Diotima reveals to him that the nature of love is not simple but complex. Neither god nor man, love has qualities of both. In other words, love is a *daemon*, that is to say a being which partakes of the divine and the human, filling the gap between the two. It is love which gives unity to the universe.

Love seeks the beautiful. Its purpose is generation through beauty. All men are fecund both physically and spiritually, for when they become adult, they feel the need to procreate. Procreation is the passage from nothing to being and the creators (in Greek *poetai*) are not only those who create poetry, but who create in every sphere. Creation is the justification of love for, through creation, mortal man participates in immortality or, more properly, becomes immortal himself, for, when he has decayed and vanished, another being, similar to himself, takes his place. Each being endows his offspring with significance for the offspring represents the renewal of life and, in this way, immortality.

Just as physical procreation is realized in the getting of children, spiritual procreation takes the form of the production of literary and artistic works. The spiritual procreator or poet seeks beauty and is inspired by the presence of beautiful bodies and beautiful souls. Entering into contact with a beautiful person, he gives birth to all the things which have existed within him. And he rears the fruit of their union with the object of his love. In this way the bonds formed between the poet and the object of his love are more intimate and more stable than those between children and parents.

At this point in the argument Diotima pauses for breath. She has already described love, its birth, its nature, its purpose and its relation to artistic and literary inspiration. But this is still only a description of love. She has not yet postulated any general principles derived from her observations.

She now begins a new survey from a different point of view. Beauty is not confined to one body alone; it exists everywhere. The poet's attachment to one object will, as he grows more mature, give way before the admiration he feels for all beautiful objects. It will not stop there, however. Beauty is not only physical. It is also spiritual. The beauty of the soul is worthy of greater reverence than the beauty of the body. Even more worthy is the beauty of science. Thus from individual beauty, Diotima comes to the idea of universal beauty.

Diotima has reached the last stage in her argument. Beauty in its ultimate form does not appear in the guise of a face, or of hands, or of science. Absolute beauty exists outside the realm of natural phenomena. It exists by itself and of itself alone, always the same, eternal and simple. All the manifestations of beauty are but shadows of beauty itself. Human life, concludes Diotima, offers nothing more noble than the contemplation of beauty. But this cannot be achieved without intuitive faculties, for, according to Plato, it is not simply a universal definition established by inductive and rational methods, proceeding from complex notions to simple ones; it is a concept outside and beyond experience and can only be apprehended by ecstasy. This is the first step towards mysticism. In this, Plato goes beyond the rationalism of Socrates and looks forward to the philosophy of Plotinus.

In the *Phaedrus*, Plato returns to the problem of beauty. Perhaps he felt that the Dionysiac atmosphere of the *Symposium* had drawn him too far towards the sensual aspect of the beautiful and he wanted now to examine in greater detail its spiritual aspect.

In the *Phaedrus* absolute or essential beauty exists together with other ideas in a realm of primary existence. The soul of man, before descending to earth to inhabit a body and be born again, knows the beautiful in all its brilliance. But when it assumes a human body, it becomes a captive of the senses and thereby loses contact with this vision. The memory of the beautiful returns, however, when the soul is confronted with beauty incarnate. At the recollection of the beautiful, it trembles as though in a trance, dominated by the fervour of love. Love, by the effect of its heat, dissolves the dry substance which constricts the wings of the soul and prevents them from growing and developing. They are then able to become bigger, spreading over the surface of the soul which experiences the greatest of all pleasures. The man who loves the beautiful desires to possess it bodily. Instinct and soul enter into conflict. Instinct seeks to enjoy the beautiful by means of the senses whereas the soul seeks to enjoy it spiritually.

As man can only enter into contact with the beautiful through his soul, any effort on the part of the senses even to approach it is doomed to failure. Art itself cannot succeed; indeed it may even become a danger for it uses tricks of imitation to deceive the beholder and the draw him away from the path of truth. In the last chapter of the *Republic*, Plato uses many examples to express his dislike of the graphic arts.

Let us take, for example, he says, a " category " composed of many particular objects, as tables constitute the category " table ". All these objects are derived from one general idea: the idea of the table. The carpenters who make tables for our use all have in their minds the idea of the essential table. Before they start to work, the idea of the table exists. It is not the carpenter who has invented the idea. It is divinely created. The carpenter has merely imitated it. Divine creation is primary, the creation of the carpenter is mimetic and technical. Let us now imagine a single " maker " who is neither carpenter, blacksmith nor artisan; yet he is somehow able to show us tables, beds, plants or animals, even humans, gods and the underworld. His work is like a mirror which, being turned hither and thither, reproduces immediately for us all the things with which we are surrounded. However, the objects shown in the mirror are not real but illusory. This "maker" is of course the painter. The reproduction he makes is inferior to the one made by the carpenter, for, while the carpenter imitates an ideal example, the painter imitates the material imitation of the carpenter.

The table of the painter is therefore of a lower order than the table of the carpenter, just as the table of the carpenter is of a lower order than the ideal table. But are the material creations of the artisan, which the painter imitates, made according to their essential nature? No, says Plato. Things, according to him, while they remain substantially the same, change in appearance if we view them from different viewpoints. Thus if the table is rectangular, it will appear different if looked at obliquely. What does the painter reproduce: the table as it is or as it appears?

Starting from this distinction between appearance and reality, Plato in the *Sophist* divides the art of his age into two schools. The first school which reproduces objects in their true proportions and with their actual colours, he calls "figurative" (*ikastic*); the second, which interprets the objects, distorting their proportions so that they appear from afar to have correct proportions (although if one views them from close to, they are clearly seen to be disproportionate) he calls "imaginative" or "fantastic." And Plato uses this latter term to define the work of decorators and painters who use perspective to give the illusion of a third dimension.[115]

According to Plato, the illusion produced by perspective is similar to the impression produced by the speeches of the sophists. For as the sophists present truth not as it is but as their listeners want it to be, so imaginative painters represent objects not exactly as they are but in the manner most agreeable to viewers.

Another point of similarity between imaginative painters and sophists is their readiness to play with all ideas without exploring any one of them thoroughly. Painters are quite prepared to make pictures of tables without being carpenters, of vases without being potters and of plants, animals and men without being gods. What could such men be? Leonardo would have answered: gods; Plato answered: fools.

The "imitator," whether painter or sophist has no proper knowledge of the object he imitates. Imitation is a sort of game devoid of seriousness. By imitations which evoke memories of natural disasters and human tragedies, poets are able to corrupt men's characters and render them vicious.

Plato therefore concludes that justice is not violated if art is excluded from the republic for it excites the passions and feeds evil instincts. If art were protected, it would be tantamount to encouraging bad men to the detriment of wise.

But in spite of this, Plato, himself a poet, tries to find an argument to justify the presence of art in the republic, to bring it back from the exile to which he has banished it. And he pursues this problem in the *Philebus*. When art, says Socrates to Protarchus, manages to avoid the usual themes, that is to say the imitation of living and material things, to present us with straight or curved figures, then the pleasure it causes is pure. Thus Plato, as we noticed in our discussion of Proto-geometric vase-painting (*see* p. 87), is an advocate of abstract art and an opponent of realism. Abstract art is akin to philosophy, and thus becomes worthy to enter the gates of his ideal republic. The reconciliation of the image with the idea, of art with philosophy, should not surprise us in the writer of the *Symposium*.

Plato, in his last work, the *Laws*, admits that the rhythm and harmony of a work of art, as well as the recognition of the object which the artist is reproducing, produce a particular joy. A work of art in his view may constitute a source of aesthetic emotion. With such theories, Plato looks forward to the *Poetics* of Aristotle which reviewed the poetic achievement of the Greeks, as well as laying down aesthetic rules.

It is fortunate that nearly all the works of Plato have survived for they constitute in a sense the spiritual testament of Athens. Belonging miraculously both to poetry and science, they give a survey of all the philosophical movements of the preceding ages: the relatavism of Heraclitus, the static monism of the Eleatics, the mathematical formalism of Pythagoras, the dialectical method of Socrates. At the same time, they try to adjust their differences in an audacious and undogmatic system where thought, feeling and intuition are blended. Plato broke the the classical synthesis of archaism, rationalism, and realism and retained only the first two elements: the archaism of the myth and the rationalism of mathematical analysis. Realism he rejected with unequivocal contempt. With his mathematical explanation of the universe and his frequent recourse to myth, Plato, uniting logic with intuition, endeavoured to cross the bounds which separate human existence from the mysteries of the unknown.

THE CRISIS OF CLASSICAL ART

THE DISTINCTION made by Plato between " figurative " and " imaginative " types of art corresponds to a real division in the art of classical Athens during the fourth century. According to W. Deonna [116] the " figurative " artists were the archaists, that is to say, those who returned to the traditions of Athenian primitivism and to the intellectual realism of the geometric period. Schmidt has observed, in many Panathenaean amphorae produced between 390 and 360, the revival of archaic features and Athenian sculpture of the same period reveals similar returns to archaic techniques.[117]

" This movement," writes Charles Picard, " is to be attributed to the fermentation of ideas, both religious and political. It was encouraged by the conservative party to whose vicissitudes the archaic movement was closely linked." [118]

Plato took a stand in favour of archaism and against modernism in art. Having personal—but no political—ties with the conservative party, he showed that he was sympathetic to its ideology when he declared that every change was a source of decay and that every tradition which survived was a demonstration of virtue. The remarkable facility with which he penetrated each technique, analyzing it with all its implications, is due to his artistic education. His biographers relate that he studied painting and poetry and was often seen in the studios of the artists. The violence of his attacks on realistic painters in the *Republic* read very like the polemics exchanged nowadays by artists of different schools. His fear of the social consequences resulting from changes of technique or style are characteristic of his artistic mentality. When Plato's anger against the " modernists " at last relented and he reflected upon what would happen if, one day, art disappeared altogether, he wrote in his *Politician* that life, already so difficult, would become completely unbearable. At the same time he saw very clearly the mortal danger threatening artistic creation if art became regimented and if experiment and research were forbidden.[119]

The " imaginative " artists whom Plato opposed to the " figurative " ones were, in fact, the " realists " of his age. It was they who abandoned the classical traditions of Phidias and Polygnotus. In sculpture they strove to penetrate more deeply into the psychology of human passions and in painting they pressed still further their pursuit of a third dimension by means of novel techniques such as perspective and the distribution of light and shade—*chiaroscuro*.

Perspective, called by the Ancients *skiagraphia*,[120] was first used in the time o Aeschylus, in stage scenery by Agatharchus who also wrote a treatise on the subject which was consulted later on by Anaxagoras and Democritus. Agatharchus was also known for his mural paintings. He undertook the decoration of the house of Alcibiades; as, contrary to his usual practice, he was somewhat dilatory in his work, Alcibiades is said to have locked him up till he had finished. Perspective was applied to painting proper by Apollodorus, hence his title of shadow-painter, *skiagraphos*. Plutarch attributes to him the innovation of " modelling " with the gradation of colours in various degrees of light and shade. In this way, he was able to heighten the impression of volume already produced by the use of perspective.[121] Apollodorus was widely attacked for his innovations by the archaists as well as by followers of Polygnotus. But he gained to his side two of the most talented painters of the fourth century: Zeuxis and Parrhasius.

We come across the name of Zeuxis in two dialogues of Plato, the *Gorgias* and the *Protagoras*. His reputation soon passed beyond the confines of Attica. He was asked by Archelaus, king of Macedonia, to decorate his palace at Pella. His realistic technique was so successful that he contrived to produce an illusion of nature—a kind of *trompe-l'œil*—so that the Ancients believed that birds tried to peck at the grapes he had painted. Zeuxis revived a theme which the classical painters had neglected: the Centaurs. In one of his compositions, he depicted a female Centaur giving suck to twin infants, while their father, the Centaur, hidden behind a rock, tries to frighten them with a lion cub which he is holding in his arms.

Parrhasius' skill as a realist was so great that he even succeeded in duping Zeuxis who mistook a garment he had painted for a real one. Some of his sketches were used in the decoration of the shield of the Athena Promachus. In his *Memorabilia*, Xenophon in a dialogue with Socrates presents Parrhasius not only as a master of *chiaroscuro* and perspective, but also as a subtle interpreter of human psychology.

Like those of Polygnotus, the paintings of Zeuxis and Parrhasius have not survived and the little we know of them is derived from written descriptions. To follow therefore the reaction of the new school of the fourth century against the classical tradition of Phidias in the flesh, as it were, we are obliged to confine ourselves to the achievements of the sculptors.

Phidias was always surrounded by a group of artists and artisans with whom he collaborated so that his work on the Parthenon, for example, was a collective work. Praxiteles, on the other hand, appears to have been a solitary figure, working in isolation without the encouragement of commissions for great public works and therefore outside the political and religious context which contributed so much to the vigour of the work with which the veterans of Salamis embellished the Acropolis.

Civil war had exhausted Athens economically and morally and all great public works had stopped in the fourth century. The only architectural monument which has survived from this period is the elegant monument of Lysicrates with its monolithic roof. It is a votive offering to commemorate the victory in a choral contest of the boys from the Akamantide tribe which Lysicrates had trained at his own expense.

The prize received by Lysicrates—a bronze tripod—stood at the top of the monument which is decorated with Corinthian columns surging from large marble slabs. The frieze on the architrave evokes the comical episode of the

Tyrrhenian pirates who, having unwittingly captured the god Dionysus and sold him as a slave, are transformed into dolphins and thrown into the sea, while the god becomes a lion. The monument of Lysicrates is the first example of Corinthian style in Athens.

Other public works which were carried out under the rule of Lycurgus (336-26)—the marble stage of the theatre of Dionysus and the Panathenaean stadium—are of historical rather than artistic interest. The artists who contributed to their decoration did not have the impression that they were taking part in an enterprise of national and religious importance as did those who worked on the monuments of the Acropolis in the time of Pericles.

Lacking the security of regular commissions at home, Athenian sculptors of the fourth century tended to seek work elsewhere in Greece and the colonies. Scopas who had left his native Paros to settle in Athens rebuilt and decorated with his sculptures the temple of Alea Athena at Tegaea which was destroyed by fire in 395. The few surviving heads from the pediments, now in the Archeological Museum of Athens, show how subjective and indrawn sculpture had become in his hands.

With three other sculptors from Athens, Timotheus, Bryaxeus and Leochares (Pl. 105), Scopas undertook the decoration of the Mausoleum of Halicarnassus, the most interesting monument erected during the first fifty years of the fourth century by Greek architects and sculptors. The fights between the Amazons with which Scopas adorned the eastern side display the most extreme realism ever shown in the history of Greek art.

PRAXITELES

THE VIOLENCE of the passions in the work of Scopas is in marked contrast with the exhaustion of the passions apparent in the human form as treated by Praxiteles. The soul, in the sculptures of Praxiteles, seems to be spread on to the surface of the bodies and its most distinctive quality is melancholy reflected on the faces of gods who seem listless and bored. A kind of cerebral sensualism gradually replaced the logical energy of the classical age and led sculpture away from solidity to delicacy, from strength to tenderness, from self-control to self-indulgence.

Praxiteles was born in Athens in about 390. His father, Cephisodotus, was the sculptor of the bronze statue of Eirene with the infant Plutus in her lap, of which a marble copy has survived, now in the Munich Glyptothek. Cephisodotus belonged to the fifth generation of a family of sculptors.[122] Praxiteles worked with his father till he reached the age of twenty-five and appears to have accompanied him to Megalopolis which was built in about 370. The most important event in his private life was his meeting with Phryne, a beautiful white-skinned hetaera who became the model for his celebrated Aphrodite. Among his first works are statues of Leto, Apollo and Artemis at Mantinea which were to influence later works: the sculptured slabs representing the Muses and the musical contest of Apollo and Marsyas, of which the latter is now in the Archaeological Museum of Athens (Pl. 117). In middle age, Praxiteles worked on the Artemisium of Ephesus, on the Adonion of Caria and at Cnidus where he made his statue of Aphrodite.

The Aphrodite of Cnidus was the first nude goddess of Grrek art. Copies and adaptations are preserved in many European museums: the little bronze version in the British Museum (Pl. 108) is one of the most passionate of the whole series.[123] It represents a small Aphrodite taking off her necklace—the only thing she is wearing—before entering the water. The movement of her hands about her neck, the inclination of the head, the turning of the right foot, the expression of modesty and candour, give grace and charm to her regular and sturdy body.

Praxiteles endowed the goddesses of Olympus with delicacy and the gods with youth. Apollo, Hermes, the Satyrs, come to life again with youthful naked bodies. They play carelessly with lizards, tortoises or babies; their hands are raised above their heads, or gripping a tree, or holding a cluster of grapes, or pouring wine from a jug. The hip over the unbent leg which supports the weight of the body is slightly raised while the other hip is tilted slightly downward over the free leg. In this attitude of repose, the body acquires fluid curving lines which are accentuated by delicate touches of the chisel on the material itself. Archaeologists are inclined to attribute to Praxiteles a bronze statue called the Ephebe of Marathon (Pl. 89)—now in the Archaeological Museum of Athens—which was hoisted up from the sea one morning in June 1925 by fishermen in the bay of Marathon.[124] It was lost in a shipwreck and remained in the sea for twenty centuries like another bronze statue called the Ephebe of Anticythera, which was found near Cape Malea and is now in the same Museum. Perhaps the Ephebe of Marathon which has all the characteristics of the great sculptor's style represents a Hermes, for a little wing protrudes above his forehead exactly in the frontal axis. No more than four feet high, this statue cannot have represented an athlete. The left hand is bent with the palm open and may have held a tortoise. The right hand is raised above the head with the thumb playing with two fingers. The eyes, made of inlaid precious stones, shine and the mouth is half open as if the statue were breathing. The head is turned and the body is relaxed, as if resting after some exertion.

The most famous work of Praxiteles is the Hermes of Olympia.[125] It is mentioned by Pausanias and was found in 1877, fallen from its pedestal and buried within the ruins of the sanctuary of the temple of Hera, at the very place where Pausanias saw it in the second century A. D. The legs are missing and only the left foot remains. The right arm is also broken off at the elbow. The little Dionysus, which Hermes is carrying, was found in pieces. The whole statue, restored with great care, is now in the museum at Olympia. It represents Hermes carrying away the infant Dionysus, born of the unlawful love of Zeus and Semele, from the jealousy of Hera, to be confided to the nymphs of Boeotia who will bring him up. He is depicted resting by the wayside, near a tree; he has plucked a bunch of grapes and, leaning against the tree, is playing with Dionysus, showing him the appetizing fruits.

After the tension which characterized Athenian sculpture in the fifth century, the Hermes of Praxiteles is markedly relaxed. A sort of autumnal feeling of decline, a romantic melancholy hovers round it, reflecting the exhaustion of Athens which had lost an empire and had suffered the humiliations of defeat. The sad beauty of the Hermes has an aura of a lost paradise.

For the first time, the marks of spiritual suffering are apparent in sculpture which in the fourth century expresses what every Athenian craved for: withdrawal from action. The Hermes is no longer a hero of Salamis or Marathon. He is a dandy. His body does not have the muscular vigour of the earlier kouroi. It is all grace and ease.

Having achieved complete mastery of their materials, the sculptors of the fourth century became skilful technicians who had turned their backs on the austere canons of tradition—a tree solved the old problem of stability and the back was left unworked—to concentrate on the face, the chest and the legs and to try to convert marble into light. Rubbing rendered the marble of the Hermes as diaphanous as alabaster and as soft as flesh itself. The marble lost its stoniness just as the forms had lost their edge: Hermes had become a wraith.[126]

Praxiteles created a new race of men in sculpture, perfecting a techinique to represent them adequately, and until the end of the fourth century, his statues were widely copied.

Scopas and Praxiteles put the stamp of their style on the art of their age. The history of classical art ends with their names and the Hellenistic age starts under their sign.

CONCLUSION

ATHENIAN CIVILIZATION, like European civilization after the Renaissance, resembles the Platonic realm of Ideas from which are derived all experience and knowledge. In politics, physics, anthropology, philosophy, literature, sculpture and painting European culture owes its starting point and its general direction to the ideas of Athens.

On the confined and barren soil of Attica, round the rock of the Acropolis the first code of social justice was promulgated by Solon in the sixth century, the first orations defining political rights were uttered by Themistocles and Pericles and the first commercial and naval empire of history was formed. Colonists from Athens, on the neighbouring shores of Ionia, discarding superstitions and myths, laid the foundations of the positive sciences and endeavoured to understand and control the forces of nature by means of experiment and deduction. The Ionian sophists and philosophers, like Anaxagoras and Protagoras, brought to Athens the message of empiricism. In the same way, Thucydides' inquiries into the causes of the war between Athens and Sparta laid the foundations of a science of history.

The poets of Athens, uniting, in a daring step, word with action, invented the theatre. Aeschylus, Sophocles, Euripides and Aristophanes gave such eloquent expression to sentiments and passions that they widened the meaning of experience.

But as man's experience deepened, so did his need for understanding. Long before Christ, Socrates asked Athenians of what avail was the conquest of the world if the soul went to perdition. In the dialogues in which he debated with the sophists, the ethics of politics were opposed to the logic of politics and it was the subtle analysis of these problems which produced the theory of Ideas by which Plato sought to reconcile the real with the spiritual world.

While Athenian thought abandoned physics to concentrate on metaphysics, Athenian art took the opposite course: it left the abstractions of geometric art and strove after the physical reality of man in painting and sculpture. Religious and monumental architecture followed suit and the Acropolis of Athens became the scene of a marriage between beauty and reason, of which the work of Phidias, Ictinus, Callicrates, Mnesicles and Philocles bear eternal witness.

The fusion of rationalism with archaism and realism which constitutes the essence of the classical ideal was dissolved by the crisis of conscience which followed the political decline of Athens after the close of the fifth century. The apologists of the new cultural movement were Praxiteles and Scopas. Their work contains the seed of one trend of European art as exemplified by Michelangelo and Rodin just as the origins of cubism and the abstract art of our age can be discerned in the theories expounded by Plato in his *Philebus* and in proto-geometric vase-painting.

It was the lot of Athens to pose for the first time the basic problems of philosophy and art which have pre-occupied Europe ever since. The history of European consciousness begins with Athens.

Notes

¹ See A. Philippson and E. Kirsten, *Die Grie-chischen Landschaften*, 1, 3, " Attica und Mega-ris," *pp.* 753-907, Frankfurt-am-Main, 1952; D. Aeginitis, *The Climate of Grèce*, 2 vols., Athens, 1907-8 (in Greek); El. Mariolopoulos, *The Climate of Greece*, Athens, 1938 (in Greek); which describe the geology, geography and climate of Attica.

² For the period of colonization and the spread of the Greeks, see J. Bérard, *L'Expan-sion et la colonisation grecques jusqu'aux guerres médiques*, Paris, 1960; M. B. Sakellariou, *La Migration grecque en Ionie*, Athens, 1958; T. J. Dunbabin, *The Greeks and their Eastern Neigh-bours*, London, 1957; C. Roebuck, *Ionian Trade and Colonization*, New York, 1959.

³ For the influence of geological structure on the political life of ancient Greek cities see G. Glotz, *Histoire grecque*, 1, " Des origines aux guerres médiques," Paris, 1949; A. Jardé, *La Formation du peuple grec*, Paris, 1938.

⁴ See A. Orlandos, *The Structural Materials of the Ancient Greeks*, 2 vols., Athens, 1955-6 (in Greek).

⁵ A study on palaeolithic Greece has not yet appeared in book form. Only papers on the results of excavations and reports on discoveries now in the Museums of Volos and Larissa exist. See R. Stampfus in *Mannus*, XXXIV, 1-2, 1942; Vladimir Milojcic, *Germania*, XXXVI, 1958, 409-417. For the pre-Ceramic findings of the early neolithic age see an article by the same author in *Germania*, XXXIV, 1956, 208-10; *Ar-chäologischen Anzeiger*, 1959; *Neue Deutsche Ausga-bungen in Mittelmeergebiet* (p. 234), 1959; D. R. Theocharis, *Transactions of the Academy of Athens*, 32, 1959 (in Greek); and " Summary of the Results " in the journal *Bulletin de Correspondence Hellénique*, LXXXIII, p. 690, 1959. See also *Ar-chaeologikon Deltion*, Vol. XVI, 1960, Text, Athens, 1962, *pp.* 186-94, Vladimir Milojcic.

⁶ See Christian Zervos, *La Naissance de la civilisation en Grèce*, 2 vols., Vol. II, Paris, 1963, *pp.* 505-6 and 529.

⁷ For the neolithic age of Sesclos and Dimini, C. Tsountas. *The Prehistoric Acropolis of Dimini and Sesclos*, Athens, 1908 (in Greek) is still the fundamental work; other useful studies include A. J. B. Wace and M. S. Thompson, *Prehistoric*

Thessaly, Cambridge, 1912; G. Mylonas, *The Neolithic Age in Greece*, Athens, 1928 (in Greek) and Christian Zervos, *La Naissance de la civili-sation en Grèce*, Vol. II, Paris, 1963, which con-tains a complete bibliography up to the date of publication. The conclusions drawn by D. R. Theocharis from his excavations of the neolithic settlements at Pyrassos in Thessaly and at Néa Makri in Attica can be found in his monograph on Pyrassos in *Thessalika*, Vol. II, Volos, 1959, *pp.* 1-15 (in Greek) and in " Excavation of the Neolithic Settlement at Néa Makri " in *Praktika*, 1953 (ed. 1956), *pp.* 114-22 (in Greek).

⁸ The results of the excavations of the Italian School on the southern slope of the Acropolis which brought to light neolithic findings of the Sesclos period were published by Doro Levi in the *Annuario*, XIII-XIV, 1930-1, *pp.* 411-98 with the title " Abitazzioni preistoriche sulle pendici meridionali dell'Acropoli." The results of the excavations of the 21 wells with neolithic find-ings of the Dimini period undertaken by the American Classical School were published in *Hesperia* by T. L. Shear (V, 1936, *pp.* 20-1, VII, 1938, *pp.* 335-8, VIII, 1939, *pp.* 221-35, XI, 1940, *pp.* 297-8) and by A. W. Parsons (XII. 1943, *pp.* 191-267). On the pre-Mycenaean Acropolis, see the two excellent doctoral theses of Spyros Jacovides, *The Mycenaean Acropolis of Athens*, 1962, and John Travlos, *The Develop-ment of Town-planning in Athens*, Athens, 1960 (both in Greek).

⁹ The results of his excavations of neolithic settlements in Athens were published by D. R. Theocharis in his article " Néa Makri, Eine grosse neolithische Siedlung in der Nähe von Marathon " in *Mitteilungen des Deutschen Ar-chäologischen Instituts*, Athenische Abteilung, LXXI, Part 1, Berlin 1956, *pp.* 1-29; by G. My-lonas, " Excavations at Haghios Kosmas," in the *American Journal of Archaeology*, XXXVIII, 1934, *pp.* 258-79, and by the same author, " The Haghios Kosmas Excavations, 1951," in the *Ar-chaeologike Ephimeris*, 1953-54, *pp.* 117-34 (in Greek).

¹⁰ Paul Kretschmer was amongst the first to make a systematic study of the place-names of Attica in his book *Einleitung in die Geschichte der Griechischen Sprache*, Göttingen, 1896.

¹¹ John Chadwick discussed his theory on the origin of the Greek language and the Greek

people in a lecture delivered at the University of Athens in 1959. This was published in the Athenian daily *Kathimerini* on 27 and 31 May 1962, by Miltis Paraskevaides.

[12] According to the ceramic evidence the chronology of the various settlements can be determined in relation to the Aegean system of dating by Sir Arthur Evans and others. Thus in broad terms, Troy I dates 3000-2600; Troy II, 2600-2300; Troy III, 2300-2200; Troy IV, 2200-2050; Troy V, 2050-1900 and all fall in the Early Bronze Age. The first half of Troy IV falls in the Middle Bronze Age and the second of Troy VI (1900-1300) together with Troy VIIa (1300-1250) and VIIb (1250-1100) fall in the Late Bronze Age. Troy VIII (700-350) and Troy IX (350 B. C.-400 A. D.) See A. J. B. Wace and F. H. Stubbings (ed.) *A Companion to Homer*, London, 1962, *pp*. 382-3 by Carl W. Blegen.

[13] For an account of how Linear B was deciphered, see John Chadwick, *The Decipherment of Linear B*, Cambridge, 1958, (2nd ed. London, 1961) and Michael Ventris and John Chadwick, *Documents in Mycenaean Greek*, with a Foreword by Alan J. B. Wace, Cambridge, 1956.

[14] Herodotus, VII, 129; Apollodorus, *Bibl.* I, 7, 2.

[15] For Greek mythology, see Pierre Grimal, *Dictionnaire de la mythologie grecque et romaine* (3rd ed.), Paris, 1963. See articles on " Deucalion " and " Hellèn," with references to the ancient sources.

[16] See D. R. Theocharis, *Askitario, The Early Helladic Acropolis at Rafina*, Athens, 1960 (in Greek) and George Mylonas, " Excavations at Haghios Kosmas " in the *American Journal of Archaeology, loc. cit.*

[17] A. J. Evans, in his great work *The Palace of Minos at Knossos*, 4 vols., London, 1921-36, reported the results of his excavations at Knossos. Excavations had begun in 1900 following his acquisition of the site in 1894. The views of Evans on Knossos and the dates of its palaces were elegantly summarized in popular form by J. D. S. Pendlebury in *A Handbook to the Palace of Minos, Knossos, with its Dependencies*, London, 1933, 1954. The excavations in Crete after 1900 brought an entirely new world to light and several excellent books have been written on the subject, such as E. M. and H. B. Hawes, *Crete, the Forerunner of Greece*, 1909; G. Glotz, *La Civilisation égéenne*, Paris, 1937; V. Gordon Childe, *The Dawn of European Civilization*, London, 1957; and N. Platon, *A Guide to the Archaeological Museum of Heraclion*, Heraclion, Crete, 1959.

[18] J. Vercoutter, in his *L'Égypte et le monde égéen préhellénique*, Cairo, 1961, examines the links between Crete and Egypt.

[19] In his *L'Art de la Crète néolithique et minoenne*, Paris, 1956, and *L'Art des Cyclades*, Paris, 1957, Christian Zervos has given the impressions of a modern art critic on the aesthetic forms of the Aegean. Both works are beautifully illustrated. For information about the latest excavations together with comments on pre-Homeric Greece, see A. Séveryns, *Grèce et Proche-Orient avant Homère*, Brussels, 1960.

[20] *Archaeologikon Deltion*, Vol. XVI, Athens, 1962. *Pp.* 254-73 refer to work of the Archaeological schools (Greek, British, Italian and French) in Crete up to 1960 (in Greek).

[21] In his *Mycenaeans and Minoans: Aegean Prehistory in the Light of the Linear B Tablets*, London, 1961, Leonard R. Palmer has rearranged Evans's dating of the Knossos tablets and has compared his results with evidence provided by the Pylos tablets. He has thus moved by 200 years the dating of Evans which has been generally accepted hitherto. Palmer's theory is convincing and does not leave a gap from 1400 to 1200 as Evans had done. According to him, not only are the Pylos tables correlated with the Knossos tablets, but Homeric sources with archaeological evidence. The chronology of Evans (1450-1400) failed to account for the participation of Knossos in the Trojan expedition.

[22] *Iliad* II, 645-52.

[23] Herodotus, I, 172. The social origin of the monarchy from the clan explains several characteristic elements of Minoan mythology: the female goddess (Potnia, snake-goddess), the queen's chamber in the royal palaces, the participation of women in entertainments and in religious ceremonies (wall-painting of Knossos) and in political events (the Ariadne myth as well as the totemic emblems of a sacrificial rite depicted on the sarcophagus of Hagia Triada which display clan symbols corresponding to the clan emblems on the Egyptian palettes of Narmer and of King Scorpius. See also A. Moret and G. Davy, *Des Clans aux empires*, Paris, 1923, which constitutes the most serious attempt to trace in social terms the transformation of the primitive clans of the east into the great agrarian empires of Egypt and Mesopotamia.

[24] A. J. B. Wace's theory on the interdependence of the Mycenaeans and Knossos is brought out in his *Mycenae, An Archaeological History and Guide*, Princeton, 1949; in his " Foreword " to Michael Ventris and John Chadwick, *op. cit.*; and more summarily in his article on " Mycenae " in *A Companion to Homer*, London, 1962, *pp*. 386-98. A description of the second cycle of Mycenaean graves uncovered by the late John Papadimitriou and Professor G. Mylonas in 1951-2 and 1953-4 is given in the latter's *Ancient Mycenae, The Capital City of Agamemnon*, London, 1957, *pp*. 128-76. A. Séveryns, *op. cit., pp*. 11-6, also discusses Wace's theory on Mycenaean influences at Knossos.

[25] The correlation of the Ivory Trio and the Eleusis bas-relief of Demeter, Persephone and Triptolemus was made by Charles Picard in a study which he contributed to *Epitaph for Christos Tsountas*, Athens, 1941, entitled " Sur un groupe d'ivoire de Mycène," *pp*. 446-51.

For the religion of the Aegean inhabitants and its survival into the religion of classical Greece, the basic work is still M. P. Nilsson, *The Minoan-Mycenaean Religion and its survivals in Greek Religion*, Lund, 1950. The conclusions drawn from the Linear B tablets about Mycenaean worship are described in the already cited *Documents in Mycenaean Greek*, pp. 125-9.

[26] See the article on " Argonautes " in Pierre Grimal, *op. cit.* For the excavations at Iolcus see *Archaeologikon Deltion* Vol. XVI. 1960, Athens, pp. 176-7 (in Greek).

[27] A summary of the institutions of Achaean society is given in Jacques Ellul, *Histoire des institutions de l'antiquité*, Paris, 1961, with relevant bibliography. For the growth of Mycnaean society until Homer, see the following works: T. B. L. Webster, *From Mycenae to Homer*, London, 1958, A. Séveryns, *op. cit.* and *A Companion to Homer*, pp. 431-559.

[28] Thucydides, II, 15; Plutarch, *Theseus*, 24; John Travlos, *op. cit.*, *p.* 24.

[29] The measurements of the hearths at Mycenae, Tiryns and Pylos are recorded in S. Marinatos, *Crete and Mycenaean Greece*, Athens, 1959 (in Greek), *p.* 59. On the relationship between the Mycenaean hearth and the monastic hearths in Byzantine and post-Byzantine Greece, see A. Orlandos, *Monastic Architecture*, Athens, 1955, *pp.* 61-70 (in Greek).

[30] C. Tsountas and J. I. Manatt, *The Mycenaean Age*, London, 1903; A. J. B. Wace, " Excavations at Mycenae," in *Annual of the British School of Archaeology at Athens*, XXV, 1921-3.

[31] In his study " The Royal Graves of Mycenae and Athenian Tradition " which appeared in the *Epitaph for Christos Tsountas*, *pp.* 415-22, Professor George Mylonas develops his theory on the relationship between the grave of Cecrops and the tombs of the Shaft Grave Dynasty of Mycenae. For Cecrops, see Thucydides, II, 15, Pausanias, *Arcadia*, II, 3, and *Attica*, 26, 5; Strabo, IX, 1, 20; and Apollodorus, III, 14, 1.

[32] Spyros Jacovides, *op. cit.*, *pp.* 55.*ff.*

[33] S. Marinatos in his preface to Spyros Jacovides, *op. cit.*, *pp.* 11-7.

[34] Herodotus, VIII, 41.

[35] Pausanias, *Attica*, I, 24, 7.

[36] M. P. Nilsson, *op. cit.*, *pp.* 279; N. Kontoleon, *The Erechtheum as a Temple of infernal worship*, Athens, 1949, *pp.* 17-20 (in Greek).

[37] Homer, *Iliad*, II, 546-51; *Odyssey*, VIII, 80-1.

[38] Apollodorus, III, 191.

[39] Pausanias, *Attica*, I, 26, 5-27, 2.

[40] Herodotus, V, 72.

[41] Charles Picard, *Erechtheion*, Paris, 1932, *p.* 34.

[42] N. Kontoleon, *op. cit.*, *pp.* 69-79. The view held by Kontoleon that the area in front of the Caryatides contained the tomb of Cecrops appears reasonable if it is borne in mind that the walling and monopteral columns of the structure are in essence features of the ancient funerary edifices of Greece.

[43] Bacchylides, *Carmina cum Fragmentis*, ed. Bruno Snell, Teubner, 1934; a French translation of *Odes* XVII and XVIII with interesting illustrative material has appeared under the title: *Thésée, Images et Récits*, présentés par Ch. Ducas et R. Flacelière, Paris, 1958.

[44] Homer, *Iliad*, X, 263-5; Hesiod, *The Shield*, 182.

[45] For an interpretation of the heroic myth and of the epic in the light of modern psychology, see Charles Baudouin, *Le Triomphe du héros*, Paris, 1952.

[46] Bacchylides, *Ode* XVII.

[47] Plutarch, *Theseus*, 19.

[48] Doubts concerning the dating of the Trojan War are described by Carl Blegen in *A Companion to Homer*, *pp.* 385-6. Our estimate of the dating is based on the reference in Thucydides (I, 12) that the Dorians and the Heraclidae began occupying the Peloponnese eighty years after the fall of Troy. Archaeologists date the Dorian conquest round about 1210, and consequently the fall of Troy (VIIa) should have occurred in 1290. A. Séveryns, *op. cit.*, *pp.* 179-81, agrees with this dating. Carl Blegen favours 1250 and George Mylonas 1183.

[49] Homer, *Iliad*, XXI, 27.

[50] Jan Six in *Journal of Hellenic Studies*, 1919, *p.* 130.

[51] James H. Breasted, *Ancient Records of Egypt*, Chicago, 1906, 5 vols., IV, sections 44, 129 and 403.

[52] A. Moret and G. Davy, *op. cit.*, *pp.* 392-3, figs. 43 and 44, and A. Moret, *Histoire de l'Orient*, Vol. II, Paris, 1936, *pp.* 578-87.

[53] See articles on " Calchas " and " Mopsos (2) " in Pierre Grimal, *op. cit.*; A. Séveryns, *op. cit.*, *p.* 178.

[54] John Chadwick, *The Decipherment of Linear B*, *p.* 104.

[55] Thucydides, II, 2; Herodotus, V, 76.

[56] Alan J. B. Wace in *A Companion to Homer*, *p.* 357.

[57] Euripides, *Ion*, 1575.*ff.*

[58] M. K. Sakellariou, *op. cit.*, *p.* 493.

[59] Thucydides III, 114-5. The translation of lines from the *Hymn to Apollo* is by Rex Warner.

[60] Herodotus II, 53.

[61] Plato, *Hipparchus*, 228 B.

[62] Cicero, *De Oratore* III, 34.

[63] J. A. Davison in *A Companion to Homer*, pp. 234-66.

[64] The basic modern works on the development of Athenian political institutions are Paul Cloché, *La Démocratie athénienne*, Paris, 1951 and C. Hignett, *A History of the Athenian Constitution*, Oxford, 1952.

[65] M. P. Nilsson, *A History of Greek Religion*, Oxford, 2nd ed., 1949, p. 10.

[66] V. R. D. A. Desborough, *Protogeometric Pottery*, Oxford, 1952; K. Kubler and W. Kraiker, *Kerameikos-Ergebnisse der Ausgrabungen*, Berlin, 1939. Eva T. H. Brann, *Late Geometric and Protoattic Pottery*, *The Athenian Agora* VIII, Princeton, 1962.

[67] G. Mylonas in *A Companion to Homer*, p. 486.

[68] John Travlos, *op. cit.*, p. 28.

[69] Alan J. B. Wace, *The Arrival of the Greeks*, New York, p. 211 and in *A Companion to Homer*, p. 357.

[70] K. A. Romeos, *The Pottery of Calydon*, Athens, 1951 (in Greek), pp. 101*ff*.

[71] For the Hecatompedon, see W. Dinsmoor, "The Hecatompedon on the Athenian Acropolis" in *American Journal of Archaeology*, LI, 1947. For the peripteral temple of Athens see H. Riemann, "Der Peisistratidlische Athena Tempel auf der Akropolis zu Athen" in *Mitteilungen des Deutschen Archäologischen Instituts zu Athen*, III, 1950. For the early architecture of the Acropolis, see G. Stevens, "Architectural Studies concerning the Acropolis of Athens" in *Hesperia*, XV, 1940; and John Travlos, *op. cit.*, pp. 43-4.

[72] Roland Martin, *L'Urbanisme dans la Grèce antique*, Paris, 1956, p. 86 and John Travlos, *op. cit.*, p. 36.

[73] John Travlos, *op. cit.*, p. 41.

[74] M. P. Nilsson, *A History of Greek Religion*, Oxford, 2nd ed., 1949, p. 9.

[75] Louis Cernet and André Boullanger, *Le Génie grec dans la religion*, Paris, 1932, pp. 11-50. For the history of the cult of Dionysus see H. Jeanmaire, *Dionysos*, Paris, 1951.

[76] The current of Dionysian worship branched out into Orphism and Pythagorianism, two streams that ran in different directions, for the former led to belief in the redemption of the soul and in repeated reincarnation until the soul was finally liberated from the animal inheritance of man, whereas the latter starting from the same ideas culminated in a superstition involving the inner significance of numbers which gave rise to a tyranny of magic formulae determining everyday conduct and behaviour. M. P. Nilsson, *A History of Greek Religion*, Oxford, 2nd., 1949, pp. 213-23.

[77] For Greek architecture the basic works are still J. Durm, *Die Baukunst der Griechen*, Stuttgart, 1910 and the first volume of A. Choisy, *Histoire de l'architecture*, XI, Paris. More recent books on Greek architecture are W. B. Dinsmoor, *The Architecture of Ancient Greece*, London, 1950; D. S. Robertson, *A Handbook of Greek and Roman Architecture*, Cambridge 1943; and A. W. Lawrence, *Greek Architecture*, London, 1957.

[78] For archaic sculpture see C. Picard, *Manuel d'archéologie grecque*, I, Paris, 1953; J. Charbonneaux, *La Sculpture grecque archaïque*, Paris, 1938; G. Lippold, *Handbuch der Archäologie, Die Griechische Plastik*, Munich, 1950; R. Lullies and M. Hirmer, *Greek Sculpture*, London, 1957.

[79] Gisela M. A. Richter, *Kouroi*, London, 2nd ed., 1960, pp. 30-58, figs. 25-125.

[80] Gisela M. A. Richter, *The Archaic Gravestones of Attica*, London, 1961, figs. 35-9.

[81] George Posener, *Dictionnaire de la civilisation égyptienne*, Paris, 1959, and P. Grimal, *op. cit.*, article on "Sphinx."

[82] Jean Charbonneaux, *op. cit.*, pp. 71-4.

[83] For the architecture and sculpture of the temple of Aphaea the basic works are still A. Furtwängler, *Aegina, Das Heiligtum der Aphaia*, Munich, 1906 and his *Die Aeginetan der Glyptothek König Ludwigs I*, Munich, 1906.

[84] Herodotus, III, 59. The excerpt from Herodotus on the temple of Aegina is as follows: "But in the sixth year they were attacked by the Aeginetans, who with the help of the Cretans beat them in an engagement at sea and reduced them to slavery. They sawed off the boars' heads which the Samian ships carried on their prows, and laid them up in the temple of Athena in Aegina."

[85] For the black-figure style of Attica vases, see J. D. Beazly, *Attic Black-figure*, London, 1956; A. Pfuhl, *Malerei und Zeichnung der Griechen*, 3 vols., Munich, 1923; A. Rumf, *Malerei und Zeichnung*, *Handbuch der Archäologie* IV, I, Munich, 1953; and more specifically F. Villard, *Les Vases grecs*, Paris, 1956, pp. 62-9; M. Robertson, *Greek Painting*, London, 1959, pp. 53-82; P. E. Aris and M. Hirmer, *Le Vase grec*, Paris, 1962, pp. 37-60, figs. 38-81.

[86] Aristotle, *Constitution of Athens* XX, where Isagoras is described as a friend of the tyrants. The likelihood of an alliance between Isagoras and the supporters of tyranny is also favoured by Paul Cloché, *op. cit.*, p. 17.

[87] Gabriel Welter, *Aegina*, I, Athens, 1962 (in Greek), p. 7.

[88] G. Welter, *op. cit.*, pp. 7-13.

[89] For descriptions of the battle see J. B. Bury, *A History of Greece to the Death of Alexander the Great*, London, 3rd ed., 1951, pp. 247-54 and G. Glotz, *Histoire grecque*, Vol. II, *La Grèce du V*e *siècle*, Paris, 1925-38, pp. 31-41.

237

[90] G. Richter, *The Archaic Gravestones of Attica*, p. 47, figs. 156-8.

[91] Chr. Karouzos, *Aristodikos*, Athens, 1961 (in Greek).

[92] Pausanias, *Boeotia*, IX, 4, 1 and *Attica* I, 50; Plutarch, *Aristides*, 20; C. Picard, *Manuel d'archéologie grecque*, Vol. II *La Sculpture. Période Classique*, 310.

[93] Pausanias, *Phocis*, X, 10, 2.

[94] C. Picard, *op. cit.*, pp. 320-2.

[95] Formerly, archaeologists believed that the statue of Zeus at Olympia was Phidias' last work, dating to the period 438-1, on the eve of the Peloponnesian War. This conjecture was based on Aristophanes, *Peace*, l. 605 and Philochorus Atthidographos (4th-3rd century, who relates that Phidias, accused of stealing gold from the statue of Athena Parthenos (438), left Athens with his family, after his condemnation, for Elis where he worked on the statue of Zeus and ended his days. Other sources contradict the story of his exile in Elis. In Plato's *Protagoras* Socrates advises his companion to go to Phidias, if he wishes to study sculpture. As the *Protagoras* seems to refer to the year 432 when Phidias was 58, he could not have been teaching sculpture to Athenians if he was either in prison or in exile in Elis. Plutarch does not mention the exile in Elis, but says that he was accused of impiety for having represented portraits of himself and of Pericles on the shield of Athena and that he was thrown into prison where he died of an illness the same year. Pausanias writes that the statue of Zeus was paid for by the treasury of the Atlis when the temple was completed in 456 or 457 by the Elian architect Libon. Moreover, the Zeus of Olympia could not have been made in the period 438-1 as Phidias was then in Athens, working on the Parthenon.

[96] Emil Kunze, *Die Ausgrabungen in Olympia*, 1952-8, Archaeological Bulletin, Vol. 16, (1960), Athens, 1962, pp. 127-34.

[97] Angelo Procopiou, *Classicisme et Primitivisme Antithèse ou Synthèse*, Recherche No. 2, Paris, 1962.

[98] For a bibliography to the sculptures of the Parthenon see C. Picard, *op. cit.*, pp. 396-521 and Reinhard Lullies, *La Sculpture grecque*, p. 56.

[99] Homer A. Thompson in *Hesperia*, XVIII, 1959, XIX, 1950, XXII, 1953, XXIII, 1954, XXIV 1955, *The Ancient Agora as a Cultural Center*, New Forms, No. 3, Athens, 1962. See also *The Athenian Agora, A Guide to the Excavations and Museum*, Athens, 1962.

[100] J. Travlos, *op. cit.*, pp. 68-70.

[101] For Hippodamus and the town plan of Piraeus, see Pierre Lavedan, *Histoire de l'urbanisme*, Paris, 1926, pp. 127-41 and Roland Martin, *L'Urbanisme dans la Grèce antique*, pp. 103-10.

[102] R. Martin, *op. cit.*, p. 108.

[103] E. Loewy, *Polygnot, Ein Buch Von Griechischen Malerei*, Vienna, 1929 and E. Pfuhl, *Meisterwerke Griechischen Zeichnung and Malerei*, Munich, 1924, p. 635.

[104] For the history of Greek art, apart from the books mentioned already, two important general works in Greek are to be noted; C. Tsountas, *History of Archaic Greek Art*, Athens, 1928 and P. Kavadias, *History of Greek Art*, Athens, 1916, which were used at Athens University by all contemporary Greek archaeologists.

[105] Barclay V. Head, *A Guide to the Principal Coins of the Greeks*, London, 1959, pp. 22, 31-5, 36, Pl. 11.

[106] B. V. Head, *op. cit.*, pp. 6-8, 26-30, 31-2, 33-6, Pls. 4 and 5.

[107] B. Papathanassopoulos, "Über die Akustic des Griechischen Theaters," in *Proceedings of the Third International Congress in Acoustics, Stuttgart, 1959*, Amsterdam, 1960.

[108] The theme of tragic fear in Aeschylus has been treated very thoroughly by Jacqueline de Romilly in *La Crainte et l'angoisse dans le théâtre d'Éschyle*, Paris, 1958.

[109] C. Hignett, *op. cit.*, pp. 195*ff.*

[110] About the invention and application of the empirical method in medicine and in history see Cochrane, *Thucydides and the Science of History*, Oxford, 1929.

[111] Robert Flacelière, *A Literary History of Greece*, London, 1964, p. 221, "Twenty-four centuries before Marx, he explains social and political history in terms of economics."

[112] All these examples are taken from the introductory section of Thucydides' *History*. Known as the "Archaeology," it sets the tone of the whole from the outset.

[113] Jacqueline de Romilly, *Histoire et raison chez Thucydide*, Paris, 1956.

[114] Thucydides' *History* breaks off at the year 411. The continuation down to 362 was written by Xenophon (430-355) in the seven books of his *Hellenica*. Like Thucydides, Xenophon was an Athenian of a wealthy family from the deme of Erchias. At the age of seventeen he became a disciple of Socrates whom he venerated throughout his life. Three of his works —The *Memorabilia*, the *Apology* and the *Symposium*—are devoted to Socrates. He accompanied Cyrus in his campaign against his brother Artaxerxes, with a contingent of Greek mercenaries whom he was to lead back to Greece after the death of Cyrus. An account of this exploit forms the subject of his best-known book, the *Anabasis*. We find him again in Asia in 396 accompanying the king of Sparta, Agesilaus, in his war against Artaxerxes. To reward him for his services, the Spartans presented him with a country seat near Olympia where

he was to spend twenty years writing his books, after he had been exiled by the Athenians for collaborating with the Lacedaemonians. But he made his peace with Athens when she joined Sparta to fight the Boeotians. At the battle of Mantinea in 362, his son Gryllus died a heroic death in the ranks of the Athenian cavalry. Xenophon left behind him a very varied literary *œuvre:* politics, philosophy, economics and history. The Ancients regarded his style as a model of Attic prose. His narratives are clear and abound in descriptions, but lack the depth and cogency of Thucydides, in spite of his efforts to imitate him.

[115] Pierre-Maxime Schuhl, *Platon et l'art de son temps*, Paris, 1952.

[116] W. Deonna, *Du miracle grec au miracle chrétien, classicisme et primitivisme dans l'art*, Basel, Vol. II, p. 112: "Le mode 'icastique,' c'est l'abstraction du primitivisme et son 'realisme logique'; le mode 'phantastique,' c'est l'imitation exacte de la réalité visuelle du classicisme."

[117] E. Schmidt, *Archäistische Kunst in Griechenland und Rom*, Munich, 1922. P. Devambez, "La Stèle de Philis et les tendances archaïsantes à Thasos" in *Bulletin de Correspondance hellénique* (École Française d'Athènes), Paris, 1931, pp. 413-22.

[118] C. Picard, "Les antécédents des 'Astragalizontes' polyclétéens" in *Revue des Études grecques*, Paris, 1929, Vol. XLII, p. 127 and *Manuel d'archéologie grecque*, Vol. II, 2, p. 557 and Vol. III, 1, p. 27.

[119] P.-M. Schuhl, *Essai sur la formation de la pensée grecque*, Paris, 2nd ed. 1949, p. 363.

[120] E. Pfuhl, "Apollodorus the *skiagraphos*" in *Jahrbuch des Deutschen Archäologischen Instituts*, XXV, 1910, pp. 13-22.

[121] For a description of the use of the perspective by the Greeks see P.-M. Schuhl, *Platon et l'art de son temps*, Paris, 1956, pp. 77-9.

[122] C. Picard, *Manuel d'archéologie grecque*, Vol. III, 2, pp. 406*ff*.

[123] *Ibid*, pp. 614-6.

[124] *Ibid*, pp. 498-509.

[125] *Ibid*, p. 504.

[126] It is not generally agreed whether the Hermes is an original work of Praxiteles or a copy. See C. Picard, *ibid.*, pp. 250*ff*. The technical execution of this work makes it abundantly clear that it is the work of a great sculptor and we have Pausanias' testimony that the sculptor was Praxiteles.

Bibliography

A. M. ANDREADES, *History of Greek Public Finances*, Cambridge (Mass.), 1933

J. ANGELOPOULOS, *Aristophane et ses idées sur Socrate*, Athens, 1933

A. AYMARD AND J. AUBOYER, *L'Orient et la Grèce*, Paris, 1953

G. BASTIDE, *Le Moment historique de Socrate*, Paris, 1939

J. D. BEAZLEY AND B. ASHMOLE, *Greek Sculpture and Painting*, Cambridge, 1932

J. D. BEAZLEY, *Attic White Lekythoi*, London, 1938
Attic Red-Figure Vase-Painters, London, 1942
The Development of Attic Black-Figure, Berkeley, 1951
Attic Black-Figure, London, 1956

H. BENGSTON AND V. MILOJCIC, *Grosser historischer Weltatlas*, 1: Vorgeschichte und Altertum, Munich, 1958

H. BENGSTON, *Griechische Geschichte*, Munich, 1950

J. BÉRARD, *La Colonisation grecque de l'Italie méridionale et de la Sicile*, Paris, 1941

M. BIEBER, *The Sculpture of the Hellenistic Age*, New York, 1954

EVA T. H. BRANN, *Late Geometric and Protoattic Pottery*, Princeton, 1962

E. BRÉHIER, *Histoire de la Philsophie*, Vol. 1, Paris, 1st ed., 1960

J. B. BURY, *A History of Greece to the Death of Alexander the Great*, London, 3rd ed., 1951

E. BUSCOR, *Griechische Vasenmalerei*, Munich, 1925

E. BUSCOR, *Griechische Vasen*, Munich, 1940

The Cambridge Ancient History, Cambridge, 1923-39

A. CAPIZZI, *Protagora*, Florence, 1955

E. CAVAIGNAC, *Le Monde méditerranéen jusqu'au IVe siècle av. J. C.*, Paris, 1929

J. CHADWICK, *The Decipherment of Linear B*. Cambridge, 1958, London, 2nd ed., 1961

J. CHARBONNEAUX, *Les Terres cuites grecques*, Paris, 1930
La Sculpture grecque archaïque, Paris, 1938
La Sculpture grecque classique, Paris, Vol. 1 1943, Vol. II 1945
Greek Bronzes, London, 1962

J. CHEVALIER, *Histoire de la pensée*, Vol. 1, Paris, 1955

F. M. CLEVE, *The Philosophy of Anaxagoras*, Oxford, 1949

P. CLOCHÉ AND P. ROUSSEL, *La Grèce et l'Orient des guerres médiques à la conquête romaine*, Paris, 1938

P. CLOCHÉ, *La Civilisation athénienne*, 5th ed., Paris, 1956
La Démocratie athénienne, Paris, 1951
Le Siècle de Périclès, Paris, 1960

E. COCHÉ DE LA FERTÉ, *Les bijoux antiques*, Paris, 1956

R. COHEN, *La Grèce et l'hellénisation du monde antique*, Paris, 3rd ed., 1948

A. AND M. CROISET, *Histoire de la littérature grecque*, 5 vols., Paris, 1887-1928

V.R.D.A. DESBOROUGH, *Protogeometric Pottery*, Oxford, 1952

P. DEVAMBEZ, *L'Art au siècle de Périclès*, Lausanne, 1955
Antiquité Classique, pp. 547-854, *Histoire de l'Art*, I: Le Monde non-chrétien, Paris, 1961

E. DERENNE, *Les Procès d'impiété intentés aux philosophes à Athènes aux Ve et IVe siècles*, Paris, 1930

W. B. DINSMOOR, *The Architecture of Ancient Greece*, London and New York, 1950

P. DUCATI, *L'Arte classica*, Turin, 1956

T. J. DUNBABIN, *The Western Greeks*, Oxford, 1948

E. DUPREEL. *Les Sophistes*, Neuchatel, 1948

J. DURM, *Die Baukunst der Griechen*, Stuttgart, 1910

V. EHRENBERG, *The People of Aristophanes: A Sociology of Old Attic Comedy*, Oxford, 1951
Sophocles and Pericles, Oxford, 1954
The Greek State, Oxford, 1960

A. J. EVANS, *The Palace of Minos at Knossos*, 4 vols., London, 1921-36

R. FLACELIÉRE, *Daily Life in the Athens of Pericles*, London, 1964
A Literary History of Greece, London, 1964

L. GERNET AND A. BOULANGER, *Le Génie grec dans la religion*, Paris, 1932

G. GIANNELLI AND S. MAZZARINO, *Trattato di storia greca e romana*, 3 vols., 1954-6

G. GLOTZ, *Le Travail dans la Grèce ancienne*, *Histoire économique de la Grèce depuis la période homérique jusqu'à la conquête romaine*, Paris, 1920

G. GLOTZ, *La Cité grecque*, Paris, 1928, (new edition revised by P. Cloché)

G. GLOTZ AND R. COHEN, *Histoire grecque*, I: Des origines aux guerres médiques, II: La Grèce au Ve siècle, III: La Grèce au IVe siècle, la lutte pour l'hégémonie, Paris, 1925-38
La Civilisation égéenne, Paris, 1952

A. W. GOMME, *A Historical Comment on Thucydides*, 3 vols., Oxford, 1945-56

P. GRIMAL, *Dictionnaire de la mythologie grecque et romaine*, Paris, 3rd ed., 1956

N.G.L. HAMMOND, *A History of Greece to 322 B. C.*, Oxford, 1959

J. HATZFELD, *Histoire de la Grèce ancienne*, Paris, 3rd ed., 1950

C. HIGNETT, *A History of the Athenian Constitution*, Oxford, 1952

I. T. Hill, *The Ancient City of Athens, its Topography and Monuments*, London, 1953

J. Imbert, G. Sautel and M. Boulet-Sautel, *Histoire des institutions et des faits sociaux, textes et documents*, Paris, 1957

S. Jacovides, *The Mycenaean Acropolis of Athens*, Athens, 1962 (in Greek)

W. Jaeger, *Paideia*, 3 vols, Oxford, 1944-51

A. Jardé, *La Formation du peuple grec*, Paris, 1938

H. Jeanmaire, *Dionysos*, Paris, 1951

A.H.M. Jones, *Athenian Democracy*, Oxford, 1957

P. Jouguet, *Les Premières Civilisations*, Paris, 1950

C. Karouzos, *Aristodikos*, Athens, 1961 (in Greek)

H. D. F. Kitto, *Greek Tragedy*, London, 2nd ed., 1950
The Greeks, London, 1962

N. Kontoleon, *The Erechtheum as a Temple of Infernal Worship*, Athens, 1949, (in Greek)

W. Kraiker, *Die Malerei der Griechen*, Stuttgart, 1958

P. Kretschmer, *Einleitung in die Geschichte der Griechischen Sprache*, Göttingen, 1896

W. Lamb, *Greek and Roman Bronzes*, Cambridge, 1929

M. Lang and C. V. J. Eliot, *The Athenian Agora*, Athens, 1954

P. Lavedan, *Histoire de l'Art*, Vol. 1, L'Antiquité, Paris, 1949

A. W. Lawrence, *Greek Architecture*, London, 1957

P. E. Legrand, *Hérodote, Introduction*, Paris, 1932

A. Lesky, *Geschichte der Griechischen Literatur*, Bern, 1958

Doro Levy, *Abitazione preistoriche sulle pendici meridionali dell'Acropoli*, Annuario, 13/14, 1930-31, pp. 411-98

G. Lippold, *Handbuch der Archäologie, Die Griechische Plastik*, Munich, 1950

R. Lullies and M. Hirmer, *Greek Sculpture*, London, 1957

V. de Magalhaes-Vilhena, *Le Problème de Socrate; Socrate et la légende platonicienne*, Paris, 1952

S. Marinatos, *Crete and Mycenaean Greece*, Athens, 1959 (in Greek)

H.-I. Marrou, *A History of Greece to 322 B.C.*, London, 1956

R. Martin, *Recherches sur l'Agora grecque, études d'histoire et d'architecture urbaines*, Paris, 1951
L'Urbanisme dans la Grèce antique, Paris, 1956

G. Mathieu, *Les Idées politiques d'Isocrate*, Paris, 1925

F. Matz, *Geschichte der Griechischen Kunst*, 1, Frankfurt-am-Main, 1949-50

F. Matz, *Le Monde égéen*, Paris, 1956

F. Matz, *Kreta, Troja, Die minoische und die homerische Welt*, Stuttgart, 1956

J. Miliadis, *The Acropolis*, Athens, 1963

V. Milojcic, *Hauptergebnisse des Deutschen Ausgrabungen in Thessalien*, 1953-8, XXIII, 75, Germania 36, 1958

G. E. Mylonas, *Ancient Mycenae, The Capital City of Agamemnon*, London, 1957
Eleusis and the Eleusinian Mysteries, Princeton, 1961

B. Niese, *Geschichte der Griechischen und Makedonischen Staaten seit der Schlacht bei Chaironeia*, 1893-1903

M. P. Nilsson, *A History of Greek Religion*, Oxford, 2nd ed., 1949

The Minoan-Mycenaean Religion and its Survivals in Greek Religion, Lund, 2nd ed., 1950
La Religion populaire de la Grèce antique, Paris, 1954
Les Croyances religieuses de la Grèce antique, Paris, 1955

L. R. Palmer, *Mycenaeans and Minoans*, London, 1961

J. D. S. Pendlebury, *A Handbook to the Palace of Minos at Knossos*, London, 2nd ed., 1955

M. Pohlenz, *La Liberté grecque, nature et évolution d'un idéal de vie*, Paris, 1955

A. Pfuhl, *Malerei und Zeichnung der Griechen*, 3 vols., Munich, 1923
Meisterwerke Griechische Zeichnung und Malerei, Munich, 1924

A. Philippson and E. Kirsten, *Die Griechischen Landschaften*, Vols I and III, Attica und Megaris, Frankfurt-am-Main, 1952

C. Picard. *La Sculpture antique*, I, Des origines à Phidias; II, De Phidias à l'ère Byzantine, Paris, 1923-6
La Vie privée dans la Grèce classique, Paris, 2nd ed., 1946
Les Religions préhelléniques, Paris, 1948
Manuel d'archéologie grecque: la sculpture, Vols. I-V, Paris, 1935-53

L. Preller, *Griechische Mythologie*, 3 vols., Berlin, 1920-6

J. Przyluski, *La Grande Déesse*, Paris, 1950

C. Ramnoux, *Mythologie de la famille olympienne*, Paris, 1962

A. Reinach, *Recueil Milliet, Textes grecs et latins relatifs à l'histoire de la peinture ancienne*, Paris, 1921

A. Rey, *La Science dans l'antiquité*, Paris, 1948

G. M. A. Richter and Milne, *Shapes and Names of Athenian Vases*, Oxford, 1955

G. M. A. Richter, *Archaic Greek Art against its Historical Background*, New York, 1949
Attic Red-figured Vases, A Survey, New Haven, 2nd ed., 1958
A Handbook of Greek Art, London, 1959
Kouroi, London, 2nd ed., 1960
The Archaic Gravestones of Attica, London, 1961

A. Ridde and W. Deonna, *L'Art en Grèce*, Paris, 1924

A. Rivaud, *Histoire de la philosophie*, Paris, 1948

G. E. Rizzo, *La Pittura ellenistico-romana*, Milan, 1929
Monumenti della pittura antica scoperti in Italia, Rome, 1935

D. S. Robertson, *A Handbook of Greek and Roman Architecture*, Cambridge, 2nd ed., 1943

M. Robertson, *Greek Painting*, Geneva, 1959

L. Robin, *La Pensée grecque*, Paris, 1923, new edition revised by P.-M. Schuhl, 1963

C. A. Robinson, *Athens and the Age of Pericles*, New York, 1959

E. Rohde, *Psyche, le culte de l'âme chez les Grecs et leur croyance en l'immortalité*, Paris, 1928

K. A. Romeos, *Pottery of Calydon*, Athens, 1951 (in Greek)

J. de Romilly, *Thucydides and Athenian Imperialism*, Oxford, 1963
Histoire et raison chez Thucydide, Paris, 1956
L'Évolution du pathétique d'Éschyle à Euripide, Paris, 1961

A. Rumpf, *Malerei und Zeichnung*, Munich, 1953

G. de Sanctis, *Storia dei Graeci dalle origini alla fine del secolo quinto*, 2 vols., Florence, 1960

M. B. Sakellariou, *La Migration grecque en Ionie*, Athens, 1958

F. Schachermeyer, *Die Altesten Kulturen Grie-chenlands*, Stuttgart, 1955

P.-M. Schuhl, *Essai sur la formation de la pensée grecque*, Paris, 2nd ed., 1949

Platon et l'art de son temps, Paris, 1952

L'Œuvre de Platon, Paris, 1954

Sereni-Outchenko, *État et classes dans l'antiquité esclavagiste*, Paris, 1957

A. Severyns, *Grèce et Proche-Orient avant Homère*, Brussells, 1960.

T. A. Sinclair, *Histoire de la pensée politique grecque*, Paris, 1953.

G. Starr, *The Origins of Greek Civilization*, New York, 1961.

C. H. V. Sutherland, *Art in Coinage*, London, 1955

G. Tenekides, *La Notion juridique d'indépendance et la tradition hellénique*, Athens, 1954.

H. Thompson, *The Athenian Agora*, Athens, 1962.

J. Travlos, *The Development of Town-planning in Athens*, Athens, 1960 (in Greek).

A. Toynbee, *A Study of History*, abridgment by D. C. Somervell, Vol II, London, 1956.

C. Tsountas and J. I. Manatt, *The Mycenaean Age*, London, 1903.

C. Tsountas, *History of Archaic Greek Art*, Athens, 1928 (in Greek).

The Prehistoric Acropoleis of Dimini and Sesclos, Athens, 1909 (in Greek).

D. Theocharis, *Pyrasos*, " *Thessalica* " (*B*), Volos, 1959 (in Greek).

P. van der Heyden and A. J. Scudder, *Atlas of Classical Antiquity*, London, 1961.

M. Ventris and J. Chadwick, *Documents in Mycenaean Greek*, Cambridge, 1956.

J. Vercoutter, *L'Égypte et le monde égéen pré-hellénique*, Cairo, 1961.

J. P. Vernant, *Les Origines de la pensée grecque*, Paris, 1962.

F. Villard, *Les Vases grecs*, Paris, 1956.

A. J. B. Wace and F. H. Stubbings (ed.), *A Companion to Homer*, London, 1962.

A. J. B. Wace, *The Arrival of the Greeks*, New York, 1954.

Mycenae, An Archaeological History and Guide, Princeton, 1949.

A. J. B. Wace and C. W. Blegen, " Pottery as Evidence for Trade and Colonization in the Aegean Bronze Age ", *Klio*, XXXII, 2, 140.

T. B. L. Webster, *From Mycenae to Homer*, London, 1958.

M. Wegner, *L'Art grec*, Basle and Paris, 1955.

C. Werner, *La Philosophie grecque*, Paris, 1962.

M. Woodhouse. *Solon the Liberator*, Oxford and London, 1938.

C. Zervos, *L'Art de la Crète néolithique et minoenne*, Paris, 1956.

L'Art des Cyclades, Paris, 1957.

La Naissance de la civilization en Grèce, 2 vols, Paris, 1963.

G. Zuntz, *The Political Plays of Euripides*, Manchester, 1955.

Index

Fig. 25 A naked warrior from the western pediment of the temple of Aphaea at Aegina of which Pl. 55 is a detail, *Glyptothek, Munich*